# the neon gobies

## The Comparative Biology of the Gobies of the Genus *Gobiosoma*, Subgenus *Elacatinus*, (Pisces: Gobiidae) in the Tropical Western North Atlantic Ocean

dr. patrick l. colin

This manuscript was originally submitted to the faculty of the University of Miami as a doctoral dissertation. It is reproduced here with the addition of color photographs. These photographs are by the author unless otherwise specified.

Frontispiece by H. Hansen, Aquarium Berlin.

ISBN 0-87666-450-8

© 1975 by T.F.H. Publications, Inc.

Distributed in the U.S.A. by T.F.H. Publications, Inc., 211 West Sylvania Avenue, P.O. Box 27, Neptune City, N.J. 07753; in England by T.F.H. (Gt. Britain) Ltd., 13 Nutley Lane, Reigate, Surrey; in Canada to the book store and library trade by Clarke, Irwin & Company, Clarwin House, 791 St. Clair Avenue West, Toronto 10, Ontario; in Canada to the pet trade by Rolf C. Hagen Ltd., 3225 Sartelon Street, Montreal 382, Quebec; in Southeast Asia by Y.W. Ong, 9 Lorong 36 Geylang, Singapore 14; in Australia and the south Pacific by Pet Imports Pty. Ltd., P.O. Box 149, Brookvale 2100, N.S.W., Australia. Published by T.F.H. Publications, Inc. Ltd., The British Crown Colony of Hong Kong.

*Dedicated to*
Duncan, Patricia and Diane Hunter
of Islamorada, Florida for the kindness they
have extended to me over the past ten years

# CONTENTS

ACKNOWLEDGMENTS ........................ 7

INTRODUCTION ........................... 9

.MATERIALS AND METHODS ................. 12

INSTRUCTIONS FOR USE OF THE KEY TO
WESTERN ATLANTIC SPECIES OF *Gobiosoma*,
SUBGENUS *Elacatinus* ......................... 18

GENERAL SPECIES ACCOUNTS .............. 24
    *Gobiosoma oceanops* ....................... 24
    *Gobiosoma evelynae* ....................... 32
    *Gobiosoma illecebrosum* ................... 47
    *Gobiosoma genie* ......................... 55
    *Gobiosoma prochilos* ...................... 66
    *Gobiosoma randalli* ....................... 75
    *Gobiosoma chancei* ....................... 82
    *Gobiosoma horsti* ......................... 87
    *Gobiosoma xanthiprora* ................... 110
    *Gobiosoma louisae* ....................... 119
    *Gobiosoma tenox* ......................... 134
    *Gobiosoma atronasum* .................... 143

FIELD AND LABORATORY COMPARATIVE
STUDIES ...................................... 158
    Density, Spacial Distribution and Bathymetric
        Distribution ......................... 158
    Coral Dwelling in Species of *Gobiosoma* ....... 199

Cleaning Behavior and Ecology of *Gobiosoma* . . 210
Sponge Dwelling and Noxious Properties of
  *Gobiosoma* . . . . . . . . . . . . . . . . . . . . . . . . . . . 235
Time of Spawning and Larval Transformation . . 247
Spawning and Larval Development . . . . . . . . . . 255
Zoogeography of Species of the Subgenus
  *Elacatinus* in the Western North Atlantic . . 269
Discussion of Relationships . . . . . . . . . . . . . . . . 284

LITERATURE CITED . . . . . . . . . . . . . . . . . . . . . . 295

INDEX . . . . . . . . . . . . . . . . . . . . . . . . . . . . . . . . 305

# ACKNOWLEDGMENTS

I thank my committee members, Drs. C. Richard Robins and James E. Bohlke, co-chairmen, Arthur A. Myrberg, Jr., Edward D. Houde, and Cesare Emiliani for their help and advice in this study. Other students and staff and faculty members at the University of Miami School of Marine and Atmospheric Sciences were of assistance with both field and laboratory work. These include: Dr. John Bunt, James N. Burnett-Herkes, Bruce Chalker, Nicholas and Anne Chitty, Dr. Eugene Corcoran, Richard Curry, Joan Fontana, Walter Goldberg, Martin F. Gomon, Charles Mayo III, Charles Messing, Francisco Palacio, Shirley Pomponi, Dr. Jon C. Staiger, William F. Smith-Vaniz, Susan J. Stevens, Dr. Robert Stevenson, Kenneth Sulak, Dennis L. Taylor, Ronald Thresher, and Robert Work. Ship operations from the Rosenstiel School of Marine and Atmospheric Sciences were aided by the following: *R/V Calanus*, Alexander McClennan, John Hines, and S. Hartshorne; *R/V Orca*, Clifford Shoemaker; and others on the *R/V Pillsbury* and *R/V Gerda*.

The field work at most locations would have been impossible without the assistance of personnel at the following laboratories: Discovery Bay Marine Laboratory, Discovery Bay, Jamaica (Norman L. Copland, Eileen Graham, John B. Heiser, Judy C. Land, Phillip Dustan, and David Barnes); Caribbean Marine Biological Institute, Piscadera Baai, Curacao, Netherland Antilles (Ingvar Kristensen, Rolf de Bak, Hans de Kriujf, Bart de Bor, Franciso Palacio, Jan Kees Post, Peter Cruetzberg); Bellairs Research Institute, St. James, Barbados (Finn Sander, Bruce Ott, Charles Hollingsworth, Howard Powles); West Indies Laboratory, St. Croix, U.S. Virgin Islands (John C. Ogden, H.G. Multer, C. Bowman); Port Royal Marine Laboratory, Port Royal, Jamaica (M. Itzkowitz, W. Simms, J. Munro, P. Reeson); Smithsonian Tropical Research Institute, Balboa, Canal Zone (C. Birkeland, D. Meyer). The field work in Colombia was made possible by Franciso Palacio and the staffs of the INDERANA, Cartagena and the Instituto Colombo-Aleman, Santa Marta. The Colombian field work was also assisted by C. Roessler and J.K. Post. Field work in British Honduras (now Belize) during the Nekton

7

Beta project was made possible by Dr. Robert N. Ginsburg and Dr. Noel P. James. Field work at the Dry Tortugas was made possible by Gary E. Davis and the staff of the Fort Jefferson National Monument. Additional field work at Discovery Bay, Jamaica was carried out during the Nekton Gamma project, and participation was made possible by Dr. Lynton S. Land. Dr. Richard Slater and Mr. Richard T. Davies were most helpful during both Nekton projects. Catherine Engel assisted in some aspects of the field work.

Photos of specimens were loaned by Dr. Paul R. Ehrlich, Carl Roessler, and Roger Hanlon. Drs. James E. Tyler and C. Lavett Smith of the American Museum of Natural History offered advice and loaned specimens of *Gobiosoma*. In addition, they freely loaned unpublished data. Dr. James E. Bohlke of the Philadelphia Academy of Natural Sciences also loaned specimens. Robert C. Work and Dr. Willard Hartman assisted in identifying sponge specimens.

This work was supported by a variety of different sources. The most important was NSF grant GA 29333, C. Richard Robins principal investigator, which supported a major portion of the field work and without which this study would not have been carried out. During the study the author was supported first by a NSF Traineeship and later by NSF grant GB 28400X, Continuing Studies of Oceanic Fishes, C. Richard Robins, principal investigator, both of which are gratefully acknowledged. Observations on the Jamaican Nekton Gamma project were supported by NSF grant GA 35111, Lynton S. Land, principal investigator, and on the British Honduras Nekton Beta project by Robert N. Ginsburg through NOAA. Ship operations from RSMAS were supported by NSF grant GD 31576 for ship operating funds.

The assistance of the Ministry of Fisheries and Agriculture of the Bahamas is gratefully acknowledged in connection with several different research cruises by *R/V Calanus* and *R/V Gerda*.

# INTRODUCTION

The gobies comprise the largest family, in terms of numbers of species, of marine fishes in the world. Estimates vary, but there are probably over 1000 species in this group and, for the vast majority of these, their biology is very poorly known. The genus *Gobiosoma*, a New World group possessing seven spines in the first dorsal fin, has been divided into 5 subgenera (*Gobiosoma, Austrogobius, Garmannia, Tigrigobius,* and *Elacatinus*) by Bohlke and Robins (1968). The subgenus *Elacatinus*, popularly called "neon gobies," has the following characters: 1) no segment of lateral canal (therefore no pores) above opercle; 2) preopercular canal with two pores; 3) spinous dorsal fin without prolonged or filamentous anterior spines; 4) precaudal vertebrae 11, caudal vertebrae 17; 5) lateral stripe from eye to posterior margin of head and usually extending along body to caudal base; 6) no vertical bars or bands on body; and 7) body without scales (all Atlantic species) or with two modified basicaudal scales.

Although most ichthyologists concerned with western Atlantic reef fishes were aware of the existence of several species of gobies very similar to the well known neon goby, *Gobiosoma oceanops*, it was not until recently that a review of the group was published by Bohlke and Robins (1968), who dealt with all western Atlantic gobies possessing seven spines in the first dorsal fin. They described nine new species of *Gobiosoma* in the subgenus *Elacatinus* and removed a tenth from synonymy, thus recognizing a total of 12 species within the subgenus from the western Atlantic. They broadened the definition of the genus *Gobiosoma* and relegated to subgeneric rank such genera as *Austrogobius, Tigrigobius, Garmannia,* and *Elacatinus.* Two species usually referred to *Gobiosoma* were removed to other genera, *Ginsburgellus* and *Nes* respectively.

Three species of the subgenus *Elacatinus* had been described previous to Bohlke and Robins' work. *Gobiosoma oceanops* was described as *Elacatinus oceanops* in 1904 by David Starr Jordan from 5 specimens collected at Dry Tortugas. These specimens were sent to him by Joseph C. Thompson, a surgeon then stationed at the U.S. Naval Station at Garden

9

Key. Thompson noted the presence of *G. oceanops* on living coral heads, and this was recorded by Jordan (1904) and Jordan and Thompson (1905). Next, Metzelaar (1922) described *Gobiosoma horsti* from Curacao and noted that the type specimens were from sponges. Beebe and Tee-Van (1928) provided the first extensive field information on this species during the survey of fishes in Port-au-Prince Bay, Haiti, but confused the sponge-dwelling *G. horsti* with coral-dwelling members of subgenus *Elacatinus*. Finally, *Gobiosoma chancei* was described by Beebe and Hollister (1931) from Grenada; this species was incorrectly synonymized with *G. horsti* by Ginsburg (1933). The distinctiveness of the species was not recognized until the study by Bohlke and Robins (1968).

For most of the new species of *Gobiosoma* described by Bohlke and Robins (1968), few data were available regarding life habits and coloration. Their study, however, provided the impetus and starting point for the present work. The present study attempted to gather basic information concerning the biology of the 12 species to help formulate relationships within the subgenus. During this study all 12 species have been observed and collected and most have been maintained in laboratory aquaria for varying periods of time.

The members of the subgenus *Elacatinus* are of particular interest biologically since they have unusual ecological and behavioral adaptations. The first is their association with certain invertebrate organisms. Seven of the 12 species are associated with living scleractinian corals; six of these seven species spend much of their time sitting on the surface of the corals. In addition, at night some individuals rest on the corals, often beneath the expanded polyps.

The remaining 5 species of the subgenus are associated with large massive and tubular sponges, spending all of their juvenile and adult lives in this relationship. These species remain with the sponges both day and night.

Six of the coral-dwelling species engage in cleaning behavior or the removal of ectoparasites from the body, mouth, and gills of larger fishes. This phenomenon is becoming increasingly well known in the aquatic environment. Parasite picking behavior was first described for the subgenus *Elacatinus* by Longley (1918:81) for the species *G. oceanops*. The eastern Pacific members of the subgenus also engage in cleaning behavior (Feder, 1966; Bohlke and Robins, 1968).

The first section of this report provides a general account of each of the 12 species in the subgenus *Elacatinus*. Topics covered for each species include a synonymy, any alterations of the systematics of the species since the paper of Bohlke and Robins (1968), distribution, life coloration, general habits, food habits, and reproductive habits. Comments on the methods used in the study and a key to the species with instruction for use also are provided. Few attempts are made to compare the species in this first section. The intention of the study was to gather and interpret on a comparative basis biological information on the group. Some systematic problems arose during the study and are commented upon at the appropriate place.

The second section is comparative ecology. Some aspects of the life history for the different species, such as larval development, cleaning behavior, and sponge dwelling, are dealt with in greater detail and the zoogeography of the subgenus is discussed with reference to present and past oceanographic conditions.

Throughout the body of this report the subgenus *Elacatinus* will be referred to as *Elacatinus* without reference to its subgeneric status.

# MATERIALS AND METHODS

The major emphasis was to study all species of *Elacatinus* in the field. Field observations were made either snorkeling or SCUBA diving. The field operations had seven major objectives: 1) determination of species present at a given locality and their general habits; 2) determination of type of substrate and species of organisms inhabited (coral, rock, sponges, other), bathymetric range, and population structure; 3) assessment of populations within quadrats in specific localities; 4) photographic documentation; 5) collection of specimens for preservation and for study in laboratory aquaria; 6) long term observation of specific locations to detect changes in populations with seasons; and 7) detailed observation of behavioral interactions such as cleaning behavior. It is useful to consider the methods used in carrying out each of these seven objectives separately.

When a new locality was visited, the first few dives were spent attempting to locate the species of *Gobiosoma* present in a variety of habitats. Notes were recorded on underwater slates or a tape recorder in a watertight case. Life coloration was noted and, if necessary, collections were made to determine the species present.

After determining which species were present, other field information was obtained. The species of corals or sponges inhabited, numbers and sizes of individuals present on a given coral head or sponge, and the depth distribution of said species were recorded. Such observations were made in selected areas and were not intended to determine population densities for comparative analysis.

If time and conditions allowed, the number and types of individuals within quadrats of $(10 \text{ m})^2$ were determined. The area to be surveyed was marked with premeasured weighted lines set using a compass. The entire area was carefully searched in one pass, with the unsearched portion undisturbed by not having been swum over by the observer. The observer's diving partner also stayed at least 10 m away so as not to disturb any fishes in the quadrat. Again the number present at a station and the substrate inhabited were recorded. One quadrat normally required 20 minutes to 1 hour to establish and survey.

Photographic documentation was obtained both underwater and in the laboratory. Underwater color photographs of the fishes in their natural environment and undisturbed coloration were taken using a variety of cameras and flash equipment. The most satisfactory results were obtained with a 35 mm reflex camera using close-up lenses and an electronic flash for illumination. Laboratory photographs were taken both in aquaria, simulating natural conditions, and in artificial arrangements. The photographs taken in artificial arrangements were of live, anesthetized, and fresh dead specimens.

The method for collection of specimens was determined by the species to be collected and the situation encountered. Generally coral-dwelling species were collected using a quinaldine-alcohol solution (anesthetic) and a hand net. The fishes were placed in a live-bait bucket where they quickly recovered from the effects of the anesthetic. Sponge-dwelling species were collected by a variety of methods. Quinaldine-alcohol was sprayed into the osculum of the sponge, but this was not effective since the currents produced by the sponge opposed the passage of the anesthetic to the fish. The outer surface of the sponge was sprayed with anesthetic which was pumped by the action of the sponge water currents into the lumen of the sponge. The fish inside the sponge lumen were thus anesthetized and often expelled from the sponge by its water currents. This was a particularly effective method for collecting from massive sponges such as *Neofibrularia massa*, which are irritating for humans to touch. Fish inhabiting tubular sponges of soft consistency were collected most efficiently and simply. The portion of the sponge below the goby could be squeezed shut with a hand so that the goby could not pass deeper into the lumen. A plastic bag was placed over the osculum and the goby forced upward by squeezing the sponge progressively higher until the goby exited the lumen into the plastic bag. This method had the advantage of not disturbing chemically either the goby or the sponge.

Occasionally entire sponges and their fish populations were simply enclosed in large plastic bags, the holdfast of the sponge broken and the bag sealed. The sponges and all their contained organisms were brought to the surface together. The entire community could thus be determined. This destruction of habitat should not be used for just obtaining specimens!

Specimens for stomach analysis were collected with anesthetic and placed immediately underwater into 50% formalin for quick fixation. Later the specimens were transferred to 10% formalin. This technique was termed R.I.P. for "rapid and immediate preservation." Technically

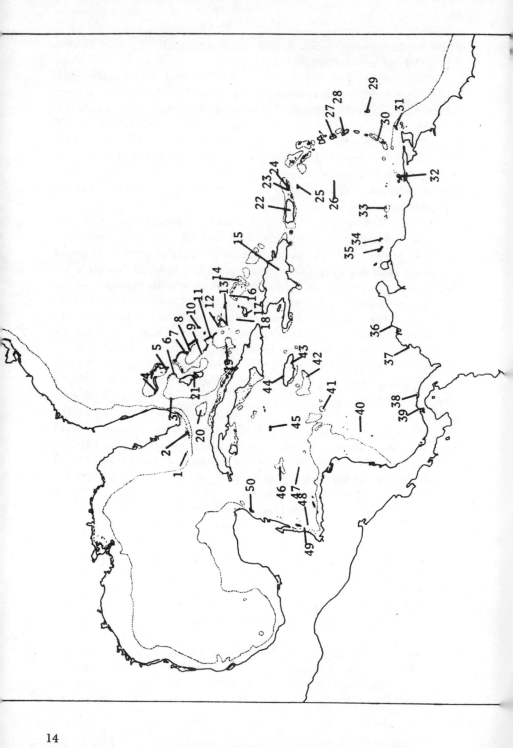

gobies do not have true stomachs, so it is convenient to use the term "gut" in discussions of food analysis.

Quadrat surveys were carried out at Jamaica, Curacao, Bahamas, Barbados, St. Croix, and Panama. The number of quadrats surveyed at each locality depended on time available and logistic considerations. Data of species present, number of individuals, substrate inhabited, and depth were recorded in each quadrat. The quadrat was then photographed from above in many cases, and coral cover, types, rock present, and other factors were described. Temperature was not recorded, but the general temperature regime is known for those stations near laboratories.

Reference map of localities mentioned in the text with key as follows: 1-Dry Tortugas, 2-Marquesas Keys, 3-Bimini Islands, Bahamas, 4-Grand Bahama Island, 5-Great Abaco Island, 6-Berry Islands (Chub Cay, Whale Cay, Great Stirrup Cay, and others), 7-Eleuthera Island, 8-Little San Salvador, 9-Exuma Chain, 10-San Salvador, 11-Long Island, 12-Crooked Island, 13-Acklins Island, 14-Turks Bank, 15-Hispanola, 16-Caicos Bank, 17-Great Inagua Island, 18-Hogsty Reef, 19-Ragged Island, 20-Cay Sal Bank, 21-Andros Island, 22-Puerto Rico, 23-St. Thomas, 24-St. John, 25-St. Croix, 26-Aves Island, 27-Dominica, 28-Martinique, 29-Barbados, 30-Grenadine Islands, 31-Tobago, 32-Margarita Island, 33-Los Roques, 34-Bonaire, 35-Curacao, 36-Santa Marta, Col., 37-Cartagena, Col., 38-San Blas Islands, 39-Galeta Is., 40-Isla de Providencia, 41-Serranilla Bank, 42-Pedro Bank, 43-Port Royal, Jamaica, 44-Discovery Bay, Jamaica, 45-Grand Cayman Island, 46-Misteriosa Bank, 47-Swan Islands, 48-Glovers Reef, 49-Belize barrier reef, 50-Cozumel.

A second method involved surveys made by swimming. The observer would swim slowly over the bottom inspecting corals and sponges. If any species of *Gobiosoma* or other coral-dwelling fish was noted, the location was checked carefully and the same types of data that were taken in the quadrat survey were recorded. Obviously, no determinations of population density could be made from these data. They are useful, however, in assessing relative abundance of species in one area or depth and numbers of individuals present on individual coral heads and sponges.

At two localities an objective of the field operations was the determination of long term variation in populations. Areas were surveyed periodically (every 6 months for 2 years at Discovery Bay and at a 1 year interval at Curacao) using methods like those used in the quadrat surveys.

Additional observations were made at specific areas to obtain further information on activities such as cleaning behavior or relationships of sponge-dwelling fishes. Normally such observations were made at a distance of several meters from the object of interest. An underwater viewing scope, like that described by Emery (1968), was used on occasion and found to be effective in observing behavior that would be disturbed by the close approach of an observer.

In the laboratory, meristic and morphometric data were recorded. Measurements were made with dial calipers. Gut contents of selected specimens were removed and the identifiable items recorded.

Specimens were utilized from the collections of the University of Miami (UMML) and the Academy of Natural Sciences, Philadelphia (ANSP) and are identified in the *Material Examined* sections of the species accounts by these designations.

Live specimens, returned from numerous localities, were maintained in laboratory aquaria of 20 to 200 liters. The fishes were maintained both as groups of many individuals and as pairs for reproductive purposes. Spawnings of gobies were treated in different ways and are discussed in more detail in the section on larval development. Attempts were made to rear the young of laboratory spawnings. Non-choice hybrid situations, between two fishes of opposite sex and different species, were also maintained in an attempt to induce hybrid spawning.

# TABLE 1

## TYPES OF OBSERVATIONS MADE AT THE LOCALITIES VISITED DURING THE STUDY OF WESTERN NORTH ATLANTIC SPECIES OF *ELACATINUS*

| Area | 1 | 2 | 3 | 4 | 5 | 6 | 7 |
|------|---|---|---|---|---|---|---|
| Florida Keys | X | X | — | X | X | — | X |
| Dry Tortugas | X | X | — | X | X | — | X |
| Marquesas Keys | X | X | — | X | X | — | X |
| Belize barrier reef | X | X | — | X | X | — | X |
| Glovers Reef | X | X | — | X | X | — | X |
| Panama, Galeta Is. and Portobello | X | X | X | X | X | — | X |
| Colombia, Cartagena | X | X | — | X | X | — | — |
| Colombia, Santa Marta | X | X | — | X | X | — | — |
| Misteriosa Bank | X | X | — | X | X | — | — |
| Swan Is. | X | X | — | X | X | — | — |
| Serranilla Bank | X | X | — | X | X | — | — |
| Pedro Bank | X | X | — | X | X | — | — |
| Isla de Providencia | X | X | — | X | X | — | — |
| Discovery Bay, Jamaica | X | X | X | X | X | X | X |
| Port Royal, Jamaica | X | X | — | — | — | — | — |
| St. Thomas, Virgin Islands | X | X | — | — | — | — | — |
| St. Croix, Virgin Islands | X | X | X | X | X | — | X |
| Aves Island, Lesser Antilles | X | X | — | X | X | — | — |
| Barbados | X | X | X | X | X | — | X |
| Curacao | X | X | X | X | X | X | X |
| Bonaire | X | X | — | — | X | — | X |
| S. Bahamas | X | X | X | X | X | — | X |
| N. Bahamas | X | X | X | X | X | — | X |
| Caicos Bank | X | X | — | X | X | — | X |
| Turks Bank | X | X | — | X | X | — | X |

*Key to Types of Observations*

1—General observations of species present and coloration.
2—Notes on substrates inhabited and depth distribution.
3—Quadrat surveys.
4—Photographic documentation of specimens and habitat.
5—Collection of specimens.
6—Long term surveys of populations at specific locations.
7—Detailed observation of certain behavior.

17

# INSTRUCTIONS FOR USE OF THE KEY
# TO WESTERN ATLANTIC SPECIES OF
# *GOBIOSOMA*, SUBGENUS *ELACATINUS*

Certain difficulties may be encountered when attempting to use this key. Live, or fresh dead specimens for which life colors are known, should prove fairly simple to key to species. Problems may arise in using the key to identify preserved specimens.

The snout markings of specimens of *Gobiosoma* are important key characters but are often obscured in preserved specimens by the heavy coat of mucus which turns opaque in preservative. The mucous coating should be carefully scraped away from the area by using a scalpel or similar instrument. Mucus may obscure fin-rays, particularly those of the pectoral fin, and care must be taken in determining their number.

A number of drawings are provided to assist evaluation of certain characters; reference to the figures with the general species accounts may be of additional value.

One method for determining the extent of the connection between the snout and upper lip (rostral frenum) is to move or push the snout with a small probe or forceps. If there is a deep groove between the snout and upper lip, the snout can be moved a small amount without the upper lip moving since they are not closely attached. If there is a rostral frenum present or just a shallow groove present, the upper lip will move in connection with any displacement of the snout.

Some markings may disappear in preservative in some specimens. For example, the oval spot on the snout of large specimens of *G. louisae* may or may not be visible after preservation. Often what was a brightly colored spot in life will be represented by an area of small chromatophores on the snout, black or brown in preservative; after preservation these can often be distinguished from melanophores adjacent to them by difference in size and spacing.

Brooding males of most species become extremely dusky and their markings are often indistinguishable, both in life and in preservative.

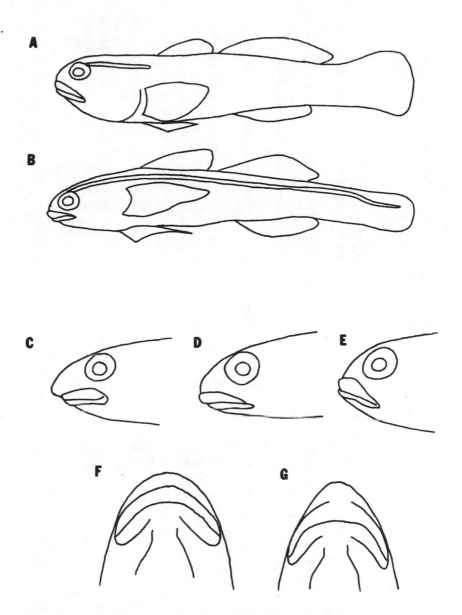

**A-G.** Drawings for use in the key to western North Atlantic species of the subgenus *Elacatinus*.

# KEY TO WESTERN NORTH ATLANTIC OCEAN SPECIES OF THE GENUS *GOBIOSOMA*, SUBGENUS *ELACATINUS*

A. Postocular colored stripe incomplete, not extending caudally beyond the pectoral fin.

  B. Body dark above, paler below, with dark area along caudal peduncle forming squarish basicaudal spot; postocular colored stripe bright yellow, no pale marking on snout .................... *chancei*

  BB. Body and fins uniformly dark slaty gray; postocular stripe yellow in life, yellow medial bar present on snout in life................................................................................. *tenox*

AA. Postocular colored (pale) stripe extending the full length of the body from the eye to the caudal fin base.

  C. Lateral pale stripe continued anterior of the eyes, forming a V on the snout.

    D. Mouth distinctly inferior, particularly in larger specimens, but the snout overhanging the upper lip even in small individuals.

      E. Rostral frenum present connecting snout and upper lip; some smaller specimens may have a slight groove between the lip and snout, but they are still closely connected. Some specimens from the southern Bahamas and possibly other localities, identified with *G. evelynae*, lack the rostral frenum. See species accounts for further information. Color of the lateral stripe in life is yellow, bluish, or bluish white; the color of the V on the snout is yellow or white. ........................................... *evelynae*

      EE. Rostral frenum absent, with upper lip separated from the snout by a deep groove. Lateral stripe white in life and the snout V yellow in life...................................................... *genie*

    DD. Mouth subterminal to terminal in position, snout does not overhang the upper lip. Lateral stripe is bluish white and the snout V white in life. ........................................................ *prochilos*

  CC. Pale marking on mid-snout absent or consisting of an oval spot or a medial bar.

    F. Pale marking on the snout an oval spot or medial bar.

      G. Pale marking on the snout consisting of a medial bar starting near the interorbit and running anteriorly to or near the upper lip. Caudal fin without a distinct oval end of the lateral dark stripe.

**H.** Mouth distinctly inferior. The lateral stripe yellow or blue in life. Medial bar yellow or white in life................................................*illecebrosum*

**HH.** Mouth distinctly subterminal to terminal.

    **I.** Pectoral fin-rays modally 19 (range 18-20), preocular area dark, medial bar starting near minimum interorbital distance and running to about the upper lip. Females with enlarged canines. Lateral stripe and medial bar yellow or white in life..........................*xanthiprora*

    **II.** Pectoral fin-rays modally 17 (range 16-18), preocular area light, medial bar starting near the anterior edge of the eyes. Females without enlarged canines. Lateral stripe and medial bar yellow in life.................................................................*randalli*

  **GG.** Pale marking on the snout consisting of an oval spot particularly evident in life, less so after preservation. Lateral dark stripe ending in a distinct oval on the caudal fin.

    **J.** Pectoral fin-rays usually 16 (range 14-17), lateral pale stripe and snout spot yellow in life.......................................................................................*atronasum*

    **JJ.** Pectoral fin-rays usually 18 (range 17-19), lateral pale stripe yellow, white, or silverish blue; snout spot yellow or white in life..................................................................*louisae*

  **FF.** Pale marking on the mid-snout absent.

    **K.** Mouth distinctly inferior. The lateral pale stripe extending slightly forward of the eyes and blue in life.............................................................................*oceanops*

    **KK.** Mouth terminal in position. Lateral pale stripe does not extend forward of the eyes and is yellow or white in life.................................................................*horsti*

# TABLE 2

## FREQUENCY DISTRIBUTIONS OF FIN-RAY COUNTS FOR WESTERN NORTH ATLANTIC SPECIES OF THE SUBGENUS *Elacatinus*

| | Dorsal Spines | | | Dorsal Rays | | | | | | Anal Rays | | | | | |
|---|---|---|---|---|---|---|---|---|---|---|---|---|---|---|---|
| | 6 | 7 | 8 | 9 | 10 | 11 | 12 | 13 | 14 | 8 | 9 | 10 | 11 | 12 | 13 |
| *Gobiosoma* | | | | | | | | | | | | | | | |
| atronasum ... | — | 30* | — | — | — | 2* | 31 | — | — | — | — | 2* | 28 | 4 | — |
| chancei ... | — | 22* | — | — | — | 10 | 12* | — | — | — | 1 | 20* | 2 | 1 | — |
| evelynae ... | — | 114* | 2 | — | — | 4 | 56 | 5* | — | — | — | — | 47* | 15 | 1 |
| genie ... | — | 30* | — | — | — | 2 | 27* | 1 | — | — | — | — | 25* | 2 | — |
| horsti† ... | — | 39* | — | — | — | 2 | 26* | 11 | — | — | — | 1 | 27* | 10 | — |
| illecebrosum ... | — | 18* | — | — | — | 2 | 16* | — | — | — | — | 1 | 16* | 1 | — |
| louisae ... | — | 20* | — | — | — | 3 | 16* | 1 | — | — | — | 1 | 17* | 2 | — |
| oceanops‡ ... | — | 38 | 1 | — | — | 1 | 19 | 17 | 2 | — | — | 1 | 11 | 20 | 7 |
| prochilos .. | — | 35* | 1 | — | — | 2* | 34 | — | — | — | — | — | 35* | — | — |
| randalli ... | — | 20* | — | — | — | 1 | 17* | — | — | — | — | 1 | 18* | — | — |
| tenox ... | — | 6* | — | — | — | — | 6* | — | — | — | — | 4* | 2 | — | — |
| xanthiprora ... | — | 12* | — | — | — | 5 | 5* | 2 | — | — | — | 1 | 11* | — | — |

| | Pectoral Rays | | | | | | | | |
|---|---|---|---|---|---|---|---|---|---|
| | 13 | 14 | 15 | 16 | 17 | 18 | 19 | 20 | 21 |
| *Gobiosoma* | | | | | | | | | |
| atronasum ... ... ... ... ... | — | 2 | 14 | 47* | 7 | — | — | — | — |
| chancei ... ... ... ... ... | — | — | — | — | — | 12 | 24* | 9 | — |
| evelynae ... ... ... ... ... | — | — | 2 | 55 | 70* | 3 | — | — | — |
| genie ... ... ... ... ... | — | — | — | 21 | 37* | 2 | — | — | — |
| horsti† ... ... ... ... ... | — | — | — | — | 9 | 46 | 20* | 1 | — |
| illecebrosum ... ... ... ... | — | — | — | 7 | 36* | 4 | — | — | — |
| louisae ... ... ... ... ... | — | — | — | 1* | 9 | 28* | 2 | — | — |
| oceanops‡ ... ... ... ... ... | — | 1 | — | 19 | 44 | 11 | 1 | — | — |
| prochilos ... ... ... ... ... | — | — | — | — | 19 | 53* | 14 | — | — |
| randalli ... ... ... ... ... | — | — | — | 2 | 29* | 9 | — | — | — |
| tenox ... ... ... ... ... | — | — | — | — | 3* | 1 | 6 | 2 | — |
| xanthiprora ... ... ... ... | — | — | — | — | 2 | 9 | 9 | 4* | — |

*holotype.

†Does not include counts from Belize material.

‡No additional counts were made since Bohlke and Robins (1968); the counts reported are from their work.

# INTRODUCTION TO GENERAL ACCOUNTS
# OF THE WESTERN ATLANTIC SPECIES OF
# *GOBIOSOMA*, SUBGENUS *ELACATINUS*

On the basis of habitat, the western Atlantic members of *Elacatinus* can be divided into 3 groups, and the species are presented in this section in that order. The first group includes 6 species (*G. oceanops, G. evelynae, G. illecebrosum, G. genie, G. randalli,* and *G. prochilos*) which dwell on living coral heads, on rock surfaces, and occasionally on the outer surface of sponges and share the habit of removing ectoparasites from larger fishes. The second group contains 5 species (*G. horsti, G. chancei, G. xanthiprora, G. tenox* and *G. louisae*) which are associated throughout their life, exclusive of larval stages, with massive and tubular sponges. None engages in parasite removal. The third group consists of a single species, *G. atronasum*, which is a plankton feeder and does not associate with sponges or engage in parasite picking behavior. This species is also found associated with living corals.

Basic information is presented for each of the 12 species, particularly regarding any alterations or additions needed in the systematic descriptions of Bohlke and Robins (1968), geographic and bathymetric distribution, life coloration, general habits, food habits, and reproductive habits. Some species have more than one color form, and in most subsequent discussion the color form concerned is differentiated by a capital letter in parentheses for each color form in the species account.

# GENERAL SPECIES ACCOUNTS

The first six species dealt with form a natural ecological unit in that they are largely coral-dwelling fishes which share the habit of ectoparasite removal.

*Gobiosoma oceanops* (Jordan)                                    Neon goby

The following synonymy includes those references cited by Feddern (1967) and Bohlke and Robins (1968).

> *Gobiosoma oceanops*, Ginsburg, 1933: 2, 19, 21-22; Briggs, 1958: 228; Duarte-Bello, 1959: 123; Hildebrand, Chavez and Compton, 1964: 124; Bohlke and Robins, 1968: 101-103, 148; Robins, 1971: 254; Collette and Talbot, 1972: 123; Valenti, 1972: 477-482; Greenberg, 1972: 95 (color photos: 61-62, 96).
>
> *Elacatinus oceanops* Jordan, 1904: 542, pl. 2, fig. 3; Jordan and Thompson, 1905: 252; Reighard, 1908: 297, 299, 302-303, 309; Longley, 1918: 81; Jordan, Evermann and Clark, 1930: 442; Longley and Hildebrand, 1941: 226; Boyd, 1956: 391-396; Simkatis, 1958: 104, 165-167; Bailey *et al.* 1960: 35; Randall, 1962: 43, 46; Axelrod and Vorderwinkler, 1963: 199, 264-265; Phillips, 1964: 49-51; Schroeder, 1965: 110-112; Eibl-Eibesfeldt, 1967: fig. 1; Starck and Davis, 1966: 340; Starck, 1968: 27; Stephens, 1968: 155-157; Valenti, 1968: 116-117; O'Connell, 1969: 104-105; Axelrod and Emmens, 1969: 354; Faulkner and Smith, 1970: 144 (color photo: 103).
>
> *Elecatinus oceanops*, Herald, 1961: 235, pl. 100; Limbaugh, 1961: 43.
>
> *Lactinus oceanops*, Straughan, 1959: 140-144; Straughan, 1964: 165-169.

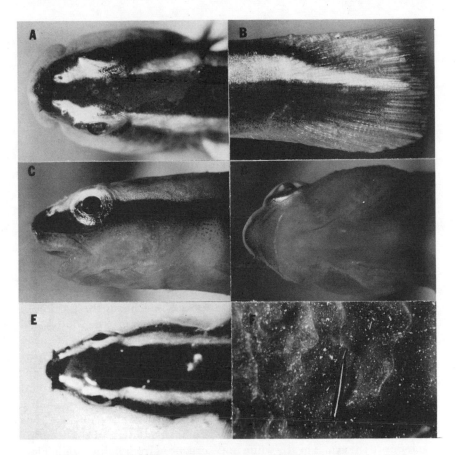

**A.** *Gobiosoma oceanops.* Dorsal view of the head of a female, 30.4 mm S.L. from Florida (anesthetized, UMML 31391).

**B.** *Gobiosoma oceanops.* Lateral view of the caudal fin of a female, 30.4 mm S.L. from Florida (anesthetized, UMML 31391).

**C.** *Gobiosoma oceanops.* Lateral view of the head of a female, 30.4 mm S.L. from Florida (anesthetized, UMML 31391).

**D.** *Gobiosoma oceanops.* Ventral view of the head of a female, 30.4 mm S.L. from Florida (anesthetized, UMML 31391).

**E.** *Gobiosoma oceanops.* Dorsal view of the head of a Bellze specimen.

**F.** *Gobiosoma oceanops.* Specimen at Marquesas Keys, Florida resting on the outer surface of the sponge *Xestospongia muta.*

*Lactinus oceahops*, Fisher, 1955: 36-37, 70; Straughan, 1956: 157.

Possibly *Elacatinus oceanops*, Wickler, 1962: 201-205.

Not *Elacatinus oceanops*, Breder, 1927: 83; Fowler, 1944: 451; Eibl-Eibesfeldt, 1955: 207-209.

Not *Gobiosoma oceanops*, Erdman, 1956: 335.

*Systematics:* This species is the best known western Atlantic member of *Elacatinus*. The fin-ray formula of D VII, 11-14 (usually 12-13); A 10-13 (almost never 10); P 16-19 (usually 16 or 17) need not be modified. Nor is modification needed in the description given by Bohlke and Robins (1968). In young specimens the mouth is more terminal in position than that found in the adults, which have distinctly inferior, shark-like mouths.

*Coloration:* The coloration of *G. oceanops* is basically as described by Bohlke and Robins (1968) and other authors. The pale lateral stripe of preserved specimens is blue in life. In Florida specimens the portion of the colored stripe on the upper surface of the eyeball may be whitish and on the caudal fin may be colorless. The iridescent blue stripe in life gives rise to the common name of the species, neon goby. There is consistent difference in life coloration between individuals from Belize and Florida. Florida individuals have the entire pale area between the dark lateral stripe and the dark dorsal area iridescent blue. Specimens from Belize have the iridescent blue confined to the center half of the pale area, thus appearing as a blue line within a pale stripe. In addition, the pale stripe anterior to the eyes is nearly white in *G. oceanops* from Belize, while Florida specimens have an iridescent blue anterior portion of the stripe.

A number of abnormally patterned individuals of *G. oceanops* from Florida have been observed. Some individuals have one or both lateral stripes with gaps and abrupt deviations in width of the stripe.

**A.** *Gobiosoma oceanops.* Specimens on the coral *Colpophyllia natans*, Florida.

**B.** *Gobiosoma oceanops*. Individual on the coral *Montastrea cavernosa*, Florida.

**C.** *Gobiosoma oceanops*. Lateral view of a live individual from Belize.

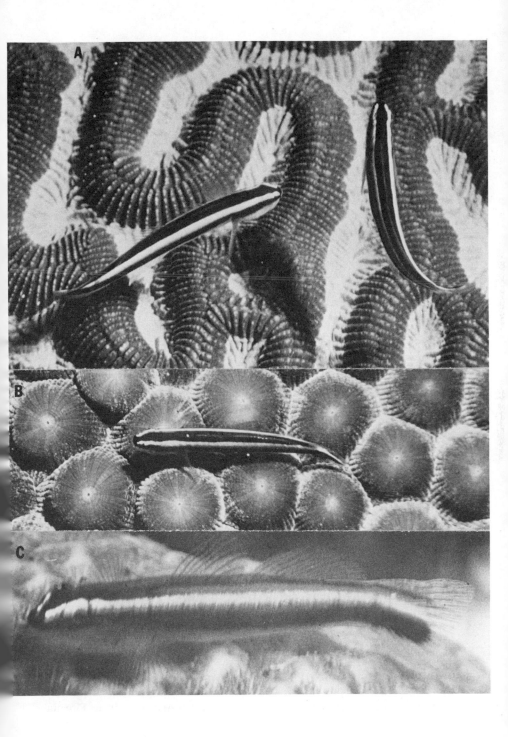

*Distribution: Gobiosoma oceanops* is known from throughout the Florida reef tract north to Broward County; from Alacran Reef, Yucatan (Hildebrand *et al.*, 1964), Belize, and off the Texas coast (C. Cashman, MS). To the south, it has not been collected from off the Honduran coast, Swan Islands, Misteriosa Bank, Rosario Bank, Cuba, or any part of the Bahama Islands. Its known depth distribution is between 1 and 40 m.

*General Habits:* Several authors have discussed the habits of *G. oceanops.* Jordan (1904) recorded the species from coral heads. Longley (1918) and Hildebrand (1941) recorded the parasite-picking activities of the species, and this has been cited by numerous authors including Limbaugh (1961), Feder (1966), and Stephens (1968). Feddern (1967) added some notes on the natural history of *G. oceanops* in a paper describing early larval development of the species. He felt that the spawning season was confined to February through March in Florida waters. Feddern (1967) also recorded the smallest juveniles found on coral heads as about 10 mm S.L. and the maximum size of adults as 34 mm S.L.

The neon goby dwells on living corals and on rock substrates. The species is also occasionally found on the outer surfaces of large sponges. A summary of the species of corals that *G. oceanops* is associated with is presented in a subsequent section.

*Gobiosoma oceanops* has been seen singly and in groups of as many as 20 individuals on a single coral head. On one occasion at Alligator Reef, more than 30 individuals were observed together in a small cave along a ledge at a depth of 8 m.

In Florida waters, *G. oceanops* does not occupy the same range as any other cleaning member of *Elacatinus*, so it is the only cleaning goby in the Florida area. However, in Belize *G. oceanops* is often found on the same coral heads as *G. prochilos*, and the two species will clean the same fish simultaneously. The cleaning activities of *G. oceanops* are discussed in a subsequent section.

Neon gobies are also capable of resting at night associated with expanded corals. The corals are often expanded to such an extent that the tentacles of the polyps cover the fishes and the gobies can be observed only by disturbing the coral so that the polyps contract. Starck and Davis (1966) found *G. oceanops* to be inactive at night on corals and in one case to shelter beneath an expanded serpulid worm. The results of the present study agree with those observations.

*Food Habits:* Nothing has been published regarding the food habits of *G. oceanops.* This is rather surprising because the parasite-removing habits of this species have been known for many years; yet it has never been confirmed in publication that the species eats parasites of fishes, based on stomach contents. The guts of several individuals from Florida

28

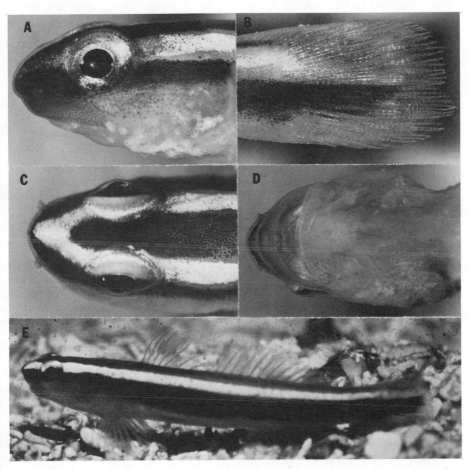

**A.** *Gobiosoma evelynae* (Y). Lateral view of the head of a female, 28.1 mm S.L. from the northern Bahamas (anesthetized, UMML 31407).

**B.** *Gobiosoma evelynae* (Y). Lateral view of the caudal fin of a female, 28.1 mm S.L. from the northern Bahamas (anesthetized, UMML 31407).

**C.** *Gobiosoma evelynae* (Y). Dorsal view of the head of a female, 28.1 mm S.L. from the northern Bahamas (anesthetized, UMML 31407).

**D.** *Gobiosoma evelynae* (Y). Ventral view of the head of a female, 28.1 mm S.L. from the northern Bahamas (anesthetized, UMML 31407).

**E.** *Gobiosoma evelynae* (Y). Lateral view of a specimen (live) from the northern Bahamas.

were examined and found to contain only larval gnathid isopod crustaceans (parasitic) and a few fish scales. The scales were all very small in size and probably ingested accidently.

*Reproductive Habits:* *Gobiosoma oceanops* is the only species of *Elacatinus* for which any definitive information on larval development exists. Numerous popular references on spawning habits have appeared in the aquarium literature, and these are summarized by Feddern (1967) and Bohlke and Robins (1968). Feddern (1967) described the eggs and newly hatched larvae. He briefly described spawning and the general behavior during spawning. Valenti (1972), in a more detailed study, also commented on general spawning behavior and assigned 20 developmental stages to the eggs of *G. oceanops* on the basis of morphology. He compared the reorientation of eggs of *G. oceanops* to that of *Bathygobius soporator* and identified a visible larval xanthophore pigment as sepiaterin.

The neon goby spawns readily in the aquarium and has hybridized with the white form of *G. evelynae* (W) in a non-choice aquarium situation. The male of *G. oceanops* guards the nest after spawning as do the other members of *Elacatinus* for which spawning has been observed. The times of spawning and larval development are considered in a subsequent section.

*Material Examined:* Most material of *G. oceanops* used in the present study was also examined by Bohlke and Robins (1968). Locality data for the Florida specimens examined are included in that earlier paper.

**A.** *Gobiosoma evelynae* (YB). Lateral view of the head of a female, 28.3 mm S.L. from Curacao (anesthetized).

**B.** *Gobiosoma evelynae* (YB). Lateral view of the caudal fin of a female, 28.3 mm S.L. from Curacao (anesthetized).

**C.** *Gobiosoma evelynae* (YB). Dorsal view of the head of a female, 28.3 mm S.L. from Curacao (anesthetized).

**D.** *Gobiosoma evelynae* (YB). Ventral view of the head of a female, 28.3 mm S.L. from Curacao (anesthetized).

**E.** *Gobiosoma evelynae* (YB). Lateral view of a live specimen from Barbados.

**F.** *Gobiosoma evelynae* (YB). Lateral view of a live specimen from the northeastern Bahamas (Bimini).

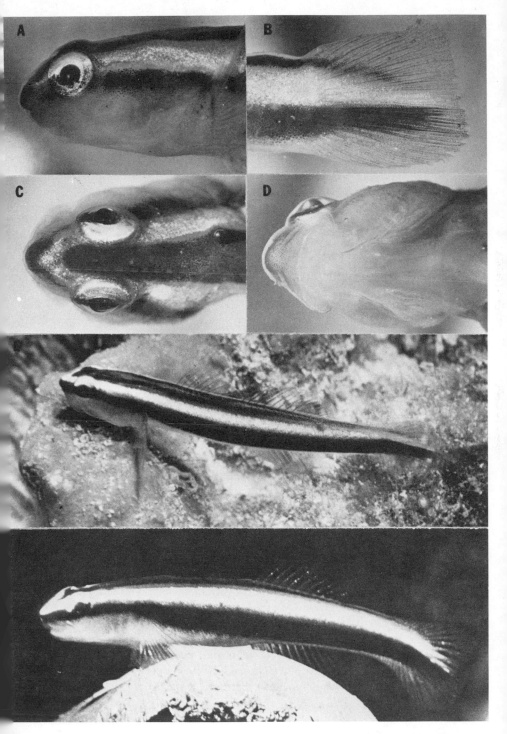

Florida: UMML 2420, 2512, 2644, 2850, 3650, 3857, 3950, 4051, 4255, 5438, 5608, 5832, 6794, 7291, 7369, 8139, 8687, 9235, 10835, 11250, 11799, 13066, 13530, 17985, 18023, 18081, 18252, 18732, 18777, 18827, 18843, 18966, 19086, 19163, 19202, 19392, 19495, 19594, 19677, 19796, 19901, 19916, 20083, 20150 (all data in Bohlke and Robins, 1968), UMML 23475, CRR-F-375; UMML 28488, CRR-F-226.

Belize: UMML 9271; UMML 31141, Queens Cay.


*Gobiosoma evelynae* Bohlke and Robins          Sharknose goby


> *Gobiosoma evelynae* Bohlke and Robins, 1968: 103-109, 112, 116-118, 148; Cervigon, 1968: 212-213; Randall, 1968: 252-253; Bohlke and Chaplin, 1968: 613, plate 34; Dammann, 1969; Colin, 1971: 23; Smith and Tyler, 1972: 131, 133-134, 139-140, 144-145, 153, 159-161, 166, 168, Figs. 141, 161; Collette and Talbot, 1972: 108-109, 112-113, 118-120, 123; Herald, 1972: 208.
>
> Probably *Gobiosoma evelynae,* Randall, 1967: 783-784; Eibl-Eibesfeldt, 1955: 296; Eibl-Eibesfeldt, 1957: 38.
>
> *Gobiosoma genie,* De Lisle, 1969: 1-81.


*Systematics:* The original description of *G. evelynae* must be somewhat modified. In some areas it is difficult to distinguish *G. evelynae* from *G. genie.* Several color forms of *G. evelynae* exist which will be discussed further under the subheading on coloration. Although in the present study these color forms are all grouped under *G. evelynae,* subsequent discussion of the species will in most cases refer also to the particular color form. If further study indicates that these various color forms deserve status as separate taxa, then information in this study may be properly allocated.

The three color forms listed are not separable on the basis of the fin-ray formula, and the fin-ray formula of D VII, 11-13; A 11-13; P 15-18 recorded by Bohlke and Robins (1968) is correct. The three color forms are also inseparable on the basis of morphometry or pigmentary pattern, exclusive of color. Certain individuals, tentatively identified as *G. evelynae,* from Hogsty Reef, Bahamas lack the rostral frenum typical of *G. evelynae* and resemble *G. genie* in this character. However these individuals have the typical color of *G. evelynae* and may represent hybrid forms. These specimens will be discussed in the general account of *G. genie. Gobiosoma evelynae* reaches a standard length of at least 33.2 mm.

Large male individual of *G. oceanops* hovering in front of a small cave it dug beneath the rock. The pointed tip of the genital papilla, a distinguishing sexual character, is clearly visible in this photograph.

*Coloration:* Bohlke and Robins (1968) described the life colors of one form, termed the "yellow form," from color transparencies. They found the colored stripe to be yellow throughout its entire length. They also recorded specimens from Dominica of similar color based on notes by Victor G. Springer. They also noted that other color varieties might exist based on a photograph taken near Bimini, Bahamas of the color form termed "yellow-blue form." Bohlke and Chaplin (1968) illustrated the "yellow form" of *G. evelynae* (plate 34b), but added no further information on life colors. Randall (1968:252-253) described the colored stripe of *G. evelynae* as "on head and anterior part of the body yellow, shading posteriorly to light gray." He does not state the locality from which the specimen(s) were collected to which the color notes refer, but probably they are of the "yellow-blue form."

At present specimens of *G. evelynae* can be referred to one of three color forms based on their life colors. The different color forms have discrete geographic distributions and support the view that they represent discrete stocks. These colors are quickly lost after preservation, and within a few weeks it is impossible to differentiate the color forms. The three color forms are described from notes and color transparencies taken both in the field and in laboratory aquaria.

*Gobiosoma evelynae* (Y) "yellow form" — Described first by Bohlke and Robins (1968) on the basis of material from near Nassau, Bahamas. The V on the snout is broad and bright yellow, the yellow continuing posteriorly to the caudal fin. The yellow of the lateral stripe is slightly less in-

**A.** *Gobiosoma evelynae* (W). Lateral view of the head of a female, 32.7 mm S.L. from Isla de Providencia (anesthetized).

**B.** *Gobiosoma evelynae* (W). Lateral view of the caudal fin of a female, 32.7 mm S.L. from Isla de Providencia (anesthetized).

**C.** *Gobiosoma evelynae* (W). Dorsal view of the head of a female, 32.7 mm S.L. from Isla de Providencia (anesthetized).

**D.** *Gobiosoma evelynae* (W). Ventral view of the head of a female, 32.7 mm S.L. from Isla de Providencia (anesthetized).

**E.** *Gobiosoma evelynae* (W). View of a specimen from Discovery Bay, Jamaica resting on the coral *Siderastrea* sp.

**F.** *Gobiosoma evelynae* (W). View of a specimen from Isla de Providencia resting on the coral *Diploria* sp.

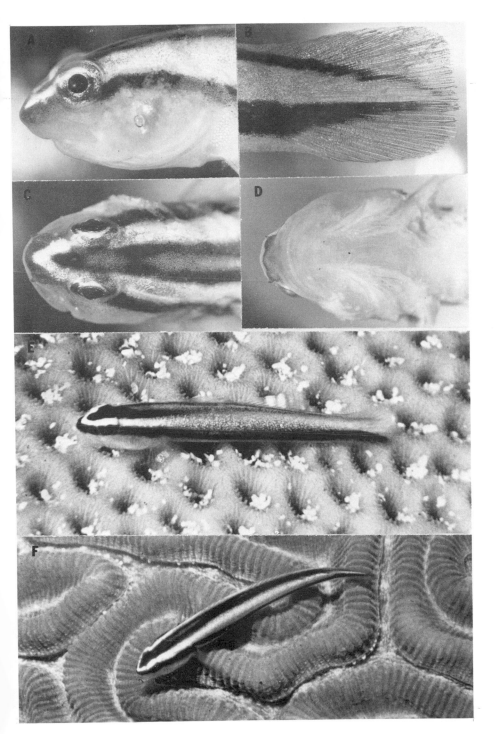

Aquarium photograph of male neon goby, *G. oceanops*, guarding its nest under the overhang of the rock.

Individual of *G. oceanops*, the neon goby, sitting on the outer surface of the sponge *Xestospongia muta,* Cosgrove Light, Florida Keys. While it is unusual for *G. oceanops* to rest on sponges, this does occasionally occur. Other fishes visible include masked gobies, *Coryphopterus personatus*, and a small striped juvenile parrotfish, *Scarus* sp.

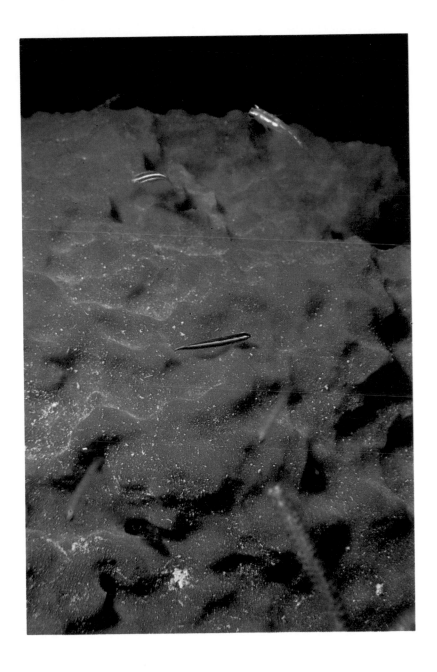

tense in color than that of the snout marking. Bohlke and Robins (1968) recorded the lateral colored stripe as occupying only one third of the width of the pale stripe formed between the dark lateral stripes of the fish. Their description was based on fresh dead material; in life the yellow of the lateral colored stripe occupies the entire area between the dark stripe. The yellow lateral stripe does not narrow or widen along its length. The yellow form of G. evelynae is more restricted in its geographic distribution than the other two color forms.

*Gobiosoma evelynae* (YB) "yellow-blue form" — There is some slight geographic variation in this color form, and individuals from different areas will be described. Individuals from the western Great Bahama Bank have the V marking on the snout bright yellow and fairly broad. In that respect they are nearly identical to the yellow form. In large males the anterior point of the V may be somewhat extended, almost producing an anterior lobe of the V. Between the opercular margin and the pectoral fin the colored stripe begins to change to light iridescent blue in color. Usually the yellow occupies the central portion of the stripe for a short distance posteriorly and the blue chromatophores lie both dorsal and ventral to the yellow chromatophores. The yellow for the colored stripe seldom continues farther posteriorly than the origin of the first dorsal fin. The blue continues posteriorly onto the caudal fin. The colored stripe widens slightly posteriorly, with its widest portion being near the second dorsal fin origin, and the blue occupies most of the area between the dark lateral stripes. An individual from Hogsty Reef in the southern Bahamas is essentially identical to those further north in the Bahamas, but there is some confusion with G. genie in this area. This problem will be discussed further under G. genie.

Individuals of G. evelynae (YB) from Curacao and Bonaire resemble those from the Bahamas. The blue color may not extend as far onto or be as intense on the caudal fin. Specimens from Barbados also closely resemble the Bahamian individuals. The yellow-blue form from Barbados has the yellow extending somewhat farther posteriorly than the first dorsal fin origin. The V on the snout may be slightly narrower than in Bahamian individuals, but there is some individual variation in the width of this marking. Photographs of individuals from Palm Island, Grenadine Islands taken by P. Ehrlich have a broad V on the snout and the yellow reaches posteriorly to about the level of the pectoral fin base. Individuals from Aves Island (west of Guadeloupe) appear identical to those from Barbados in having a slightly narrower V than Bahamian individuals of the yellow-blue form. They also seem to have a slightly narrower postocular portion of the colored stripe, and the blue of the colored stripe may not be quite as intense as in individuals from the Bahamas.

38

Specimens from St. Croix differ somewhat in coloration from specimens from the localities already discussed. The yellow of the V is generally much less intense and in some instances is just barely discernable. The V is also fairly narrow, possibly slightly more so than in individuals from Aves Island and Barbados. The blue portion of the colored stripe is also less intense, and in at least one instance there appeared to be a few yellow chromatophores scattered among the blue chromatophores all the way to the caudal fin. At most, the blue portion of the colored stripe in specimens from St. Croix could be described as pale blue. *National Geographic Magazine* (140(2):266-267) contains color photos of *G. evelynae* (YB) from St. John, Virgin Islands, and these specimens seem more typical of Bahamian or Antillean individuals of *G. evelynae* (YB) than those found in St. Croix.

*Gobiosoma evelynae* (W) "white form" — Colin (1971) recorded specimens of *G. evelynae* (W) from Jamaica having white stripes in life based on color transparencies taken in the field. The "white form" of *G. evelynae* (W) has a fairly wide distribution in the western Caribbean.

Specimens from Jamaica have a narrow V on the snout, noticeably narrower than on *G. evelynae* (Y) or (YB). The V is white in color and continues posteriorly to just past the eyes. The lateral stripe widens considerably, being widest near the second dorsal fin origin and becomes somewhat bluish green. The intensity of this bluish green is variable, and at times the lateral stripe appears mostly dull white. The white of the lateral stripe is always less intense than the white of the V-shaped snout marking. Also the angle at which the lateral stripe is viewed or photographed seems to affect the color observed.

Individuals from Pedro Bank, Serranilla Bank, Swan Island, and Isla de Providencia are apparently identically colored to Jamaican populations. Herald (1972:208) has a color photo of the "white form" of *G. evelynae* (W) also from Isla de Providencia.

*Distribution:* *Gobiosoma evelynae* is known from the Bahamas south through the Lesser Antilles to the islands off Venezuela and from many islands and banks in the western Caribbean. The distribution of the color forms is as follows. *Gobiosoma evelynae* (Y) is known from the Little Bahama Bank (Grand Bahama Island, Great Abaco Island) and from the Nassau area, the Exuma chain, Eleuthera Island, the Berry Islands, and northern Andros Island, all on the Great Bahama Bank. *Gobiosoma evelynae* (YB) is known from the the northwestern Bahamas (Bimini Islands, Sandy Cay, the Berry Islands, and Grand Bahama Island), San Salvador, Acklins Island, Crooked Island, Hogsty Reef, Caicos Bank, Turks Bank, U.S. Virgin Islands (St. Thomas, St. John, and St. Croix), through the Lesser Antilles, Aves Island (west of Guadeloupe), Barbados, and the is-

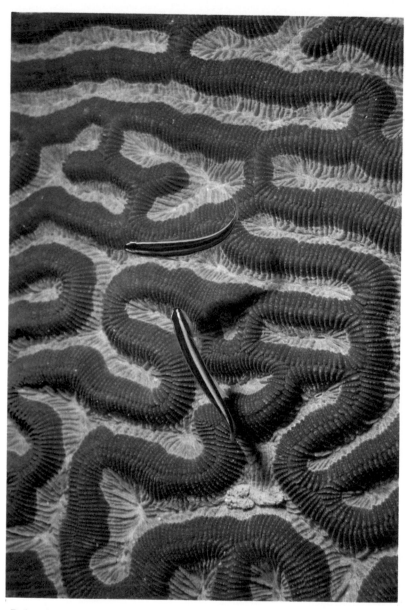

Pair of neon gobies, *G. oceanops*, near the surface of the coral *Colpophyllia natans*, Dry Tortugas, Florida.

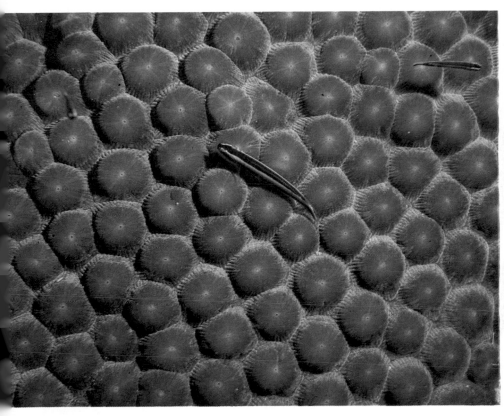

The neon goby, *G. oceanops*, on the coral *Montastrea cavernosa* at Cosgrove Light, Florida Keys. The polyps of this coral are completely retracted as they normally are during the day.

lands off of Venezuela (Isla de Margarita, Los Roques, Bonaire, and Curacao). *Gobiosoma evelynae* (W) is known from Jamaica (Discovery Bay and numerous other localities), the Pedro Banks, Serranilla Bank, Swan Island, and Isla de Providencia.

The affinities of Haitian specimens of *G. evelynae* are unknown since no life color notes are available. *Gobiosoma evelynae* has never been collected along the continental coast of North, Central, or South America. Bohlke and Robins (1968) stated that the species was unknown from Cuba or the Cayman Islands. It, or a closely related form, may occur in these areas and more comments are included in the present study under the discussion of *G. genie*. *Gobiosoma evelynae* has not been collected at a few islands and banks of the western Caribbean (Courtown Cays, Banco Chinchorro, Misteriosa Bank) where its close relative *G. illecebrosum* has been collected. Different color forms of *G. evelynae* have been collected together at a few localities. The yellow form and the yellow-blue form have been found together at the Berry Islands and recently Grand Bahama Island. The situation is unclear, but possibly interbreeding of these color varieties is occurring. These problems are discussed further in subsequent sections.

The known depth distribution of the species is between 1 and 50 m. The lower depth limit of the species is probably determined by the lower limit of reef coral growth.

*General Habits: Gobiosoma evelynae* is a coral inhabiting, parasite-removing member of *Elacatinus* as noted by Bohlke and Robins (1968). Randall (1968) briefly described cleaning behavior of this species. Collette and Talbot (1972) listed 14 species of fishes cleaned by *G. evelynae* at St. John, Virgin Islands and stated that the species occurred most often in pairs. Smith and Tyler (1972) felt *G. evelynae* was the most important cleaner on the reef they studied. They found that *G. evelynae* cleans from first light at dawn to sunset, and they listed seven species cleaned. They also recorded *G. evelynae* as retiring into reef crevices near sunset and emerging at dawn.

All three forms are occasionally found on the outer surface of living sponges or on rock surfaces, and there are no differences in behavior or in substrates inhabited. The fishes are, however, most common on corals, either singly or in groups of up to at least 19 individuals on a single head. All three forms are capable of sheltering at night beneath the expanded polyps of several species of corals, but this is apparently not an obligate relationship. Fewer individuals of *G. evelynae* were found at night on coral heads than were found there during the preceding day, and it is unknown whether the missing individuals were within reef crevices or moved to nearby coral heads for the night.

Other coral-dwelling gobies occupy the same coral heads as *G. evelynae*. Smith and Tyler (1972) recorded *G. saucrum* inhabiting the same coral heads as *G. evelynae* (YB). *Gobiosoma prochilos* occurs with *G. evelynae* (YB) and (W), while *G. genie* occurs with *G. evelynae* (Y) and (YB). *Gobiosoma randalli* inhabits the same heads as *G. evelynae* (YB), and *Coryphopterus lipernes* occurs with all three color forms. Relationships between these species are discussed further in later sections.

Some authors have suggested that the cleaning behavior of *G. evelynae* imparts an immunity from predation to it (De Lisle, 1969; Darcy *et al.*, 1974). There is some evidence that *G. evelynae* (YB) may be distasteful to predators; any assumption that its cleaning is responsible for immunity from predation should be avoided until adequate experimental evidence is available.

*Food Habits:* *Gobiosoma evelynae* is the only species of *Elacatinus* for which published food habit information exists. Randall (1967:783-784) examined 4 specimens of what is almost surely *G. evelynae* (YB) and found only one specimen with food in the gut. It contained only larval gnathiid isopod crustaceans, important parasites of reef fishes. Several specimens were examined in the present study and confirm Randall's results. A few small fish scales were also found in the gut and probably were accidently ingested.

*Reproductive Habits:* Smith and Tyler (1972) found 1 ripe individual (25.9 mm S.L.), having 321 eggs in its two ovaries, in 4 female *G. evelynae* (YB) taken in October at St. John, Virgin Islands. In the present study, spawning has not been observed in the field, but the species spawns readily in laboratory aquaria. In aquaria it spawns in plastic tubes and on undersurfaces of rocks. *Gobiosoma evelynae* (W) has also hybridized with *G. genie* and *G. oceanops* in aquaria. The eggs and larval development of *G. evelynae* are discussed further in a subsequent section.

*Material Examined:* Unless otherwise noted all collections are by P.L. Colin.

*Gobiosoma evelynae* (Y), "yellow form": UMML 29822 (1, 19.5), Berry Islands, Chub Cay, Diamond Rocks, 25 m, PLC-B-30, 9 March 1971; UMML 28848, (1, 26.9), same as above; UMML 29823 (2, 21.6-30.4), same as above; uncat., (1, 26.3), Grand Bahama Is., 15 m, PLC-B-66, 5 April 1973; uncat. (1, 23.4), Grand Bahama Is., 12 miles east of Freeport, 20 m, PLC-B-34, 10 Dec. 1971; uncat. (1, 28.4), Eleuthera Is., South end near Miller Anchorage, 23 m, PLC-B-37, 13 Dec. 1971.

*Gobiosoma evelynae* (YB), "yellow blue form": Bahamas: UMML 28483 (3, 29.7-35.8) Bimini Islands, Turtle Rocks, 10 m, PLC-B-18, 17 June 1970; UMML 28844 (1, 31.0), same as above, PLC-B-21, 8 Dec. 1970; UMML 31092 (2, 27.6-37.8), same as above, spawning pair maintained

Reef cave at 8 m (27 feet) depth, Alligator Reef, Florida Keys, with a number of *G. oceanops* clinging to the ceiling of the cave. Also visible are two cardinalfish, *Apogon maculatus*, and a number of small mysid shrimps hovering in mid-cave.

Young individual of *G. oceanops* on the coral *Montastrea cavernosa*, Florida Keys.

in aquaria, PLC-B-21; UMML 31100 (1, 26.2), Hogsty Reef, 22 m, PLC-B-46, 10 April 1972; Puerto Rico: UMML 30364 (1, 23.1), La Parguera, 18°58.4'N., 67°2.8'W., 5 June 1965; TABL; St. Croix: UMML 30358 (8, 19.7-28.3), Tague Bay back reef, 3 m, 29 Feb. 1972, J. Burnett-Herkes; uncat. (3, 14.6-28.0) same as above, 10 m, PLC,C-37, 5 June 1972; Lesser Antilles: UMML 30365 (2, 28.3-29.5), Guadeloupe, 16°12.2'N., 61°21.3'W., P-916, 11 July 1966, R/V Pillsbury; UMML 31094 (8, 15.7-28.3), Aves Island, west side, 10 m, GS-53, 12 Aug. 1972, Staiger and Colin from R/V Gilliss; UMML 31089 (13, 33.3-23.9), Barbados, St. James, 13 m, PLC-C-20b, 15 July 1972; UMML 31090 (4, 13.4-20.6), same as above, PLC-C-21, 20 July 1972; UMML 31093 (2, 22.6-28.5), Barbados, off Bellairs Research Inst., 1-5 m, PLC-C-22, 20 July 1972. Netherland Antilles: UMML 29762 (2, 15.6-22.6), Curacao, south shore, about 1 km west of Piscadera Baai, 8 m, PLC-C-1, 30 June 1971; UMML 31097 (1, 31.2), same as above, 10 m, PLC-C-33, 7 Aug. 1972; uncat. (1, 28.3) same as above, PLC-C-6, 9 July 1971; UMML 31096 (2, 18.2-19.4), Bonaire, Bachelors Beach, 10-20 m, PLC-C-30, 3 Aug. 1972.

*Gobiosoma evelynae* (W), "white form": Jamaica: all collections from the fore reef, Discovery Bay unless otherwise noted; UMML 30706 (2, 25.2-25.6), 15 m, RIP preserved, PLC-J-68, 4 July 1972; UMML 28337 (2, 17.7-20.0), 23 m, PLC-J-15, 28 Aug. 1970; UMML 28850 (1, 22.6), 25 m, PLC-J-23, 17 Feb. 1971; UMML 28383 (1, 18.5), 15 m, PLC-J-1, 8 July 1970; UMML 31099 (1, 13.8), 23 m, PLC-J-65, 2 July 1972; UMML 31098 (1, 11.2), 30 m, PLC-J-66, 2 July 1972; UMML 31091 (1, 21.2), 23 m, PLC-J-57, 24 June 1972; UMML 29761 (1, 19.7), 8 m, PLC-J-22, 16 Feb. 1971; Pedro Bank: UMML 29754 (2, 17.4-18.9), Northeast Cay, west side, 9 m, PLC-C-19, 5 Oct. 1971; Serranilla Bank: UMML 29846 (1, 26.0), 15 m, PLC-C-18, 4 Oct. 1971; UMML 30703 (4, 11.3-23.1), 15 m, PLC-C-17, 4 Oct. 1971; Swan Islands: UMML 29749 (9, 13.4-22.0), Great Swan Island, west side, 10 m, PLC-C-16, 2 Oct. 1971; Isla de Providencia: UMML 29275 (4, 10.5-18.3), 13°31.23'N., 81°20.46'W., 3 m, P-1349, 30 Jan. 1971, R/V Pillsbury; UMML 30704 (1, 33.2), same as above, PLC-C-36, 30 Jan. 1971; UMML 29286 (1, 26.7), 13°31.55'N., 81°20.55'W., 2 m, P-1350, 30 Jan. 1971, R/V Pillsbury.

*Gobiosoma illecebrosum* Bohlke and Robins

*Gobiosoma illecebrosum* Bohlke and Robins, 1968: 114-118, 148; Palacio, 1972: 90-91; Bohlke and McCosker, 1973: 609-610.

*Systematics:* Several additional collections are available beyond the material used by Bohlke and Robins (1968) in the original description. Additional material makes it necessary to modify the fin-ray formula slightly to D VII, 12; A 11-12 (usually 11); P 16-18 (usually 17). The largest specimen examined was 34.7 mm S.L.

*Coloration:* Bohlke and Robins (1968) included no information on life colors of *G. illecebrosum*. Palacio (1972) reported on observations that the colored stripe of *G. illecebrosum* was yellow in life in Panamanian specimens. He reported that Colombian specimens have a white bar on the snout and a blue lateral stripe that becomes whitish anteriorly at about the level of the opercular margin.

Bohlke and McCosker (1973) described the life colors of *G. illecebrosum* from Panama and Cozumel. They reported the snout marking and lateral colored stripe to be yellow with fine dark puncticulations in Panamanian specimens; specimens from Cozumel Island, Yucatan have the lateral stripe and snout marking white.

The three known color forms of *G. illecebrosum* are inseparable on the basis of meristic characters, morphometry, and pigmentary pattern. In the present study they are considered the same species, but often in the text will be differentiated by a capital letter in parentheses following the scientific name. The "yellow form" will be referred to as *G. illecebrosum* (Y), while the "blue form" and "white form" will be referred to as *G. illecebrosum* (B) and *G. illecebrosum* (W), respectively.

In the "yellow form" and "blue form" of *G. illecebrosum*, the colored stripe occupies only about one half to one third of the pale area between the dark stripes. The colored stripe is centrally located in the pale area and varies little in width throughout its length. The pale area, however, varies in width and is widest near the origin of the second dorsal fin.

Individuals of *G. illecebrosum* collected and observed at Misteriosa Bank appeared identical in coloration to the blue form of *G. illecebrosum*. The life colors of specimens from other localities (Yucatan, Courtown Cays) are unknown.

*Distribution: Gobiosoma illecebrosum* is known from the Caribbean coast of Panama and Colombia and from a few banks and islands of the western Caribbean. *Gobiosoma illecebrosum* (Y) has been collected from numerous localities along the Panama coast and the San Blas Islands.

A male *Gobiosoma oceanops* in the aquarium preparing a site (a plastic tube) for spawning. Sand is removed from the inside of the tube by mouth and expelled outside the opening.

Male *G. oceanops* guarding its nest in the tube after spawning. The male leaves this position every minute or so to agitate the eggs attached to the side or roof of the tube.

Female *G. oceanops* stationed near the entrance of a tube in which spawning will take place. The male, inside the tube, is completing preparation of the spawning site.

The blue form, G. *illecebrosum* (B), is known from Colombia (Cartagena, Islas del Rosario, Santa Marta) and Misteriosa Bank in the northwestern Caribbean. Additional records include the white form, G. *illecebrosum* (W), from Cozumel and fish of unspecified coloration from Banco Chinchorro and Courtown Cays in the western Caribbean. The known depth distribution is between 2 and 45 m.

*General Habits:* Gobiosoma illecebrosum is a coral-dwelling, cleaning member of *Elacatinus*. One to several individuals have been found on a single coral head. Individuals have been observed on rock substrate, and J. McCosker (pers. comm.) once observed a large pair of G. *illecebrosum* (Y) (ANSP 119227) on mangrove roots in Panama. The corals inhabited by G. *illecebrosum* are discussed in a subsequent section. Species of fish often found on the same coral heads as G. *illecebrosum* include *Gobiosoma* (*Tigrigobius*) *saucrum* and the hole-dwelling clinid *Acanthemblemaria rivasi*. Interestingly, no other species of *Elacatinus* engaging in cleaning behavior has been seen or collected with G. *illecebrosum*.

The cleaning behavior of G. *illecebrosum* has been briefly described by Bohlke and McCosker (1973). Palacio (1972) stated that G. *illecebrosum* (B) was the dominant cleaning goby of the Colombian coast. *Gobiosoma illecebrosum* does clean a wide variety of fishes, and this is dealt with in a subsequent section.

At night, individuals of G. *illecebrosum* (Y) are found sheltering on coral heads like other coral-dwelling species of *Gobiosoma*. The same coral heads are occupied at night as during the day, but it is unknown whether the same individuals shelter on the coral head at night. The nocturnal color pattern is much paler than during the day, but the color of the anterior portion of the lateral stripe is still faintly visible.

*Food Habits:* Five specimens of G. *illecebrosum* (Y) were examined for gut contents and found to contain only crustacean parasites, probably removed from fishes cleaned.

*Reproductive Habits:* Little is known of the reproductive habits of G. *illecebrosum*. Ripe females were observed in the field during Sept. 1971 off both Panama and Colombia and in Oct. 1971 at Misteriosa Bank. Such individuals are easily identified by their swollen abdomens and occasionally visible ovaries. No spawning was observed in the field and the species has not spawned in the aquarium.

**A.** *Gobiosoma illecebrosum* (Y). Lateral view of the head of a male, 34.0 mm S.L. from Galeta Island, Panama (anesthetized, UMML 31394).

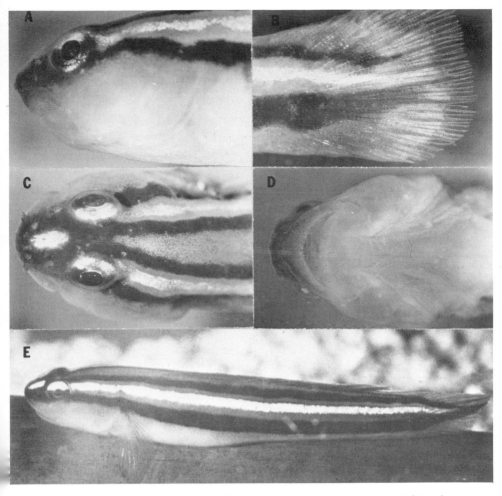

**B.** *Gobiosoma illecebrosum* (Y). Lateral view of the caudal fin of a male, 34.0 mm S.L. from Galeta Island, Panama (anesthetized, UMML 31394).

**C.** *Gobiosoma illecebrosum* (Y). Dorsal view of the head of a male, 34.0 mm S.L. from Galeta Island, Panama (anesthetized, UMML 31394).

**D.** *Gobiosoma illecebrosum* (Y). Ventral view of the head of a male, 34.0 mm S.L. from Galeta Island, Panama (anesthetized, UMML 31394).

**E.** *Gobiosoma illecebrosum* (Y). Lateral view of a live specimen from Galeta Island, Panama.

51

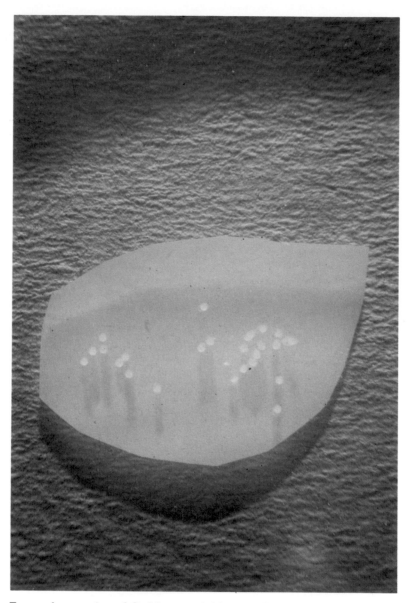

Eggs of a species of *Gobiosoma* laid on a piece of polyester drafting film. Only about 24 eggs are present in this small spawning, but the convenience of handling eggs, previously laid on the film which had been rolled up in a plastic tube, is obvious.

Newly metamorphosed individual of *G. oceanops*, Cosgrove Light, Florida Keys, associating with the coral *Siderastrea* sp. The iridescent blue stripe is still poorly developed in this specimen probably less than one week after metamorphosis.

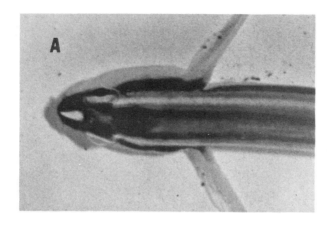

**A.** *Gobiosoma illecebrosum* (B). Dorsal view of the head of a specimen from Cartagena, Colombia.

**B.** *Gobiosoma illecebrosum* (B). Live specimen resting on the coral *Colpophyllia natans* at Islas Rosarios, Colombia. Photo by Carl Roessler.

*Material Examined:*
*Gobiosoma illecebrosum* (B), "blue form": all collections from Colombia by F.J. Palacio and P.L. Colin; UMML 29938 (1, 18.0), Castillo San Fernando, Boca Chica, Cartagena, 20 m, FJP-C-1, 30 Aug. 1971; UMML 30031 (1, 21.0), Banco de Salmedina, Cartagena, 30 m, FJP-C-2, 31 Aug. 1971; UMML 29969 (1, 19.0), Isla Tierra Bomba, 15 m, FJP-C-3, 1 Sept. 1971; UMML 29911 (2, 15.7-20.5), Islas del Rosario, north reef, 20 m, FJP-C-5, 5 Sept. 1971; UMML 29986 (1, 26.0), Islas del Tesoro, 20 m, FJP-C-8, 6 Sept. 1971; UMML 29941 (1, 16.5), Punta de Betin, Santa Marta, 15 m, FJP-C-9, 13 Sept. 1971; UMML 30028 (1, 30.2) same as above, 30 m, FJP-C-10, 14 Sept. 1971; UMML 30034 (19, 12.0-30.2) same as above, 25 m, FJP-C-11, 15 Sept. 1971; UMML 30356 (1, 24.4) Misteriosa Bank, PLC-C-15.
*Gobiosoma illecebrosum* (Y), "yellow form": UMML 29768 (12, 15.0-25.1), Portobello, mouth of the bay, west side, 4-10 m, PLC-C-14, 18 Sept. 1971; ANSP 119227 (2, 28.6-31.9), Bocas del Toro, from mangrove roots, J. McCosker; ANSP 119178; ANSP 119242; ANSP 119239; ANSP 119239; ANSP 119232.
*Gobiosoma illecebrosum* (W), "white form": ANSP 117035 (1, 34.7), Cozumel, Mexico, C. Chaplin.

### *Gobiosoma genie* Bohlke and Robins      Cleaning goby

*Gobiosoma genie* Bohlke and Robins, 1968: 109-114, 116-118,
 148; Bohlke and Chaplin, 1968: 614-615; Faulkner and
 Smith, 1970: 46.
*Elacatinus oceanops*, Breder, 1927: 83 (probably this species);
 Fowler, 1944: 451; Feder, 1966: 342-343, 360 (probably
 this species).
Not *Gobiosoma genie*, De Lisle, 1969: 1-81.

*Systematics:* The systematics of *Gobiosoma genie* are somewhat confused, particularly regarding its distinction from *G. evelynae* in certain areas. At present insufficient material with detailed color notes is available to resolve these problems, but the present discussion should be helpful.

 In the northern Bahamas *G. genie* and *G. evelynae* are quite distinct. In this area *G. evelynae* possesses a definite rostral frenum which *G. genie* lacks, and the two species are sufficiently different in coloration that field identifications can be easily made.

 In the southern Bahamas and perhaps other areas the distinctions between the species are not clear. A series of specimens from Hogsty Reef,

Three individuals of *Gobiosoma oceanops* cleaning parasites from a large green moray, *Gymnothorax moringua*, at Cosgrove Light, Florida Keys (depth 13 m).

Neon goby, *G. oceanops*, inspecting a hand held motionless near cleaning station, Cosgrove Light, Florida Keys (13 m depth).

*Gobiosoma oceanops* in an aquarium resting on the Indo-Pacific organ-pipe coral, *Tubipora musica*. Photo by Douglas Faulkner.

Bahamas for which color transparencies in life were taken is most revealing. One individual possesses a definite rostral frenum and had typical coloration of *G. evelynae* (YB). This specimen was identified as *G. evelynae* (YB) without hesitation. A second individual lacks the rostral frenum; its coloration was like that of northern Bahamian specimens of *G. genie*. A third collection of 2 specimens also lacked the rostral frenum like *G. genie*, but was colored exactly like *G. evelynae* (YB). What these intermediate forms represent is not presently known. They could be hybrid offspring of the two species concerned. They may represent a different form of either *G. genie* or *G. evelynae* that has previously always been identified as *G. genie* since its life colors, similar to *G. evelynae,* were unknown. *Gobiosoma evelynae* is more complex than originally thought, with at least three color forms, and may represent a complex of species presently inseparable on the basis of preserved material. A similar situation may exist for *G. genie*, and the *G. genie* and *G. evelynae* species groups may represent a single complex. In the present discussion, information referred to *G. genie* will deal only with material from the northern Bahamas where there is no doubting its identity. It is not necessary to modify the fin-ray formula presented by Bohlke and Robins (1968) of D VII, 11-12 (usually 12); A 11-12 (usually 11); P 16-18 (rarely 18). The species reaches at least 36 mm S.L. and the smallest known juvenile is 9.3 mm S.L.

*Coloration:* Bohlke and Robins (1968) described the life colors of *G. genie* from transparencies of aquarium specimens. Bohlke and Chaplin (1968: 614) also described the life colors, stating "the V on the snout, the upper half of the eye, and the pale stripe for a distance behind the eye are all bright yellow, fading out posteriorly".

The V on the snout and the anterior portion of the lateral stripe are bright yellow in life. Normally the stripe is yellow no further posteriorly than the opercular margin, where it becomes whitish. The yellow V on the snout is much narrower than that found on Bahamian individuals of *G. evelynae* (Y) and (YB). The pale lateral stripe widens considerably and is widest near the second dorsal fin origin. The pale color of the lateral stripe does not reach to the caudal fin margin, which is transparent.

*Distribution:* *Gobiosoma genie* is known from the Bahamas and Grand Cayman Island. There is some confusion regarding the systematic status of the population in the southern Bahamas and possibly in the Cayman Islands. Therefore, the distribution listed for *G. genie* should be regarded as tentative. The known depth distribution of *G. genie* is between 1 and 30 m.

*General Habits:* *Gobiosoma genie* often inhabits living coral heads and engages in cleaning behavior. The corals inhabited by *G. genie* are

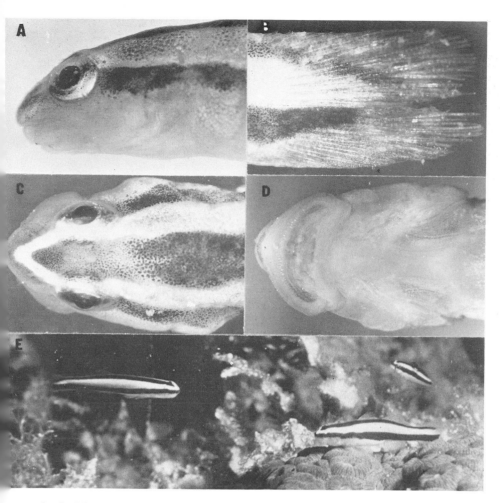

**A.** *Gobiosoma genie.* Lateral view of the head of a female, 32.9 mm S.L. from the northern Bahamas (anesthetized, UMML 31396).

**B.** *Gobiosoma genie.* Lateral view of the caudal fin of a female, 32.9 mm S.L. from the northern Bahamas (anesthetized, UMML 31396).

**C.** *Gobiosoma genie.* Dorsal view of the head of a female, 32.9 mm S.L. from the northern Bahamas (anesthetized, UMML 31396).

**D.** *Gobiosoma genie.* Ventral view of the head of a female, 32.9 mm S.L. from the northern Bahamas (anesthetized, UMML 31396).

**E.** *Gobiosoma genie.* Two individuals in life in the northern Bahamas. A young *Thalassoma bifasciatum,* which bears a resemblance to *G. genie*, is in the upper right corner.

Individual of *G. evelynae* (YB) on the coral *Montastrea cavernosa*. The transition from yellow to blue in the lateral stripe is clearly shown. Photo by Carl Roessler.

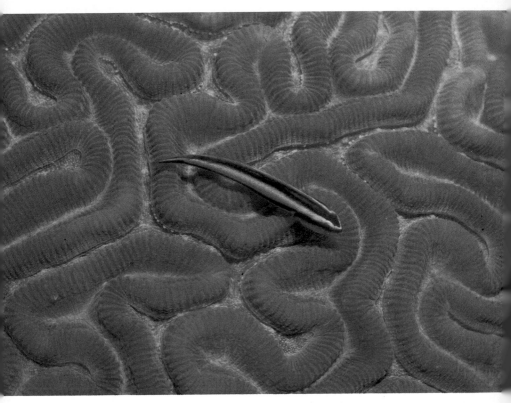

Individual of *G. evelynae* (W) from Isla de Providencia on the coral *Diploria strigosa*. The white color of the snout which becomes bluish-white laterally, is clearly visible.

Specimen of *G. evelynae* (YB) from Barbados resting on a rock substrate. This individual has the yellow of the lateral stripe extending somewhat further posteriorly than most specimens and there appears to be some slight geographic variation in the extent of the yellow chromatophores.

discussed in a subsequent section. The goby is also found on rock substrates, often under ledges, and on the outer surfaces of sponges. It has been observed on sponges inhabited by G. *horsti* (Y) and on corals inhabited by G. *evelynae* (Y) and (YB). Generally, G. *genie* is found in shallower water than G. *evelynae.*

*Gobiosoma genie* has been observed to clean a number of other species of fishes. It coexists with G. *evelynae* and both species sometimes clean the same fish.

At night, at least some individuals of G. *genie* shelter on corals like other coral-dwelling members of *Gobiosoma.* Individuals of G. *genie* from the northern Bahamas have well developed swim bladders, which are lacking in most other species of *Elacatinus.*

*Food Habits:* No published information exists on the food habits of G. *genie.* During the present study nearly all collected specimens of G. *genie* were retained alive for some period and could not be used for gut analysis. The guts of two Bahamian specimens were examined and found to be empty.

*Reproductive Habits:* Spawning by G. *genie* has not been observed in the field, but the species spawns readily in the aquarium. When brooding, males of G. *genie* are very dusky, as is typical for all species of *Elacatinus* that have spawned in aquaria.

In one case, G. *genie* hybridized with G. *evelynae* (W). The eggs hatched and the larvae lived for several days, but no attempt was made to rear them. The reproductive habits of G. *genie* are discussed in a subsequent section.

**A.** *Gobiosoma genie.* Two individuals approaching the photographer to engage in cleaning behavior.

**B.** *Gobiosoma genie.* An individual resting on the coral *Colpophyllia natans*, northern Bahamas.

**C.** *Gobiosoma genie.* Specimens resting at night on the coral *Montastrea cavernosa*, aquarium photograph.

Individual of *G. evelynae* on a coral of the genus *Agaricia*. While not unknown, the coral-dwelling members of *Gobiosoma* associate with *Agaricia* much less than with many other Atlantic reef corals.

*Gobiosoma evelynae* (YB) on coral head, *Colpophyllia natans*. Visible in the background is the blackcap basslet, *Gramma melacara*. Photographed at Landrail Point, Crooked Island, Bahamas, 20 m (66 feet) depth.

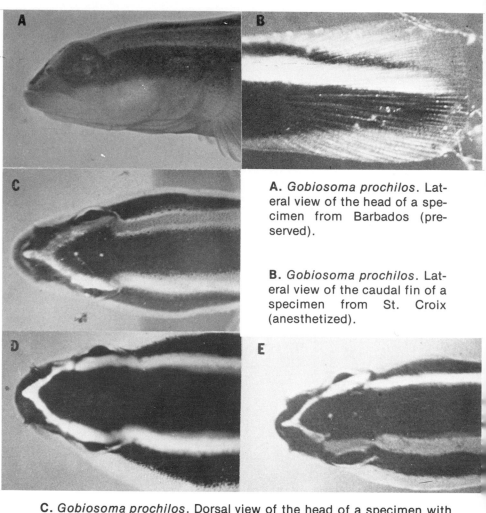

A. *Gobiosoma prochilos*. Lateral view of the head of a specimen from Barbados (preserved).

B. *Gobiosoma prochilos*. Lateral view of the caudal fin of a specimen from St. Croix (anesthetized).

C. *Gobiosoma prochilos*. Dorsal view of the head of a specimen with an elongated anterior lobe of the snout V, Barbados (anesthetized).

D. *Gobiosoma prochilos*. Dorsal view of the head of a specimen without an elongated anterior lobe of the snout V, St. Croix (anesthetized).

E. *Gobiosoma prochilos*. Dorsal view of the head of a specimen with a narrow snout V, Barbados (anesthetized).

*Material Examined:* Bahamas: UMML 28845 (1, 26.5), Chub Cay, south side, 8 m, PLC-B-28, 8 March 1971; UMML 29085 (1, 29.8), Cay Sal Bank, SW shore Cotton Cay, L.R. Rivas, Nov. 1949; UMML 31101 (1, 28.1), Hogsty Reef, NW Cay, 3 m, PLC-B-45-2, 10 April 1972; UMML 31102 (1, 23.0) same as above, 30 m, PLC-B-44, 10 April 1972; uncat., same as above, PLC-B-45-1.

## *Gobiosoma prochilos* Bohlke and Robins

*Gobiosoma prochilos* Bohlke and Robins, 1968: 97-101, 117, 148; Colin, 1971: 23.
*Gobiosoma horsti,* Caldwell, 1966: 70.

*Systematics:* The original description of *G. prochilos* by Bohlke and Robins (1968) needs only minor modifications. The fin-ray formula of D VII, 11-12 (usually 12); A 11; P 17-19 (modally 18) needs only to be modified by the occurrence of one individual with VIII dorsal spines, an unusual but not unique occurrence in the subgenus. The figure of *G. prochilos* in the original description (:98) shows only 9 anal rays in the holotype, but the text and table of fin-ray counts indicate this number should be 11. The species reaches a length of 27.4 mm S.L.

*Coloration:* Bohlke and Robins (1968) did not have any information regarding the life colors of *G. prochilos.* The species has only one color pattern, only slightly variable, throughout its fairly extensive range. The colored V on the snout is always white on specimens from Belize, Jamaica, St. Croix, and Barbados. There is some variation in the shape and width of the snout marking among different localities and among individuals at one locality. Often individuals have an anterior extension at the apex of the V. Other individuals from the same locality may not have any anterior extension of the V. The lateral portion of the colored stripe is white to bluish white and widens only slightly posteriorly. The coloration of *G. prochilos* most closely resembles that of the white form of *G. evelynae* (W). In *G. prochilos* the lateral stripe and V are narrower than in *G. evelynae* (W) and the mouth is subterminal in position in *G. prochilos,* rather than inferior as in *G. evelynae.*

*Distribution: Gobiosoma prochilos* is known from the Lesser Antilles, Barbados, St. Croix, Jamaica, Belize, Yucatan, and possibly the northern Gulf of Mexico (Cashman, MS). The known depth distribution of the species is from 1 to 34 m.

*General Habits: Gobiosoma prochilos* dwells most often on the surfaces of living corals and sponges and also engages in cleaning behavior.

*Gobiosoma evelynae* (YB) on the coral *Siderastrea* sp. Photo by Carl Roessler.

*Gobiosoma evelynae* (Y) resting on the coral *Colpophyllia natans* at Eleuthera Island, Exuma Sound, Bahamas, 21 m (70 feet) depth.

*Gobiosoma evelynae* (W) on the coral *Siderastrea,* Discovery Bay, Jamaica, 12 m.

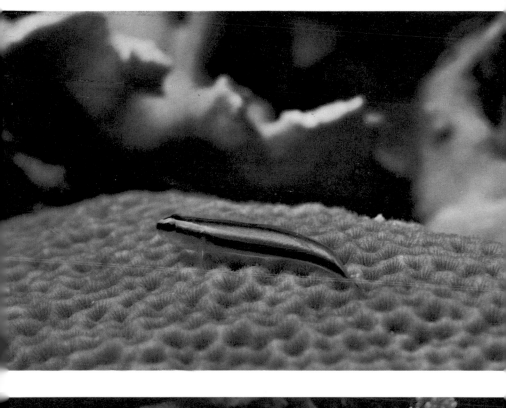

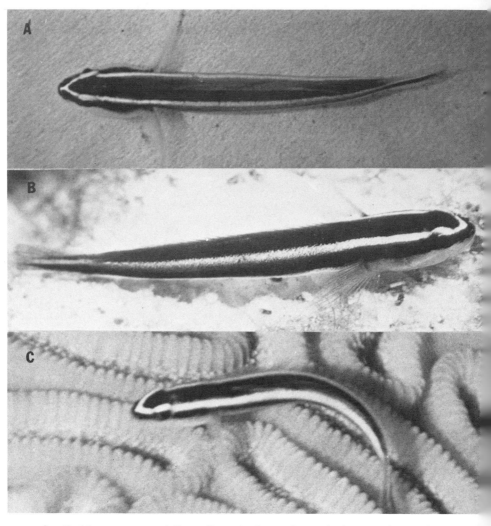

**A.** *Gobiosoma prochilos*. Dorsal view of a whole specimen from Belize.

**B.** *Gobiosoma prochilos*. Dorso-lateral view of a specimen from Barbados.

**C.** *Gobiosoma prochilos*. View of a live specimen resting on the coral *Diploria* sp., St. Croix.

The species is not limited to sponges as are *G. horsti* and *G. chancei*, but large numbers of individuals have been observed and collected from the surface of massive sponges, particularly large *Xestospongia muta*. As many as 45 individuals of *G. prochilos* and several specimens of *G. evelynae* (YB) have been observed on a single specimen of *X. muta*. These sponges and also corals are important cleaning stations. *Gobiosoma prochilos* cleans fishes alone or in conjunction with *G. evelynae* (YB).

When *G. prochilos* dwells on coral heads, it has been found with *Coryphopterus lipernes*, *G. saucrum*, and *G. oceanops* (Belize only). As many as 11 individuals of *G. prochilos* have been observed on a single coral head. Occasionally specimens have been observed resting on rock substrates.

Individuals of *Elacatinus* were found sheltering on living corals at night at St. Croix, and *G. evelynae* (YB) is the only other member of the subgenus that might be present. It is likely that *G. prochilos* was observed at night in St. Croix, but due to its similar appearance to *G. evelynae* at night, this can not be definitely stated.

*Food Habits:* Several specimens of *G. prochilos* from Barbados (UMML 31106) were examined and the guts were found to contain only parasitic copepod larvae.

*Reproductive Habits:* The spawning of *G. prochilos* has not been observed in either the field or aquaria. Several females collected in Barbados in July 1972 were ripe or had developing ova.

A pair of *G. prochilos* was observed on the barrier reef in Belize in Oct. 1972 engaged in what appeared to be nest preparation behavior. One fish, later determined to be the male, was removing sand with its mouth from an abandoned burrow in a living coral head. The second fish, later determined to be a ripe female, was stationed immediately outside the opening.

*Material Examined:* Belize: UMML 31135 (2, 21.7-23.0), Tobacco Reef, PLC-C-44, 28 Oct. 1972; uncat. (1, 18.5), Queens Cay, PLC-C-40, 26 Oct. 1972; Jamaica: UMML 28363 (1, 18.9), 2 miles west of Ocho Rios, 12 m, PLC-J-9, 17 Aug. 1970; St. Croix: UMML 31105 (1, 22.2) Cane Bay, 13 m, PLC-C-37-1, 5 June 1972; UMML 30357 (3, 14.7-23.0), Tague Bay, back reef, 3 m, 29 Feb. 1972, J. Burnett-Herkes; Lesser Antilles: UMML 30371 (2, 19.5-27.4), 16°12.2'N., 67°28'W., P-916, 11 July 1969, R/V Pillsbury; UMML 29766 (1, 22.0), 17°51.5'N., 62°38.7'W., 37 m, P-949, 22 July 1969, R/V Pillsbury; Barbados: uncat. (10, 9.9-26.0), 1 km SW of Bellairs Research Inst., St. James, 12-14 m, PLC-C-20b, 15 July 1972; UMML 31106 (13, 12.0-22.5) same as above, 12-14 m, PLC-C-21, 20 July 1972; UMML 31103 (1, 17.8), off Bellairs Research Inst., St. James, 3 m, PLC-C-22, 20 July 1972. Unless otherwise noted all collections by P.L. Colin.

Juvenile individual of *G. evelynae* (Y) photographed at Freeport, Grand Bahama Island, on the coral *Diploria labyrinthiformes.*

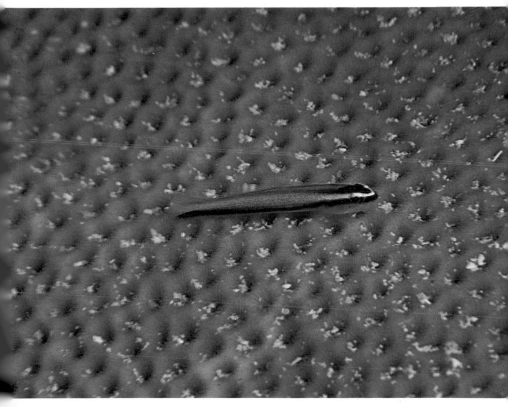

White color form of *G. evelynae* photographed on *Siderastrea,* Discovery Bay, Jamaica.

Juvenile of *G. evelynae* (YB) on the coral *Colpophyllia natans* photographed at Freeport, Grand Bahama Island, Bahamas on April 5, 1973. This color form of *G. evelynae,* the yellow-blue form, was not observed on the Little Bahama Bank in 1971-1972, but occurred there in 1973.

Individuals of *Gobiosoma prochilos* on the sponge *Xestospongia muta*. Photo taken at 12 m depth about 0.5 km offshore (W. coast), 1 km south of the Bellairs Research Institute.

*Gobiosoma randalli* Bohlke and Robins          Yellownose goby

*Gobiosoma randalli* Bohlke and Robins, 1968: 94-97, 100, 148-149; Cervigon, 1968: 212.

*Systematics:* The description of *G. randalli* does not need to be modified from that of Bohlke and Robins (1968). Some comments are needed regarding differences between *G. randalli* and *G. xanthiprora*. The fin-ray formula for the species, D VII, 12; A 11; P 17-18, does not need to be modified.

*Coloration:* The life colors of *G. randalli* were described by Bohlke and Robins (1968), and the specimens examined in the present study agree with their description except for coloration. The only difference concerns the color on the snout adjacent to the rostral bar. Bohlke and Robins (1968) record the area adjacent to the rostral bar to be pale on females, but dark on males. No specimens, including many males examined, were observed with dark snouts. Even in preservative these specimens still have a pale area around the rostral bar.

*General Habits:* The yellownose goby dwells on living coral heads and engages in cleaning behavior. Bohlke and Robins (1968) collected it from coral heads. Cervigon (1968) also recorded it on living corals and described the species as abundant on the coast of Isla de Cubagua. He stated that 4 or 5 individuals could be seen on the same coral head; when disturbed they fled to protected locations in the coral head, reappearing a short time later. I encountered *G. randalli* only in Curacao and Bonaire. Individuals are found on living corals, often sharing the same head with *G. evelynae* (YB) and *Coryphopterus lipernes*. *Gobiosoma randalli* is more variable in its abundance than *G. evelynae* (YB) at Curacao and Bonaire. Near Piscadera Baai on the south shore of Curacao the ratio of *G. evelynae* (YB) to *G. randalli* is about 10:1. *Gobiosoma randalli* seems relatively more abundant on Bonaire, nearly equaling *G. evelynae* (YB). These comparisons are discussed in a subsequent section. In addition to being found on the same coral heads as *G. evelynae* (YB), *G. randalli* cleans the same species of fishes, often in conjunction with *G. evelynae* (YB).

*Gobiosoma randalli* has not been definitely observed at night, but probably shelters on living corals as do the other coral-dwelling species of *Elacatinus*.

*Distribution: Gobiosoma randalli* is known from the islands off Venezuela (Curacao, Bonaire, Gran Roque, Cubagua), the coast of Venezuela near Cumana, St. Vincent, Dominica, and Puerto Rico. The Puerto Rican specimen is of interest since only the single individual is known from the island and from a relatively great depth (53 m). The species may be uncommon there.

Individual of *G. evelynae* (Y) sitting on the coral *Montastrea cavernosa*. Photographed at Highborn Cay, Exuma Islands, Bahamas, depth 30 m (100 feet).

Specimen of *G. evelynae* (W) on unidentified encrusting sponge at Discovery Bay, Jamaica.

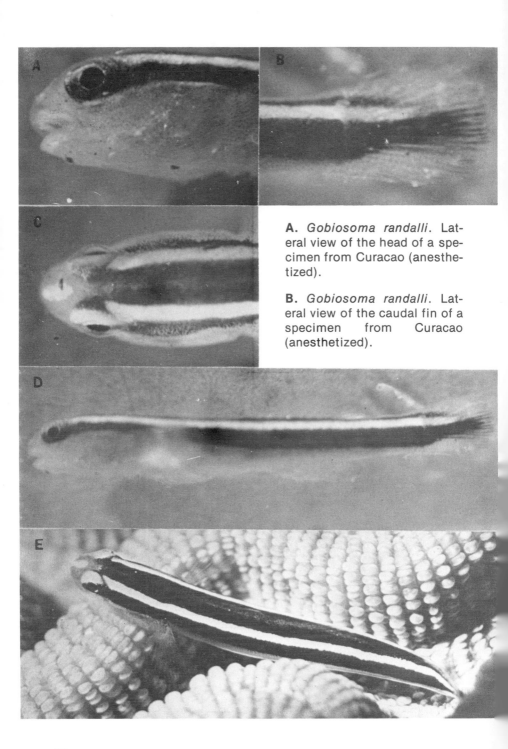

**A.** *Gobiosoma randalli*. Lateral view of the head of a specimen from Curacao (anesthetized).

**B.** *Gobiosoma randalli*. Lateral view of the caudal fin of a specimen from Curacao (anesthetized).

An unusual coral-dwelling *Gobiosoma* was observed at Buck Island, St. Croix. It appeared similar to individuals of *G. prochilos,* a common species in that area, in having a white lateral stripe, but instead of having a white V on the snout, characteristic of *G. prochilos,* the specimen had a medial bar similar to *G. randalli,* also white in color. The lateral stripe appeared narrower than that of typical *G. prochilos.* The Buck Island specimen was not collected. Whether a white-stripe population of *G. randalli* exists in St. Croix and possibly Puerto Rico or whether these individuals are aberrant individuals of *G. prochilos* cannot be determined without more material for which life colors are known. The yellow population of *G. randalli* is apparently centered around the islands off Venezuela.

*Food Habits:* The food habits of *G. randalli* have not been examined, but due to the species' cleaning behavior, large numbers of fish parasites can be expected.

*Reproductive habits:* Little is known of the reproductive habits of *G. randalli.* Bohlke and Robins (1968) noted differences in the color patterns of males and females, but whether this is a definite difference is not presently known.

At Awa de Ostpunt, Curacao, on 5 Aug. 1972 one ripe female was observed in the field. *Gobiosoma randalli* has never been observed spawning in the field and has not spawned in laboratory aquaria.

*Material Examined:* UMML 29763 (5, 13.7 17.4), 1 km west of the Caribbean Marine Biological Inst., Piscadera Baai, Curacao, PLC-C-2, 30 June 1971; UMML 31180 (2, 20.0-24.7), Bachelors Beach, Bonaire, PLC-C-30, August 1972, all collected by P.I.. Colin.

•　　•　　•　　•

The next five species dealt with form a natural ecological unit in that they are exclusively associated with massive and tubular sponges throughout their life cycle, exclusive of the larval stage. None engages in parasite removing behavior.

**C.** *Gobiosoma randalli.* Dorsal view of the head of a specimen from Curacao (anesthetized).

**D.** *Gobiosoma randalli.* Lateral view of a specimen from Curacao (anesthetized).

**E.** *Gobiosoma randalli.* Live specimen resting on the coral *Diploria* sp. at Bonaire. Photo by Carl Roessler.

Yellow color form of *G. evelynae* sitting on a colony of *Agaricia* coral. The species of *Agaricia* are used only occasionally by *Gobiosoma*, which is found most often on massive and head corals. Photographed at Highborn Cay, Exuma Islands, Bahamas.

Aquarium photograph of the white form of *G. evelynae* resting on the coral *Isophyllia sinuosa*. The fish is from Discovery Bay, Jamaica.

Specimens of cleaning *Gobiosoma* resting at night on corals. The *Montastrea cavernosa* in the photograph was deliberately caused to contract its polyps to render the gobies more visible. Photographed at Acklins Island, Bahamas.

*Gobiosoma chancei* Beebe and Hollister          Shortstripe goby

*Gobiosoma chancei* Beebe and Hollister, 1931: 87-88, Fig. 17; Ginsburg, 1933: 25; Bohlke and Robins, 1968: 81-83, 100, 148; Bohlke and Robins, 1969: 14; Tyler and Bohlke; 1972: 606, 608-609, 610, 616-617, 620, 634-635, 639-641.

*Gobiosoma horsti,* Collette and Talbot, 1972: 123; Smith and Tyler, 1972: 132, 136-137, 140, 149, 151, 160-162, 165, 167, 168. Figs. 129, 138, 139, 164.

*Systematics:* The redescription of *G. chancei* by Bohlke and Robins (1968) does not need to be modified beyond a slight expansion of the fin-ray formula to D VII, 11-12; A 9-12 (usually 10); P 18-20 (modally 19). The largest known specimen is 43.3 mm S.L. (Tyler and Bohlke, 1972: 635) and the smallest specimen collected is 9.0 mm S.L. (UMML 30712).

*Coloration:* The life coloration is basically as described by Bohlke and Robins (1968) and Tyler and Bohlke (1972). The post-ocular stripe is yellow and reaches only to the level of the opercular margin. The preorbital area is often pale yellowish, but is somewhat variable. One specimen from St. Croix had a small spot of iridescent yellow on the snout. A similar spot has been seen in some specimens of *G. horsti* (Y) from Curacao, but the spot, much smaller than the pupil, is lost in preservative.

Juveniles of *G. chancei* have a color pattern similar to larger individuals. A 9.0 mm S.L. individual from St. Croix (UMML 30712) and a 12.4 mm S.L. specimen from Hogsty Reef, Bahamas (UMML 29769) had the post-ocular stripe pattern typical of larger individuals.

Smith and Tyler (1972: Figs. 64a, 64b, 68) incorrectly show a pale stripe running the length of the body of the goby, rather than the short stripe of *G. chancei.*

*Distribution:* The shortstripe goby is known from the southern Bahamas, Caicos Islands, Puerto Rico, the Virgin Islands, the Lesser Antilles, Aves Island (west of Guadeloupe), and some of the islands off of Venezuela. In the southern Bahamas it is known from Hogsty Reef, Crooked

A. *Gobiosoma chancei.* Lateral view of the head of a male, 38.2 mm S.L., Provencales, Caicos Bank (anesthetized, UMML 31395).

B. *Gobiosoma chancei.* Lateral view of the caudal fin of a male, 38.2 mm S.L., Provencales, Caicos Bank (anesthetized, UMML 31395).

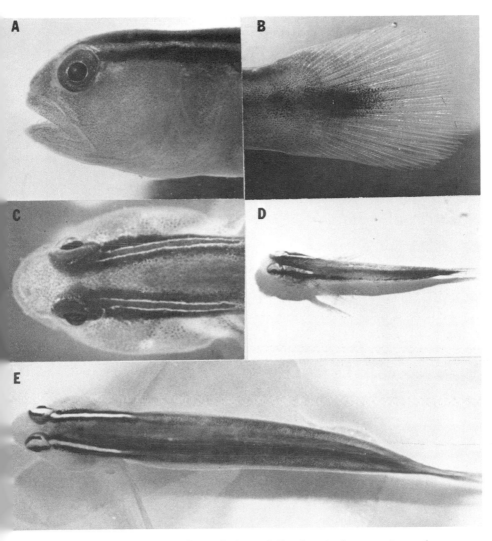

**C.** *Gobiosoma chancei*. Dorsal view of the head of a specimen from Barbados (anesthetized).

**D.** *Gobiosoma chancei*. Dorsal view of a 12.4 mm S.L. specimen from Hogsty Reef, Bahamas (UMML 29769).

**E.** *Gobiosoma chancei*. Dorsal view of a specimen from Barbados.

*Gobiosoma evelynae,* yellow-blue form, on the large barrel-like sponge *Xestospongia muta* near Freeport, Grand Bahama Island, Bahamas, at a depth of 12 m (40 feet).

*Gobiosoma evelynae* (Y) on an unidentified sponge, Eleuthera Island, Exuma Sound, Bahamas, 15 m (50 feet) depth.

Island, Acklins Island, Samana Cay, Plana Cays, Great Inagua, and Long Island. It is known no farther north or west than Long Island. In the south it has been recorded from Los Testigos and the Gulf of Cariaco (Cervigon, 1966) but is unknown from the nearby Netherlands Antilles. Its distribution is apparently exclusive of, but complementary to, the distribution of *G. horsti*. It has been observed and collected between 4 and 65 m.

*General Habits: Gobiosoma chancei* is a sponge dweller as pointed out by Bohlke and Robins (1968) and Tyler and Bohlke (1972). The species normally sits just inside the osculum of a tubular or massive sponge, but occasionally individuals sit on the outside of the sponge near the osculum. Tyler and Bohlke (1972) dealt with the species of sponges inhabited by the shortstripe goby, and this will be discussed in a subsequent section.

Smith and Tyler (1972) dealt with the general habits of *G. chancei*, which they misidentified as *G. horsti*. They found that one individual of *G. chancei* remained within its sponge during both day and night. They also observed a hamlet, *Hypoplectrus puella*, attack and attempt to eat a live specimen of *G. chancei*. The goby was rejected, and this was attributed to possible noxious properties of the mucus of *G. chancei*.

At Barbados, Aves Island, St. Croix, Hogsty Reef, and Acklins Is., in the present study *G. chancei* was always found associated with tubular sponges. In occupied sponge tubes only a single individual of the shortstripe goby was usually present, but on a few occasions two individuals were observed in the same tube. Other species of fishes found in the same tube as *G. chancei* included *Phaeoptyx xenus* (Apogonidae) and *Risor ruber* and *G. louisae* (Gobiidae). The shortstripe goby did not exhibit any cleaning behavior toward other fishes, and no fishes attempted to solicit cleaning behavior from *G. chancei*.

Nocturnal observations of *G. chancei* at Acklins Island showed both large and small individuals within the lumens of sponges and agree with the observations of Smith and Tyler (1972; 160). The noxious properties of species of *Gobiosoma* will be dealt with later.

*Food Habits:* Smith and Tyler (1972) reported that the guts of 3 of 8 specimens of *G. chancei* examined were found to be packed with a polychaete worm, *Syllis (Haplosyllis) spongicola* Grube, a cosmopolitan parasite of sponges in temperate and tropical seas. Three specimens from UMML 29012 were examined during the present study. One fish had the gut packed with *S. spongicola*. The second individual contained a number of the worms, and the third contained only a few of the polychaetes. These specimens were collected at mid-day.

*Reproductive Habits:* The spawning and eggs of *G. chancei* have not been observed. Ripe females were taken during Oct. (St. John by

Smith and Tyler, 1972), June (St. Croix, UMML 29711), and July (Antigua, UMML 27012). The shortstripe goby has not spawned in the aquarium. In the field it probably lays its eggs in the lumen of the sponge hosts in a manner similar to other sponge-dwelling species of *Gobiosoma*.

*Material Examined:* Virgin Islands: St. Croix, UMML 30712 (3, 9.0-14.7), Cane Bay, 15 m, PLC-C-37-2, 5 June 1972; UMML 30711 (1, 27.2), Cane Bay, 65 m, PLC-C-38, 6 June 1972; St. John: uncat. (1, 23.9), Lameshur Bay, 10 m, 11 Oct. 1970, J. Tyler and J. Marston; Lesser Antilles: Aves Island (west of Guadeloupe), UMML 30713 (4, 14.3-29.2), west side of the island, 9 m, PLC-C-39, 12 Aug. 1972, J. Staiger and Colin; Antigua: UMML 28586 (2, 23.7-29.0), 17°15.5'N., 62°02.2'W., P-967, 20 July 1969, R/V Pillsbury; UMML 27012 (3, 26.7-30.1), 17°29.4'N., 61°55.3'W., (between Antigua and Barbuda), P-975, 21 July 1969, R/V Pillsbury; Barbados: UMML 30709 (2, 20.2-25.0), 1 km SE of the Bellairs Institute, St. James, 15 m, PLC-C-20-b, 15 July 1972; UMML 30710 (1, 25.4), same as above, 12 m, PLC-C-21, 20 July 1972; Bahamas: UMML 29769 (1, 12.4), Hogsty Reef, NW Cay, 25 m, P-1431, 22 July 1971; UMML 30354 (1, 28.5), same as above, 23 m, PLC-B-31b, 22 July 1971. Unless otherwise noted, all collections by P.L. Colin.

## *Gobiosoma horsti* Metzelaar

> *Gobiosoma horsti* Metzelaar, 1922: 139, Fig. 2; Beebe and Tee-Van, 1928: 224; Jordan, Evermann and Clark, 1930: 446; Beebe and Hollister, 1931: 88; Ginsburg, 1933: 22-25; Fowler, 1944: 472; Fowler, 1952: 109; Briggs, 1958: 288; Bailey *et al.*, 1960: 36; Bohlke and Robins, 1968: 78-81, 100, 148; Bohlke and Chaplin, 1968: 612; Bohlke and Robins, 1969: 14; Bailey *et al.*, 1970: 52; Colin, 1971: 23; Tyler and Bohlke, 1972: 601, 606-608, 614-616, 633-634, 638-639, 641-642.
>
> *Gobiosoma evelynae,* "sharknose goby," Starck and Starck, 1972: 871 (color photo identified by common name only).
>
> Not *Gobiosoma horsti,* Collette and Talbot, 1972: 123; Smith and Tyler, 1972: (see *G. chancei* for pagination).

*Systematics:* A number of new collections of *G. horsti* are available since Bohlke and Robins (1968) treated this species. The fin-ray formula must be expanded slightly to D VII, 12-13 (usually 12); A 10-12 (usually 11); P 17-20 (usually 18 or 19).

Individuals of *Gobiosoma* sheltering at night between the expanded polyps of *Montastrea cavernosa* at night, Acklins Island, Jamaica Bay, Bahamas.

Jamaican specimen of *G. evelynae* (W) on a plastic tube in an aquarium.

Aquarium photograph of *G. evelynae* (Y) from the northern Bahamas.

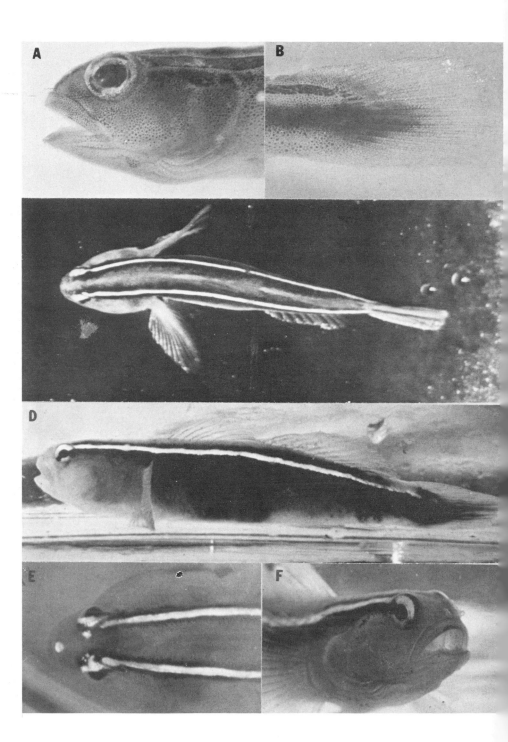

At least two color forms of *G. horsti* exist, and each is described in the coloration subsection; one consists of two geographically disjunct populations.

The two color forms, termed the "yellow form" and the "white form," are inseparable based on meristic data, morphometry, and general pigment pattern. The color of the lateral stripe in life is the only detectable difference, and this is quickly lost in preservative. Bohlke and Robins (1968) undoubtedly dealt with both color forms as preserved material and found no basis to distinguish them. The type locality of *G. horsti* is Caracas Bay, Curacao, and indicates that the type material of *G. horsti* was almost surely the "yellow form." Beebe and Tee-Van (1928: 224-226) recorded the lateral stripe as bluish white to turquoise based on specimens from Haiti; these are surely what is called the "white form" in the present study.

Collections of *G. horsti* from Isla de Providencia (Tyler and Bohlke, 1972: 615-616) are typical of *G. horsti*, but color notes indicate that the specimens may differ from other color forms of *G. horsti*. One specimen (ANSP 112621) of 29.6 mm S.L. was quite unusual in having the lateral stripes extended anteriorly to near the upper lip. *Gobiosoma horsti* has also recently been collected in Panama and, although life colors are unknown, these specimens seem typical of *G. horsti*.

**A.** *Gobiosoma horsti* (Y). Lateral view of the head of a female, 27.0 mm S.L. from Eleuthera Is., Bahamas (anesthetized, UMML 31390).

**B.** *Gobiosoma horsti* (Y). Lateral view of the caudal fin of a female, 27.0 mm S.L. from Eleuthera Is., Bahamas (anesthetized, UMML 31390).

**C.** *Gobiosoma horsti* (Y). Dorsal view of a specimen from Chub Cay, Berry Is., Bahamas in an aquarium.

**D.** *Gobiosoma horsti* (Y). Lateral view of a specimen from Curacao in an aquarium.

**E.** *Gobiosoma horsti* (Y). Dorsal view of the head of a specimen from Curacao (southern population) with accessory pigment spots.

**F.** *Gobiosoma horsti* (Y). View of the snout of a Curacao specimen (southern population) with accessory pigment spots.

"Mated pair" of *G. evelynae* (YB) from Turtle Rocks, Bimini, Bahamas. The male (lower fish in tube) is guarding the eggs produced by the female (upper fish). The transition from yellow to blue in the lateral colored stripe in the "yellow-blue" form of *G. evelynae* is clearly visible.

Small *G. evelynae* (YB) cleaning (on upper portion of soft dorsal fin) the squirrelfish *Holocentrus* at Freeport, Grand Bahama Island.

Immediately post-metamorphic individual of *G. evelynae* on the coral *Montastrea cavernosa* at Discovery Bay, Jamaica. This fish has not developed a visible lateral colored stripe, but the dark stripe in its initial Y-shaped pattern is apparent. Length of the fish is approximately 8 mm.

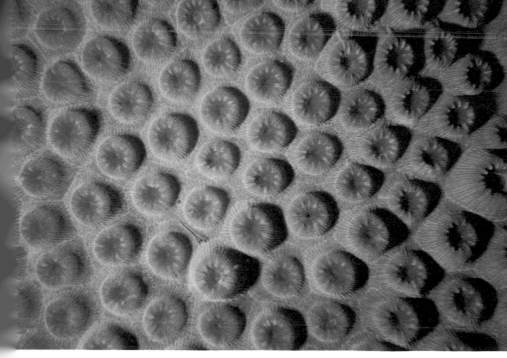

The two color forms of *G. horsti* have resulted in its being named "whiteline goby" (Bailey et al., 1960) and subsequently "yellowline goby" (Bailey et al., 1970). Obviously neither is completely correct nor incorrect, though yellowline is appropriate for populations in waters of the United States.

A series of specimens from Belize does not agree with the white form of *G. horsti* yet is very similar to it in almost every respect. These specimens, however, have a medial bar on the snout which specimens of *G. horsti* from other localities lack. On the basis of lateral stripe pattern and snout bar the specimens would be closest to *G. xanthiprora*, but they differ in several characters from *G. xanthiprora* which, like *G. horsti*, has a white and a yellow color form. Until more specimens are available from the western Caribbean, these individuals are identified with *G. horsti*.

*Coloration:* The yellow form of *G. horsti* has a bright yellow lateral stripe from the eye to the caudal peduncle. The two populations of this form are alike in this regard. There is, however, one possible difference. A few individuals from Curacao and Bonaire (southern population) had a small spot or streak of yellow on the snout. One spotted individual also had some small, bright yellow spots medially on the upper surface of the eyeball. These small spots are not visible after preservation. No individuals from the northern populations of the yellow form have shown as yet any snout marking or extra yellow pigment spots; these are the only detectable differences in the two populations, and their taxonomic value is doubtful. Henceforth, the yellow form will be referred to as *G. horsti* (Y).

Many small individuals of the yellow form lack completely developed lateral stripes, so that the yellow pigment does not extend to the caudal

**A.** *Gobiosoma horsti* (Y). Dorsal view of a juvenile specimen, 8.5 mm S.L., from Curacao (UMML 31131).

**B.** *Gobiosoma horsti* (Y). Dorsal view of a juvenile specimen, 10.4 mm S.L. from Curacao (UMML 31131).

**C.** *Gobiosoma horsti* (Y). Dorsal view of a juvenile specimen, 18.0 mm S.L. from Curacao (UMML 31131).

**D.** *Gobiosoma horsti* (Y). Specimen at the top of a tubular sponge at Berry Islands, Bahamas, 20 m depth.

**E.** *Gobiosoma horsti* (Y). Specimens on and in tubular sponges at Grand Cayman Island. Photo by A. Crook.

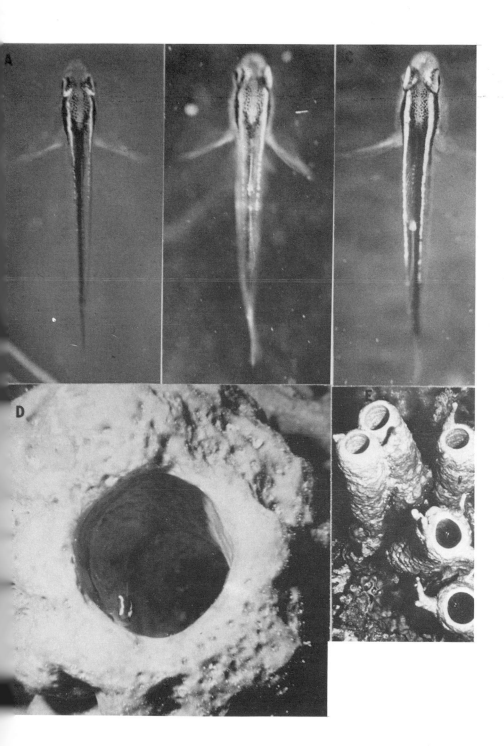

95

Sharknose goby, *G. evelynae* (YB), removing parasites from a large tiger grouper, *Mycteroperca tigris*, in the Netherlands Antilles. Photo by Carl Roessler.

Creole wrasse, *Clepticus parrai,* being cleaned in its characteristic head-down posture by *G. evelynae* (YB) at Curacao, Netherlands Antilles (depth 11 m).

Yellow goatfish, *Mulloidichthys martinicus*, being cleaned by *G. evelynae* (YB) at Curacao, Netherlands Antilles (depth 11 m).

peduncle. Three individuals from Curacao, of 8.5, 10.4 and 18.0 mm S.L., all show the posterior portion of the colored stripe as not being completely developed. Usually the stripe is complete and continuous to just past the pectoral fin base. More posteriorly the stripe may be interrupted with individual chromatophores plainly visible. The colored stripe may end near the second dorsal fin. Small individuals of *G. horsti* (Y) could be easily confused with *G. chancei*, which lack a full length colored stripe in both juveniles and adults. The stripe in young *G. horsti* (Y) usually goes beyond the pectoral fin origin, the point where it ends in *G. chancei*. If the extent of the colored stripe is noticed, then young *G. chancei* should not be confused with *G. horsti* (Y).

The white form of *G. horsti* has a brilliant white stripe from the eyes to about the pectoral fin base. More posteriorly the stripe becomes somewhat bluish white and reaches slightly onto the caudal fin base. In life the colored stripe is noticeably narrower in the white form than in the yellow form, but this distinction is lost in preservative. No snout markings or accessory pigment have been observed in any individual of *G. horsti* (W). Developing ova in females are sometimes clearly visible through the integument.

Tyler and Bohlke (1972) state that color notes on a specimen of *G. horsti* from Isla de Providencia indicate the colored stripe over the eye was bright yellow and the post-ocular stripe silver blue throughout its entire length. How these specimens relate to the other forms of *G. horsti* is unknown, and further collections with color notes and preferably color photographs are needed. Where they have been observed in detail, the two varieties of *G. horsti* are consistently colored throughout their range except as previously noted in the text. That is, color does not vary locally.

Another problem exists with the population of what is considered *G. horsti* from off of Belize. The specimens are identical in every respect to *G. horsti* (W) except they have a bar of brilliant white on the snout, running from in front of the anterior edge of the eyes to near the upper lip. The geographic range and relationship of this form to the others are unknown and must await future collections. At present, it is best to consider these specimens as *G. horsti*.

*Distribution: Gobiosoma horsti* is widely known throughout the Caribbean, but a consideration of the distribution of the color forms is much more revealing. *Gobiosoma horsti* (Y) consists of 2 widely separated populations. The northern population of this form is found in the northern Bahamas (Grand Bahama Island, Andros Island, Berry Islands, Great Abaco Island, Eleuthera Island, and the Exuma Chain), Grand Cayman Island, and probably the west coast of Florida. It has not been taken in the southern Bahamas. The southern population of *G. horsti* (Y) is

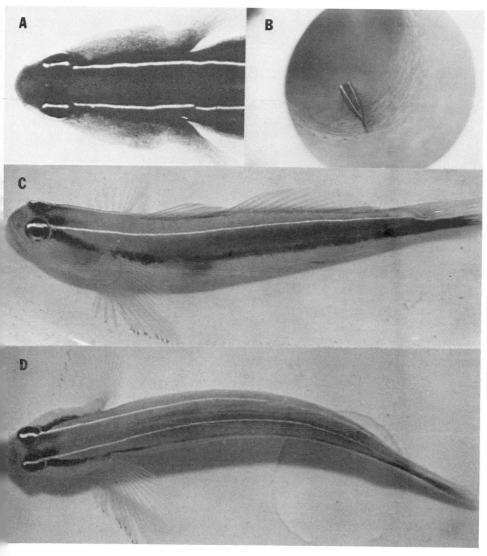

**A.** *Gobiosoma horsti* (W). Dorsal view of the head of a specimen from Discovery Bay, Jamaica.

**B.** *Gobiosoma horsti* (W). Specimen sitting head inward in a *Verongia* tubular sponge, Discovery Bay, Jamaica.

**C.** *Gobiosoma horsti* (W). Dorso-lateral view of a specimen from Discovery Bay, Jamaica.

**D.** *Gobiosoma horsti* (W). Dorsal view of a specimen from Discovery Bay, Jamaica.

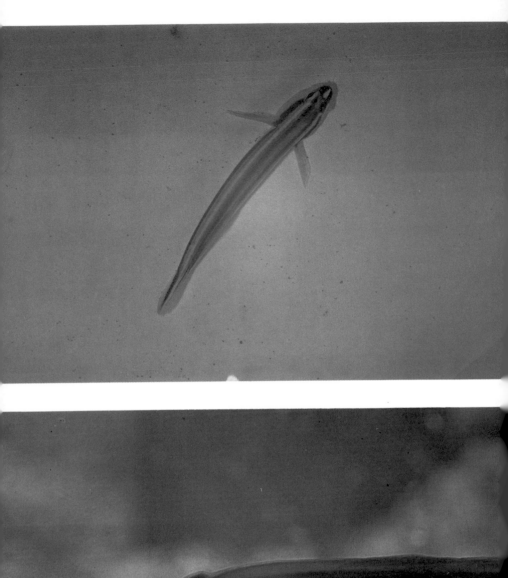

Dorsal view of a specimen of the blue color form of *G. illecebrosum* from Boca Chica, Cartagena, Colombia.

Individual of *G. illecebrosum* (W) from Islas Rosarios, Colombia on the coral *Colpophyllia natans*. The white of the medial bar on the snout and the anterior portion of the lateral stripe is clearly visible. Photo by Carl Roessler.

Aquarium photograph of *G. illecebrosum* (Y) from Galeta Island, Panama. Notice that the lateral yellow stripe does not occupy the entire extent between the upper and lower dark stripes.

known from Curacao and Bonaire, Netherlands Antilles, off the Venezuelan coast. It is unrecorded from the coast of Venezuela, any of the Lesser Antilles, or Hispanola.

*Gobiosoma horsti* (W) is known from Haiti, Jamaica, and Serranilla Bank. Its distribution does not overlap that of *G. horsti* (Y). Individuals of *G. horsti* (W) having a white bar on the snout are known from Belize and are of uncertain systematic status. *Gobiosoma horsti* is also known from Isla de Providencia and Panama, but no truly comparative color notes are available.

The known distribution of both color forms of *G. horsti* is mutually exclusive of the closely related *G. chancei*. The range of *G. chancei* essentially separates the yellow form populations of *G. horsti* by a straight line distance of 1200 km or a distance of about 2100 km over the shortest shallow water route.

The known depth distribution of *G. horsti* is between 1 and 40 m.

*General Habits:* It is well known that *G. horsti* inhabits sponges. The type specimens were collected by Metzelaar (1922: 139) from a sponge. Beebe and Tee-Van (1928) dealt with *G. horsti* (W) in detail, but they confused other coral-dwelling species of *Elacatinus* with *G. horsti* (W).

Tyler and Bohlke (1972) dealt with *G. horsti* at length. They questioned whether small *G. horsti* are sponge dwellers since the smallest individual that they were certain came from a sponge was 20.5 mm S.L. Small individuals commonly have been observed on or in sponges during the present study; the smallest known sponge-inhabiting individual of *G. horsti* is 8.2 mm S.L. Several others in the 8-12 mm S.L. range are known from sponges.

*Gobiosoma horsti* is found in both tubular and massive sponges. The species of sponges with which it is associated will be discussed later. Individuals of *G. horsti* are found on the outer surface, particularly if other individuals are occupying a single tube of the sponge. As many as five have been observed on or in a single tube. If the tubular sponge consists of more than one tube, the gobies move freely from one lumen to another. In tubular sponges like *Verongia* spp. the gobies within the lumen rest on the sponge wall with the head pointed either inwards or outward. If disturbed, they move to the base of the lumen.

The behavior of *G. horsti* in large, massive, barrel-shaped spong such as *Neofibrularia massa* differs considerably. As many as 15 individuals have been observed in a single sponge approximately 1 m in diameter. Most individuals actively swim against the current produced by the sponge. When swimming the gobies normally do not contact the inner surface of the sponge, and if disturbed retreat deeper into the numerous galleries and chambers of the sponge that are not visible from the outside.

102

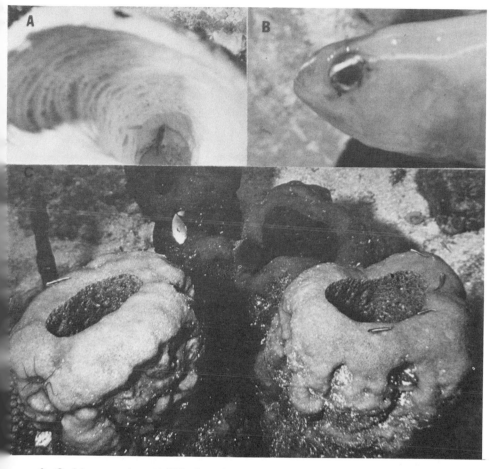

**A.** *Gobiosoma horsti* (W). Specimen at night in a tubular sponge with *Apogon lachneri* (Apogonidae) at Discovery Bay, Jamaica.

**B.** *Gobiosoma horsti* (W)? Specimen from Belize with white bar on snout. This form is provisionally placed in *G. horsti*.

**C.** *Gobiosoma horsti* (W). Specimens on the upper surface of a *Neofibrularia massa* sponge at a depth of 25 m, Discovery Bay, Jamaica.

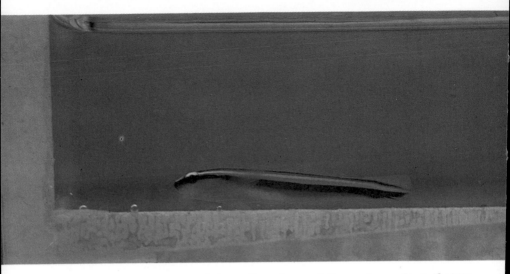

Aquarium photograph of the yellow form of *G. evelynae* from Galeta Island, Panama. The narrowness of the lateral yellow stripe is quite apparent.

*Gobiosoma illecebrosum* (B) engaged in removing parasites from a large gray angelfish, *Pomacanthus arcuatus*, at Islas Rosarios, Colombia. Photo by Carl Roessler.

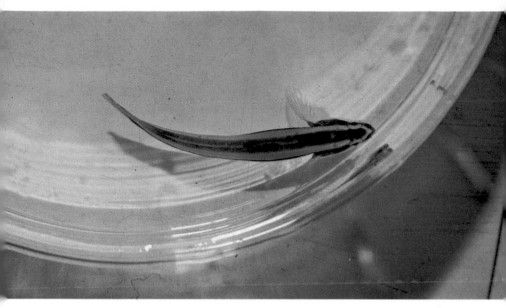

Specimen from Hogsty Reef, Bahamas, possessing coloration typical of *G. evelynae* (YB) but lacking the rostral frenum as in *G. genie*. The status of this specimen is not known at present.

Aquarium photo of *G. genie*, Chub Cay, Berry Islands, Bahamas.

*Gobiosoma horsti* is found with other sponge-dwelling fishes. *Gobiosoma horsti* (W) has been found in the same sponge with *G. louisae* and *Risor ruber* (Gobiidae) and *Phaeoptyx xenus* (Apogonidae). The fishes collected with *G. horsti* (Y) include *Phaeoptyx xenus, Risor ruber, G. louisae* (northern population of *G. horsti* (Y) only), *Starksia hassi* (Clinidae) and *Kaupichthys nuchalis* (Xenocongridae). *Gobiosoma genie* and *G. evelynae* occasionally have been seen on the surface of sponges inhabited by *G. horsti.*

*Gobiosoma horsti* does not clean other fishes. Extensive observations of this species to determine its general habits have not produced a single instance of it engaging in cleaning behavior. The species sometimes displayed itself conspicuously on the top of its sponges, but showed no behavior which could be interpreted as soliciting hosts for cleaning behavior. Under normal conditions, no host fishes were ever observed to pose for *G. horsti* to clean them. The approach of several species of fishes commonly cleaned by *G. evelynae* resulted in retreat or flight behavior into the sponge by individuals of *G. horsti* that were previously on the outer surface of their sponge.

Both color forms of *G. horsti* possess a noxious mucus on the body that apparently makes them distasteful to other fishes. This interesting aspect of some species of *Elacatinus* was first noted by Smith and Tyler (1972: 160) for *G. chancei* when an attack by *Hypoplectrus puella* on *G. chancei* failed due to the predator rejecting the prey after it had been engulfed. *Gobiosoma horsti* has a similar noxious property, and this is discussed in more detail later.

At night *G. horsti* remained within its sponges and was inactive. More than one individual may be found in a single tube or sponge at night. Occasionally other species of fishes were observed with *G. horsti* in sponges at night. In one instance, an individual of *Clepticus parrai* and one of *Chromis multilineata* were found with a single *G. horsti* in a single tube of a *Verongia* sp. sponge.

The type of area where *G. horsti* is found is variable. They have been collected in fairly flat areas and also on steep slopes. Vertical faces seem to have relatively more individuals of *G. louisae*, but *G. horsti* sometimes occurs in such areas.

*Food Habits:* The guts of 8 specimens of *G. horsti* were examined and two contained food. The only item found in guts was the polychaete *Syllis (Haplosyllis) spongicola*, a parasite of sponges. The gut of *G. horsti* is fairly short but not atypical of *Elacatinus*. No swim bladder could be seen in the specimens examined.

*Reproductive Habits:* *Gobiosoma horsti* lays its eggs near the base of the lumen of the sponges it inhabits. One spawning was collected in the Berry Islands, Bahamas at 25 m depth on 9 March 1971. The spawn was guarded by a large male *G. horsti* (Y). The eggs may have come from two females because the embryos were in two distinctly different developmental stages, with one group a few days older. The number of eggs in the spawning was not determined because they were kept alive to attempt rearing the young, but the eggs surely numbered well over 1000 and probably closer to 2000.

*Material Examined:* Except as noted, all collections by P.L. Colin.

*Gobiosoma horsti* (Y), "yellow form," northern population.— Bahamas: UMML 28492 (1, 51.0), Andros Island, ¼ mile NE of Goat Cay, off Fresh Creek, Torito-19, 17 Dec. 1969, W. and J. Starck, P. Hopper; UMML 29759 (1, 39.1), Berry Islands, Chub Cay, Diamond Rocks, 27-46 m, PLC-B-30, 9 March 1971; UMML 29825 (1, 46.6) same as above, 27-30 m; UMML 31035, same as above; Florida: UMML 29804 (1, 42.1), Anclote Light, near Tarpon Springs, 7 Dec. 1947.

*Gobiosoma horsti* (Y), "yellow form" southern population.— Curacao: UMML 29755 (1, 46.6), 1 km west of the Caribbean Marine Biological Lab., Piscadera Baai, 20 m, PLC-C-3-1, 3 July 1971; UMML 29756 (1, 22.5) same as above, 12 m, PLC-C-2, 30 June 1971; UMML 29757 (1, 15.1), same as above, PLC-C-1, same as above; UMML 29758 (3, 25.8-28.0), Vaersenbaai, 9 m, PLC-C-7, 10 July 1971, UMML 29760 (1, 44.8), Kaap St. Marie, 27 m, PLC-C-4-1, 5 July 1971; UMML 30237 (2, 44.9), 1 km west of Car. Mar. Bio. Inst., Piscadera Baai, PLC-C-3-2, 3 July 1971; UMML 31129 (2, 26.6-36.3), Eastpoint, 12 m, PLC-C-31, 5 Aug. 1972; UMML 31131 (3, 8.5-18.0), Vaersenbaai, 6 m, PLC-C-27, 29 July 1972; UMML 31132 (2, 19.7), Kaap St. Marie, 27 m, PLC-C-4-2, 5 July 1971; UMML 31037 (1, 33.1), Vaersenbaai, PLC-C-9, 11 July 1971; Bonaire: UMML 31130 (4, 17.0-39.9), Bachelors Beach, 12 m, PLC-C-30, 3 Aug. 1972.

*Gobiosoma horsti* (W), "white form."—Jamaica: all collections from the fore reef, Discovery Bay; UMML 28373 (1, 23.0), 23 m, PLC-J-17, 31 Aug. 1970; UMML 28853 (1, 30.2), 39 m, PLC-J-26, 20 Feb. 1971; UMML 29811 (1, 8.3), 22 m, PLC-J-14, 27 Aug. 1970; UMML 30705 (1, 18.4), 15 m, PLC-J-68, 4 July 1972; UMML 30707 (2, 11.9-33.3), 13 m, PLC-J-53-1, 5 Feb. 1972; UMML 30708 (1. 8.2), 13 m, PLC-J-53-2, 5 Feb. 1972; UMML (1, 46.7), 15 m, PLC-J-68b, 4 July 1972; UMML 31128 (2, 44.3-46.1), 13 m, PLC-J-57, 24 June 1972; Caribbean Sea: UMML 28583 (1, 47.2), 17°41'N., 75°41'W., Albatross Bank, 33 m, P-1191. ½ July 1970, R/V Pillsbury; UMML 29847 (2, 26.5-28.4), Serranilla Bank, 15 m, PLC-C-18, 4 Oct. 1971; uncat. (1, 27.8), same as above, PLC-C-17; Haiti: UMML 28813 (1, 26.8) 17°52.7'N.,71°41.2'W., south coast, 20-27 m, P-1272, 18 July 1970 R/V Pillsbury.

*Gobiosoma horsti* (W)?; UMML 30716 (6, 26.0-47.1) Tobacco Reef, 20-27 m, PLC-C-41, 26 Oct. 1972.

Two individuals of *Gobiosoma genie* with a small *Montastrea cavernosa* coral in the Berry Islands, Bahamas (depth 12 m). Also visible are some small bluehead wrasses, *Thalassoma bifasciatum*, which are cleaners like *G. genie.*

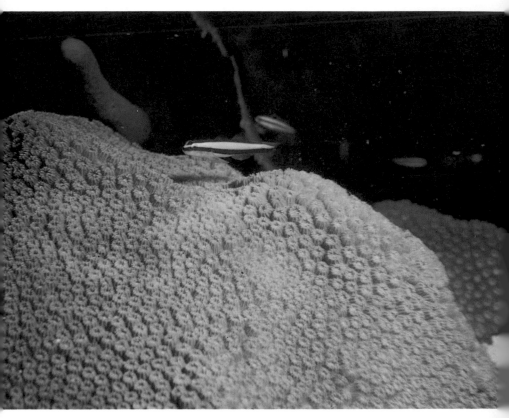

The cleaning goby, *G. genie*, above star coral, *Montastrea annularis*. Whale Cay, Berry Islands, Bahamas.

*Gobiosoma genie* on the coral *Colpophyllia natans,* Whale Cay, Berry Islands, Bahamas (10 m depth).

*Gobiosoma xanthiprora* Bohlke and Robins

*Gobiosoma xanthiprora* Bohlke and Robins, 1968: 85-87, 100,
148; Bohlke and Robins, 1969: 14; Tyler and Bohlke, 1972:
620.
*Gobiosoma* sp., Starck, 1968: 27; Tyler and Bohlke, 1972:
619, 633-634, 639, 641.
*Gobiosoma horsti*, Briggs, 1958: 228 (in part: Tortugas record);
Bailey *et al.*, 1960: 36 (Tortugas record).
*Elacatinus horsti*, Longley and Hildebrand, 1941: 227.

*Systematics:* Several new collections of this species have been obtained since the study by Bohlke and Robins (1968). The fin-ray formula in
the original description of *G. xanthiprora* needs to be expanded to D
VII, 11-13; A 10-11; P 17-20. The only species with which *G. xanthiprora* is easily confused is *G. randalli*. The differences between these two species are discussed in the section on coloration. The known size range of *G.
xanthiprora* is 19.7-37.2 mm S.L.

A. *Gobiosoma xanthiprora* (Y). Lateral view of the head of a male, 34.7
mm S.L. from the shelf edge off Nicaragua, P-1342 (freshly killed,
UMML 28865).

B. *Gobiosoma xanthiprora* (Y). Lateral view of the caudal fin of a male,
34.7 mm S.L. from the shelf edge off Nicaragua, P-1342 (freshly killed,
UMML 28865).

C. *Gobiosoma xanthiprora* (Y). Dorsal view of the head of a male, 34.7
mm S.L. from the shelf edge off Nicaragua, P-1342 (freshly killed,
UMML 28865).

D. *Gobiosoma xanthiprora* (Y). Dorsal view of the head of a female,
36.2 mm S.L. from Dry Tortugas, Florida (UMML 31120).

E. *Gobiosoma xanthiprora* (Y). Lateral view of a female, 36.2 mm S.L.
from Dry Tortugas in an aquarium (UMML 31120).

F. *Gobiosoma xanthiprora* (Y). Specimen within the lumen of the
sponge *Callyspongia plicifera* at a depth of 13 m at Dry Tortugas,
Florida.

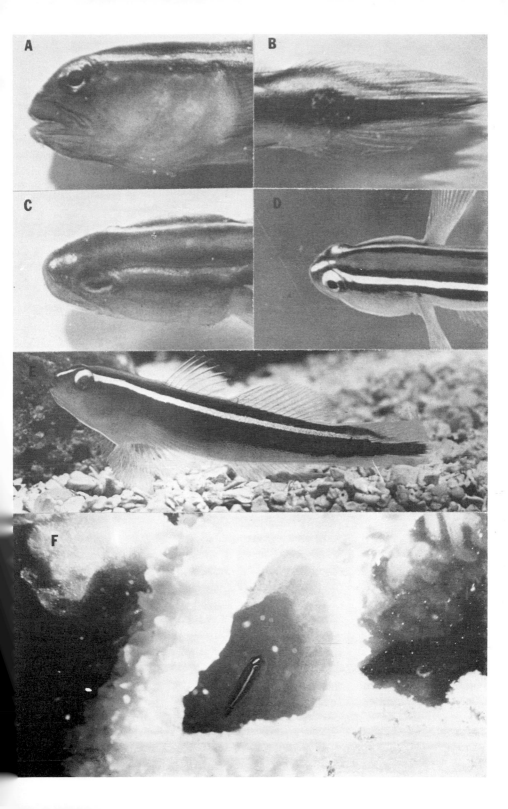

*Gobiosoma genie* clinging to the roof of a small rock cavern, depth 3 m (10 feet).

Male *G. genie* guarding eggs in a plastic tube.

Aquarium photograph of *G. genie* resting at night on the coral *Montastrea cavernosa*. The polyps of the coral are retracted so the fish are more visible.

*Coloration:* Bohlke and Robins (1968) described the coloration of a live individual of *G. xanthiprora* from the Florida Keys as having a yellow lateral stripe and mid-rostral bar. Subsequent live collections from the Dry Tortugas and along the continental shelf edge of Nicaragua (UMML 28865) agree closely with the Florida Keys specimen in coloration. Other collections have shown the presence of a second color variety of *G. xanthiprora* in the Caribbean. A color variety with a white snout bar and white lateral stripe was collected at Serranilla Bank. The "white form," will hereafter be designated as *G. xanthiprora* (W), the "yellow form" as *G. xanthiprora* (Y).

Some individuals of *G. xanthiprora* (W) have possessed a thin stripe of iridescent blue beneath the lateral dark stripe on the head which runs from directly beneath the eye to the opercular margin. This blue stripe is diffuse on its lower margin. Although none of the Florida specimens of *G. xanthiprora* (Y) have had this stripe, photographs of specimens of the yellow form collected off Nicaragua (UMML 30714) show a pale area which may have been blue in life. Otherwise *G. xanthiprora* (Y) and (W) are identical except for the color of the lateral stripe and snout marking.

*Gobiosoma xanthiprora* can be easily confused with *G. randalli*, both when alive and when preserved; therefore a comparison of coloration of the two is worthwhile. In life, *G. xanthiprora* has the following characteristic coloration: 1) dorsal surface of body anterior to the dorsal-fin origin is much paler than the area above the colored lateral stripe and this predorsal area is often gray in color; 2) anterior portion of the upper lip is dusky; 3) snout adjacent to the rostral bar is dark; and 4) the rostral bar is narrow, often its length 4 or more times its width and often beginning at the point of minimum interorbital distance. *Gobiosoma randalli* possesses the following characters in life: 1) the predorsal area is dark, similar in intensity to the area immediately dorsal of the colored lateral stripe; 2) upper lip is pale, sometimes with some pigment on the anterior portion but much less than that found in *G. xanthiprora*; 3) snout adjacent to the rostral bar generally pale yellow in life; and 4) rostral bar wide, its length 2 or 3 times its width, starting at or just posterior to the anterior margin of the eyes. After preservation these characters usually are still present, but there are cases where confusion exists. One additional character which is useful, but not definitive, is that in *G. randalli* the rostral bar begins some distance from the anterior interorbital pore in most individuals, but in *G. xanthiprora* the posterior origin of the rostral bar reaches to or even beyond the anterior interorbital pore.

When brooding eggs, males of *Gobiosoma* become very dusky and the lateral colored stripe and snout markings are nearly invisible. If preserved in this state the pigmentary characters on the body are lost and

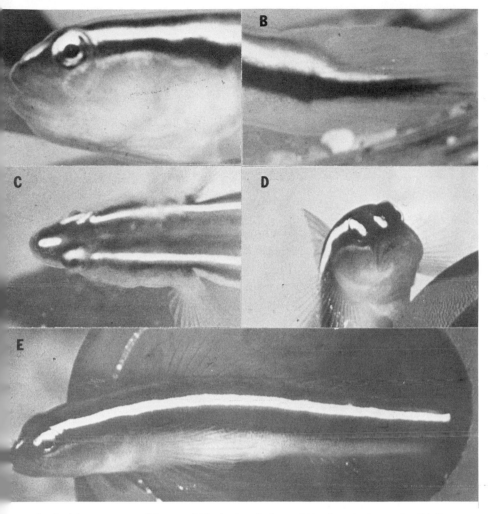

**A.** *Gobiosoma xanthiprora* (W). Lateral view of the head of a male, 34.6 mm S.L. from Serranilla Bank (UMML 30714).

**B.** *Gobiosoma xanthiprora* (W). Lateral view of the caudal fin of a male, 34.6 mm S.L. from Serranilla Bank, (UMML 30714).

**C.** *Gobiosoma xanthiprora* (W). Dorsal view of the head of a female, 27.0 mm S.L. from Serranilla Bank (UMML 30714).

**D.** *Gobiosoma xanthiprora* (W). View of the head of a male, 34.6 mm S.L. from Serranilla Bank (UMML 30714).

**E.** *Gobiosoma xanthiprora* (W). Lateral view of a male specimen from Serranilla Bank.

Red hind, *Epinephelus guttatus*, being cleaned by *G. genie*.

Two individuals of *G. genie* approach the photographer to solicit cleaning. Whale Cay, Bahamas.

This brave *G. genie* is cleaning between the teeth of a tiger grouper, *Mycteroperca tigris*, Grand Bahama Island, Bahamas (depth 13 m).

such specimens are difficult to identify. When brooding eggs, *G. xanthiprora* (W) is an overall slate gray, paler ventrally, but without a distinctive colored stripe or snout bar.

Tyler and Bohlke (1972) recorded the stripe and rostral bar color of *G. xanthiprora* from Isla de Providencia as silvery blue. This color is apparently very similar or identical to what is termed *G. xanthiprora* (W).

*Distribution:* *Gobiosoma xanthiprora* is known from Florida and some areas of the western Caribbean. The yellow form has been taken in the Florida Keys, the Dry Tortugas, and on the edge of the continental shelf off Nicaragua. *Gobiosoma xanthiprora* (W) has been collected at Serranilla Bank and probably Isla de Providencia. The coloration of one specimen taken at Lime Cay, Jamaica is unknown. The known depth distribution of the species is between 4 and 25 m.

*General Habits:* Bohlke and Robins (1968) reported this species to be a sponge dweller. Subsequent collections have been from sponges or areas rich in sponges in the case of the trawled specimens. In most instances, specimens were first observed within the lumen of the sponge. In one case at Dry Tortugas, Florida, a specimen was observed resting on top of a gray, globular sponge for several minutes. During the attempt to collect this specimen (UMML 30715), it fled from the gray sponge, which did not have oscula sufficiently large for it to enter, to a nearby tubular sponge where it sought shelter. Generally *G. xanthiprora* was found singly in sponges, but in two instances occurred with a single specimen of the apogonid *Phaeoptyx xenus*.

No cleaning behavior was exhibited by *G. xanthiprora*. The Dry Tortugas specimen (UMML 30715) was observed for several minutes and, although numerous fishes were nearby, the goby made no attempt to clean or attract potential cleanees. When a moderate-sized grouper, *Mycteroperca* sp., approached, the specimen of *G. xanthiprora* (Y) moved to a crevice between the gray sponge it was sitting on and a rock, where it remained for about one minute. Both *G. xanthiprora* (Y) and (W) were maintained in aquaria for a number of months, and these individuals made no attempt to clean their tankmates.

Usually *G. xanthiprora* has been collected in areas of flat or moderately sloping bottom. It has been collected at Serranilla Bank immediately adjacent to sponges containing *G. horsti* (W). The two species have not been collected from the same sponge, however.

*Gobiosoma xanthiprora* has not been observed at night.

*Food Habits:* No published information regarding the food habits of *G. xanthiprora* exists. Since the specimens in the present study were maintained alive for varying periods after collection, no attempt was made to examine the gut contents of these specimens. The sponges inhabited by *G. xanthiprora* possess large numbers of the polychaete worm *Syllis spongicola*, and this probably constitutes a large portion of the diet of *G. xanthiprora* as it does for other sponge-dwelling members of *Gobiosoma*.

*Reproductive Habits:* *Gobiosoma xanthiprora* lays its eggs within the lumen of tubular sponges. On 4 Oct. 1971, a single male *G. xanthiprora* (W) was collected from a sponge at Serranilla Bank and the sponge lumen was found to contain 624 eggs. The eggs were arranged in a compact mass near the base of the sponge lumen. The male fish was in the dark color phase typical of brooding fish. Other members of this species were found in other sponges within a few meters, but no female was associated with the brooding male.

*Gobiosoma xanthiprora* (W) spawned readily in aquaria. The four individuals collected at Serranilla Bank were retained alive and spawned several times in the laboratory. The reproductive activity, eggs, and larvae of this species are discussed in a subsequent section on reproduction.

*Material Examined:*

*Gobiosoma xanthiprora* (Y), "yellow form:"  Florida, Dry Tortugas: UMML 30715 (1, 22.7), 1 km NE of Garden Key, 12 m, PLC-F-38, 25 Feb. 1973; UMML 31120 (1, 36.2), reef off Long Cay, 12 m, PLC-F-40, 22 Feb. 1973; Nicaragua: UMML 28865 (2, 22.7-34.6), 13°43.3'N., 82°00.5'W., 27 m, P-1342, 29 Jan. 1971, R/V Pillsbury.

*Gobiosoma xanthiprora* (W), "white form:"  Serranilla Bank: UMML 30714 (3, 27.0-34.6), 15 m, PLC-C-17, 4 Oct. 1971 (maintained alive for several months).

*Gobiosoma xanthiprora* (W)?; Isla de Providencia, collected by J. and H. Tyler: ANSP 112623, 112624 (2, 27.5-35.6), Cat Rocks, NW of Morgans Head on east side of Santa Catalina Island, 11-13 m, 21 Aug. 1968; ANSP 112625, 112628 (5, 19.5-37.2), SW end of Catalina Hbr., 6 m, Aug. 1968; ANSP 112626, 112627 (2, 26.0-28.7), midway between Morgans Head and Fort Aury on SW coast of Santa Catalina, 5-7 m, Aug. 1968.

### *Gobiosoma louisae* Bohlke and Robins         Spotlight goby

> *Gobiosoma louisae* Bohlke and Robins, 1968:  90-94, 100-101, 148; Bohlke and Chaplin, 1968:  611; Bohlke and Robins, 1969:  14 (record referred to young *G. louisae*, probably refers to *G. atronasum*); Tyler and Bohlke, 1972:  601, 606-608, 617-619, 635-637, 639-641.

*Systematics:* The description of *G. louisae* by Bohlke and Robins (1968) does not need modification. The fin-ray formula of the species is D

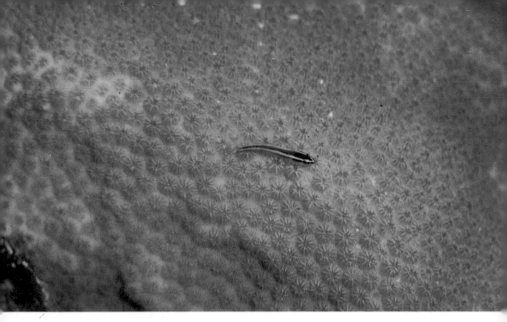

Small individual of *G. prochilos* on the coral *Montastrea annularis* photographed at Tague Bay Reef, St. Croix, Virgin Islands. This species occurs with *G. evelynae* (YB) at St. Croix.

An unusual specimen of *G. prochilos*. This individual (UMML 31105) has the gill opening severely restricted ventrally due to the branchiostegal membrane being fused to the jugular area of the fish. This condition, noted only in this specimen, causes the opercula to protrude more than normal.

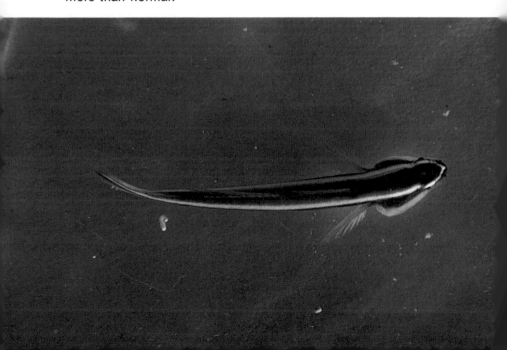

The cleaning gobies of Barbados. *Gobiosoma prochilos* (lower fish) occurs abundantly there together with *G. evelynae* (YB), the upper fish.

Detail of a *G. prochilos* from Barbados with an anterior extension of the snout 'V' which is occasionally found in this species.

VII, 12-13 (usually 12); A 10-12 (usually 11); P 17-19 (usually 18). The largest known specimen is 50.8 mm S.L., and the smallest is 9.0 mm S.L. (Tyler and Bohlke, 1972: 617).

*Coloration:* Bohlke and Robins (1968: 92) recorded the oval spot on the snout of *G. louisae* as yellow in life, but had no other life color notes. Tyler and Bohlke (1972: 618-619) confirmed that the snout marking was yellow and recorded that the lateral stripe over the eye was yellow in the live material they examined. They also found the lateral stripe posterior to the eye to vary in color. Some were yellow or yellowish green anteriorly, silvery to silver blue posteriorly. Tyler and Bohlke (1972) also noted that some individuals possessed snout markings confluent with the anterior portion of the lateral stripe.

Jamaican specimens also have the snout spot and the lateral stripe yellow at the eyes with the postocular lateral stripe greenish yellow. Individuals have been observed from Jamaica and the Bahamas with one or both of the lateral stripes joined to the snout spot. Bahamian specimens agree with Tyler and Bohlke's (1972) observation on life colors. Small specimens (up to about 20 mm S.L.) have a pale yellow snout with an iridescent yellow spot on the pale area. In some smaller individuals the iri-

**A.** *Gobiosoma louisae* (Y). Lateral view of the head of a male, 39.7 mm S.L. from the Bahamas (anesthetized, UMML 31392).

**B.** *Gobiosoma louisae* (Y). Lateral view of the caudal fin of a male, 39.7 mm S.L. from the Bahamas, fin slightly damaged (anesthetized, UMML 31392).

**C.** *Gobiosoma louisae* (Y). Dorsal view of the head of a male, 39.7 mm S.L. from the Bahamas (anesthetized, UMML 31392).

**D.** *Gobiosoma louisae* (W). Dorsal view of the head of a male, 50.8 mm S.L. from Glovers Reef, Belize (UMML 30717).

**E.** *Gobiosoma louisae* (Y). Dorsal view of the head of a female, 30.3 mm S.L. from the Bahamas (anesthetized, UMML 31393).

**F.** *Gobiosoma louisae* (Y). Lateral view of the caudal fin of a female, 30.3 mm S.L. from the Bahamas (anesthetized, UMML 31393).

**G.** *Gobiosoma louisae* (Y). Lateral view of a male specimen from the Berry Islands, Bahamas.

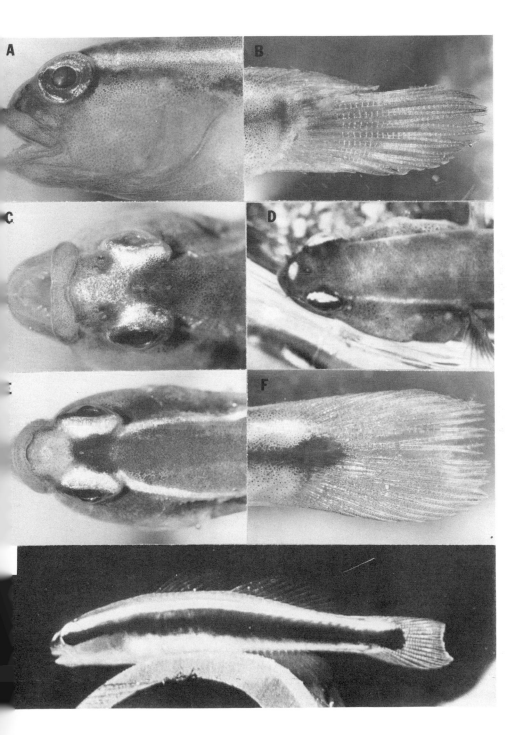

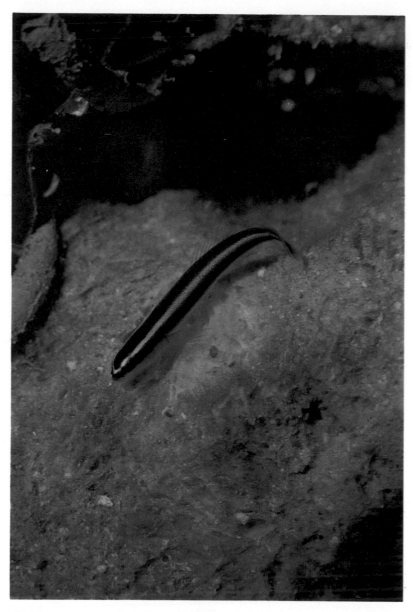

*Gobiosoma prochilos* from Barbados photographed in an aquarium.

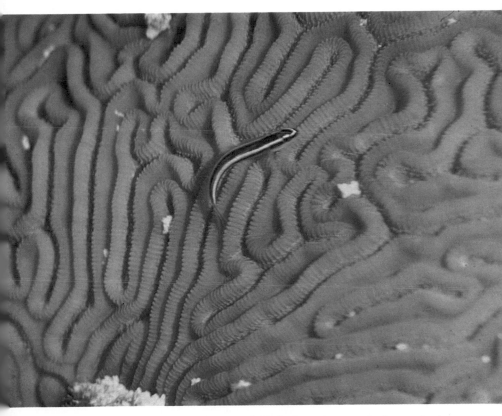

Specimen of *G. prochilos* on the coral *Diploria strigosa*, photographed at 3 m depth (10 feet), Tague Bay Reef, St. Croix, Virgin Islands.

descent spot is difficult to observe, although the individual is otherwise easily identifiable as G. louisae. One large individual from the Bahamas was observed to have several small breaks in the lateral stripe at about the mid-point of the body on one side only.

A single individual (UMML 30717) from Glovers Reef, Belize, differed considerably in having a white snout spot and lateral stripe. The snout marking was smaller than that found in adult G. louisae that have a yellow marking, and the lateral stripe posterior to the eye is slightly narrower than that found in G. louisae from other localities. The portion of the lateral stripe on the eye is white and becomes somewhat paler posteriorly. The Belize individual has counts typical of the yellow form of G. louisae, and there is no basis for separating the two forms at present.

*Distribution:* Gobiosoma louisae is known from the Bahamas, Grand Cayman, Jamaica, Isla de Providencia, Glovers Reef, Belize, and probably Haiti. The non-types of G. louisae noted by Bohlke and Robins (1968) probably represent individuals of G. louisae with the lateral pale stripe connected to the oval snout marking. Such a pattern occurs in some individuals from areas where considerable numbers of live individuals have been observed. The known depth distribution of the species is between 15 and 106 m.

*General Habits:* Gobiosoma louisae inhabits large tubular shaped and massive sponges. Individuals of all sizes have been observed on the outer surfaces and within the osculum of such sponges. The species of sponges with which individuals of G. louisae are associated are dealt with in a subsequent section.

Often more than one individual of G. louisae is found per individual chimney of large, multiple tubed sponges. Other species of sponge-dwelling fishes may be found in the same tube as G. louisae. These species include G. horsti, G. chancei, and Phaeoptyx xenus. In the Bahamas, individuals of G. evelynae (YB) also have been observed resting on the outside of large tube sponges adjacent to individuals of G. louisae. On one occa-

**A.** Gobiosoma louisae (Y). Dorso-lateral view of a specimen from the Berry Islands, Bahamas.

**B.** Gobiosoma louisae (Y). Dorso-lateral view of a specimen from Discovery Bay, Jamaica.

**C.** Gobiosoma louisae (Y). Dorso-lateral view of a male, 40.5 mm S.L. from Hogsty Reef, Bahamas (freshly killed, UMML 30355).

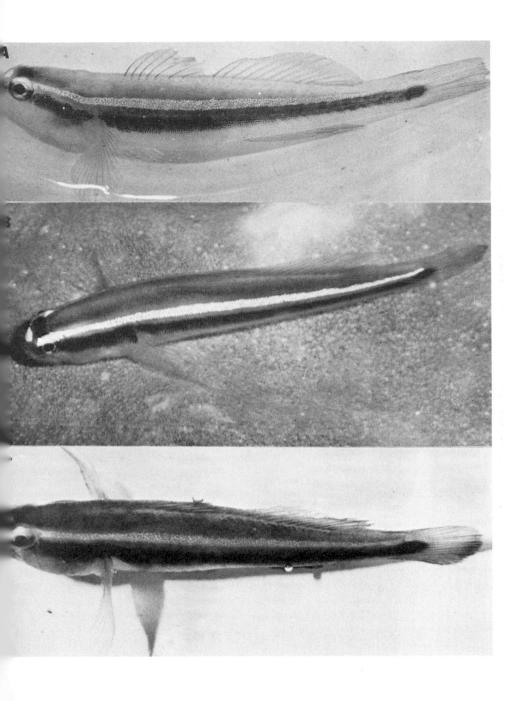

Colony of *Montastrea cavernosa* at Piscadera Baai, Curacao, occupied by both G. *randalli* (upper fish) and G. *evelynae,* yellow-blue form (lower fish). Not only will these two species occupy the same coral head, they will even clean the same host fish simultaneously.

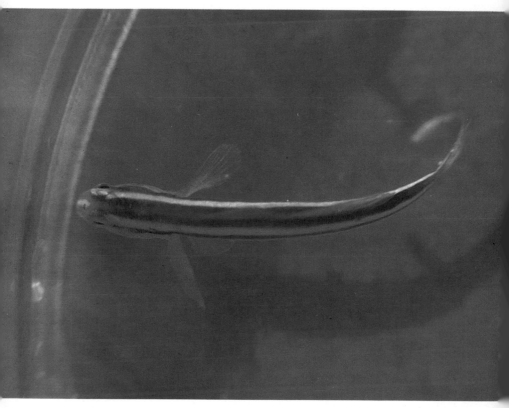

Dorsal view of *Gobiosoma randalli* from Curacao, Netherlands Antilles. The pale snout area adjacent to the medial snout marking is readily apparent.

*Gobiosoma randalli* on the coral *Diploria strigosa* in the Netherlands Antilles. The yellowish snout area with the bright yellow medial bar is plainly visible. Photo by Carl Roessler.

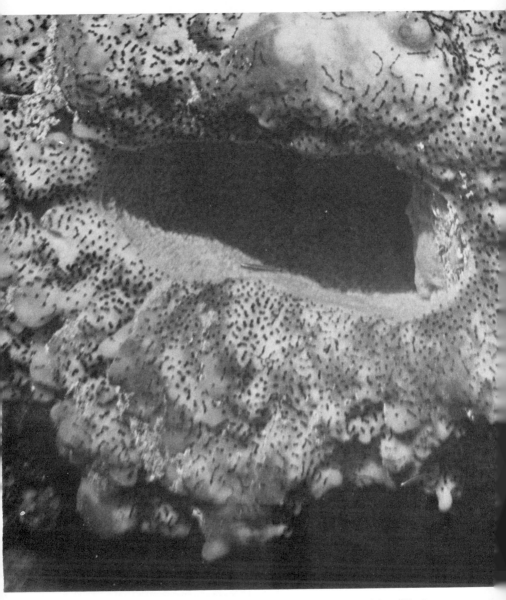

Three specimens of *Gobiosoma louisae* (Y) on an unidentified sponge at 106 m depth off Discovery Bay, Jamaica.

sion 8 individuals of *G. louisae* were observed at night in the lumen of a sponge consisting of a single chimney.

The spotlight goby has the deepest distribution of any species of *Elacatinus*. It has been observed at 106 m at both Glovers Reef, Belize and Discovery Bay, Jamaica from the submersibles Nekton Beta and Gamma. The observed gobies were on the outer surfaces of sponges and retreated into the lumen when disturbed by the submersibles. As many as 3 individuals were observed on a sponge at 106 m. Sponges that appear suitable for individuals of *G. louisae* were observed to at least 120-130 m depth, and it seems likely that these sponges may have *G. louisae* associated with them.

The nocturnal habits of *G. louisae* are similar to the other sponge-dwelling members of *Elacatinus*. At night they are found within the lumen of the sponges, sometimes with other fishes. In one instance, a small individual of *Clepticus parrai* was observed at night resting head down, a common behavior, within the lumen of a tubular sponge which also contained a *Gobiosoma*, probably *G. louisae*, at 25 m at Acklins Island, Bahamas. Such sharing of a sponge between a species of *Gobiosoma* and larger unrelated fish has not been previously noted.

Tyler and Bohlke (1972: 618) felt that the size at which *G. louisae* takes up residence in sponges is variable. Their evidence for young *G. louisae* inhabiting corals was probably based on specimens of *G. atronasum*. In this study *G. louisae* was collected only in association with sponges, and it is believed that individuals associate with sponges immediately after metamorphosis. Individuals of *G. louisae* have never been observed to engage in cleaning behavior in the field or laboratory aquaria. No attempt has been made to determine if *G. louisae* possesses noxious properties as in the other sponge-dwelling species, *G. chancei* and *G. horsti*.

*Food Habits:* The only identifiable remains in the guts of two large Jamaican specimens of *G. louisae* were the polychaete worm *Syllis spongicola*. *Gobiosoma louisae* apparently is similar to the other sponge-dwelling species of *Gobiosoma* in its food habits.

*Reproductive Habits:* *Gobiosoma louisae* lays its eggs deep within the lumen of the tubular sponges it inhabits. On 10 April 1972, a spawn consisting of 859 eggs was discovered near the base of the lumen of a sponge collected at a depth of 35 m at Hogsty Reef, Bahamas. The eggs occupied an area approximately 27 by 35 mm, and the sponge lumen also contained a single dusky male *G. louisae*, 46.9 mm S.L., which was probably guarding the eggs. No female was observed or collected in the vicinity of the spawn or the guarding male.

Individuals of *G. louisae* also have spawned within PVC plastic tubes in laboratory aquaria, and in all cases the male vigorously defended the spawning.

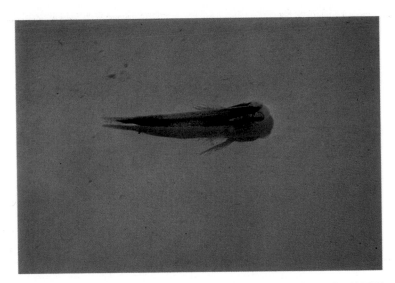

Small individual (12.4 mm S.L.) of *G. chancei* (UMML 29769) collected from a sponge at Hogsty Reef, Bahamas.

Specimen of *G. chancei* (center) from Barbados, collected from a sponge. On the side is *G. prochilos*, a cleaning species.

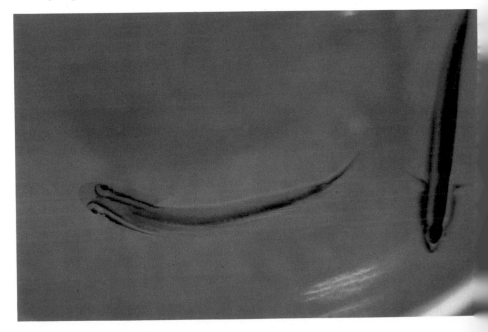

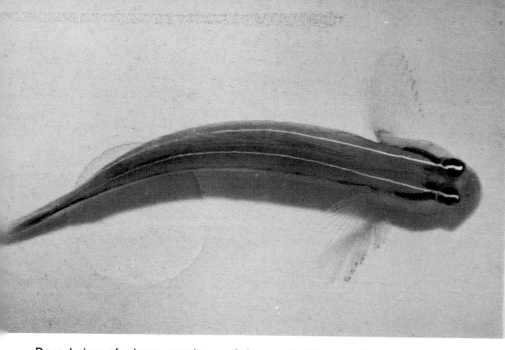

Dorsal view of a large specimen of *G. horsti* (W) from Discovery Bay, Jamaica. The fish is quite pale in its "fright" coloration.

Dorso-lateral view of a large specimen of *Gobiosoma horsti* (W) from Discovery Bay, Jamaica. The individual is considerably paler than undisturbed field specimens due to handling.

*Material Examined:* Bahamas: UMML 31111 (3, 27.2-28.8), Hogsty Reef, near NW Cay, on drop-off, 21-24 m, PLC-B-46, 10 April 1972; UMML 31112 (1, 16.9), Eleuthera Island, Miller Anch., 46 m, PLC-B-38, 14 Dec. 1971; UMML 31113 (1, 20.2), Great Abaco Island, south tip, on drop-off, 27-30 m, PLC-B-36, 12 Dec. 1971; UMML 31114 (1, 30.0), San Salvador, west side, 23 m, PLC-B-41, 8 April 1972; UMML 31115 (1, 13.5), Eleuthera Island, south tip, Miller Anch., 23 m, PLC-B-40, 14 Dec. 1971; UMML 29765 (1, 30.9), Hogsty Reef, 27 m, P-1431, 22 July 1971, R/V Pillsbury; UMML 30348 (2, 18.7-22.3), Eleuthera Island, Miller Anch., 24 m, PLC-B-39, 14 Dec. 1971; UMML 30355 (1, 39.8) Hogsty Reef, NE Cay, 24 m, PLC-B-31b, 22 July 1971; Jamaica: UMML 28843 (1, 32.3), Discovery Bay, fore reef, 39 m, PLC-J-18, 12 Feb. 1971; UMML 28852 (1, damaged), Disc. Bay, fore reef, 42-50 m, PLC-J-25, 19 Feb. 1971; UMML 31108 (1, 39.5), Disc. Bay, fore reef, 42 m, PLC-J-55, 8 Feb. 1972; UMML 31109 (5, 22.0-35.0), Disc. Bay, fore reef, 30 m, PLC-J-66, 2 Feb. 1972. Belize, "white form": UMML 30717 (1, 50.8), Glovers Reef, 37 m, PLC-C-42, 27 Oct. 1972. Except where noted all collections by P.L. Colin.

### *Gobiosoma tenox* Bohlke and Robins                     Slaty goby

*Gobiosoma tenox* Bohlke and Robins, 1968: 83-85, 100, 148; Bohlke and Robins, 1969: 14; Palacio, 1972: 92; Tyler and Bohlke, 1972: 620.

*Systematics:* Bohlke and Robins (1968) described this species from one specimen (ANSP 110688) collected off Dominica. Five additional specimens have been taken and expansion of the fin-ray formula is needed to D VII, 12; A 10-11; P 17-20. The largest known specimen is 31.7 mm S.L.

*Coloration:* The life colors of *G. tenox* were not described by Bohlke and Robins (1968). In life the post-ocular stripe is yellow, not blue as had been suggested by Bohlke and Robins (1968). The species also has a yellow medial bar on the snout starting at about the point of the least interorbital distance and running nearly to the upper jaw. This bar is often lost in preservative, but is visible in the material from Aves Island. As with other *Gobiosoma*, the snout marking may or may not be visible after preservation. The body and fins of live specimens of *G. tenox* are generally slaty gray as described by Bohlke and Robins (1968) for preserved material.

*Distribution:* *Gobiosoma tenox* is known from Dominica (Bohlke and Robins, 1968), Nevis, Aves Island (west of Guadeloupe), and the San

**A.** *Gobiosoma louisae* (Y). Male specimen with snout marking and lateral stripe (right) merged.

**B.** *Gobiosoma louisae* (Y). Specimen with head barely protruding from the osculum of a *Verongia* sponge at Discovery Bay, Jamaica.

**C.** *Gobiosoma louisae* (Y). Juvenile specimen, 17.4 mm S.L., from San Salvador, Bahamas.

Aquarium photograph of a typical specimen of the southern population of *G. horsti* (Y). This sponge-dwelling individual was collected in Curacao, Netherlands Antilles.

Anterior view of *G. horsti* from Curacao showing the terminal position of the mouth.

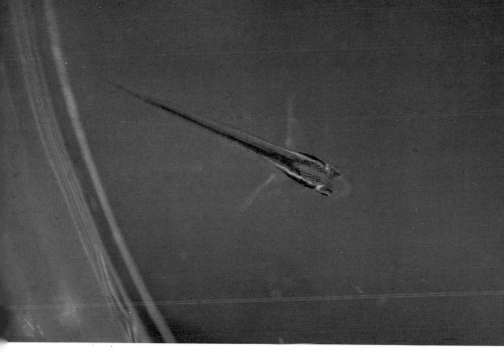

Dorsal view of a juvenile *G. horsti* (Y), 8.5 mm S.L., from Curacao. The yellow stripe reaches only about one half of the length of the fish.

Juvenile specimen of *G. horsti* (Y), 18.00 mm S.L., from Curacao. Even at this size the lateral yellow stripe has not reached its full length.

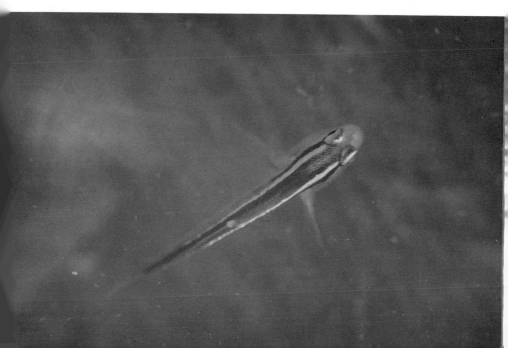

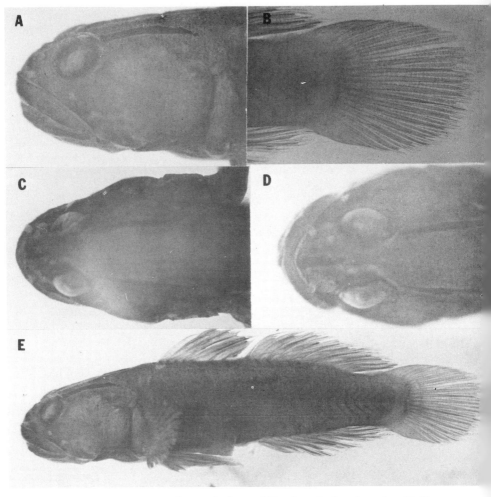

**A.** *Gobiosoma tenox.* Lateral view of the head of a female, 31.7 mm
S.L. from Aves Island (Lesser Antilles) (preserved, UMML 30701).

**B.** *Gobiosoma tenox.* Lateral view of the caudal fin of a female, 31.7
mm S.L. from Aves Island (Lesser Antilles) (preserved, UMML 30701).

**C.** *Gobiosoma tenox.* Dorsal view of the head of a female, 31.7 mm
S.L. from Aves Island (Lesser Antilles) (preserved, UMML 30701).

**D.** *Gobiosoma tenox.* Dorso-anterior view of the head of a female, 31.7
mm S.L. from Aves Island (Lesser Antilles) showing the snout bar,
dark in preservative (UMML 30701).

Blas Islands, Panama (Palacio, 1972). Its known depth distribution is between 15 and 70 m.

*General Habits:* The slaty goby is an inhabitant of sponges. Bohlke and Robins (1968) thought that *G. tenox* was a sponge dweller. Tyler and Bohlke (1972) discussed the types of sponges present at the type locality and added that they probably were a species similar to, but not identical with, *Speciospongia vesparia.* They also mentioned that a number of *G. chancei* were collected in the same station as the holotype of *G. tenox.*

*Gobiosoma tenox* was observed and collected at Aves Island (west of Guadeloupe). A male and a female were taken from the same osculum of a large specimen of the sponge *Neofibrularia* sp. (UMML 30701). A third individual that was facing outward was collected from just inside the osculum of a separate specimen of the same sponge species (UMML 30702).

Nothing is known of the nocturnal habits of *G. tenox.*

*Food Habits:* The gut contents of two specimens from Aves Island (UMML 30701) and one from Panama (UMML 26112) were examined. All contained only *Syllis spongicola,* the gut being nearly full, but not packed with the polychaete worms. The specimens all were collected in the mid to late afternoon.

*Reproductive Habits:* Very little is known of spawning by this species, but it probably lays its eggs within its sponges as do other sponge-dwelling *Gobiosoma.* The female of UMML 30701 had developing ova and was collected during August, 1972. This collection (UMML 30701) may have represented a spawning pair of fishes since they were taken in the same osculum.

*Material Examined:* UMML 26112 (1, 21.8), 9°33.8'N., 78°36.2'W., San Blas Islands, 70 m, P-422, 19 July 1966, R/V Pillsbury; UMML 28638 (1, 24.1), 17°10.0'N., 62°38.5'W., 27 m, P-959, 19 July 1969, R/V Pillsbury, UMML 30701 (2, 29.7-31.7), Aves Island (west of Guadeloupe), west side, 52 m, PLC-C-35, 12 Aug. 1972, P.L. Colin; UMML 30702 (1, 18.2), same as above, 53 m, PLC-C-34.

This final species of *Elacatinus* in the western North Atlantic, *G. atronasum,* represents a third ecological type and is quite different from the two groups covered previously.

E. *Gobiosoma tenox.* Lateral view of a female, 31.7 mm S.L. from Aves Island (Lesser Antilles) (UMML 30701).

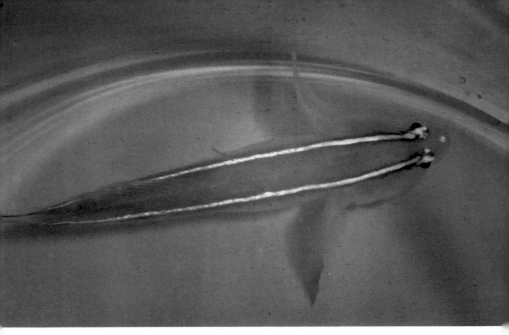

Unusual individual of *G. horsti* (Y) from Curacao. This specimen has a superficial spot of iridescent yellow pigment on the snout and some others on the upper surface of the eyeball. This accessory pigment has been observed rarely in the southern population of *G. horsti* (Y), but is not known in the northern population.

Aquarium photograph of a female *G. horsti* (W) with developing ova (white) clearly visible through the ventral abdomen wall.

Female *G. horsti* (W) from Jamaica.

Male *G. horsti* (W) from Jamaica guarding eggs in a "pseudosponge," a plastic tube stuck nearly vertically into the aquarium bottom. This male has extremely dusky coloration typical of brooding *Gobiosoma*.

*Gobiosoma atronasum* Bohlke and Robins

*Gobiosoma atronasum* Bohlke and Robins, 1968: 88-90, 100, 148.

*Gobiosoma louisae,* Bohlke and Robins, 1969: 14 (in part, the statement "young of *G. louisae* said to school in deep water" undoubtedly refers to *G. atronasum*); Tyler and Bohlke, 1972: 618 (in part, record from C.R. Gilbert of young of *G. louisae* dwelling on corals is almost surely attributable to *G. atronasum*).

*Systematics:* Three additional collections have been taken since the study by Bohlke and Robins (1968). Fin-ray counts from these specimens do not greatly modify ranges listed by Bohlke and Robins (1968), and the fin-ray formula for this species is D VII, 11-12; A 10-12; P 14-17. The original description needs no other modification except for coloration as discussed later. The species grows to 24.5 mm S.L. (UMML 30350) and the smallest specimen examined is 12.3 mm S.L. (UMML 30349).

**A.** *Gobiosoma atronasum.* Lateral view of the head of a specimen from Eleuthera Island, Bahamas (preserved, UMML 30350).

**B.** *Gobiosoma atronasum.* Lateral view of the caudal fin of a specimen from Eleuthera Island, Bahamas (preserved, UMML 30350).

**C.** *Gobiosoma atronasum.* Dorsal view of the head of a specimen from Eleuthera Island, Bahamas.

**D.** *Gobiosoma atronasum.* Specimen exhibiting the sigmoid flexure used in feeding.

**E.** *Gobiosoma atronasum.* Lateral view of a specimen from Eleuthera Island, Bahamas in an aquarium.

**F.** *Gobiosoma atronasum.* Lateral view of a specimen from Eleuthera Island, Bahamas which has the break in the lateral stripe at the level of the caudal peduncle.

**G.** *Gobiosoma atronasum.* Anterior view of a specimen showing the oval snout marking.

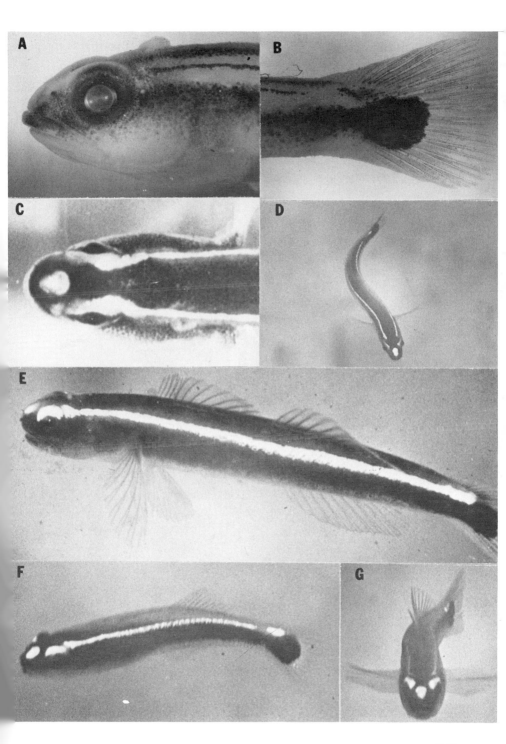

Several *G. horsti* (W) sitting on the sponge *Neofibrularia massa* at 25 m (85 feet) depth, Discovery Bay, Jamaica. This sponge should not be touched or handled since it produces an acute dermatitis in humans.

The sponge *Verongia fistularis* with three individuals of *G. horsti* (Y) visible, two in the oscula and the third on the outer surface of the tube, Grand Cayman Island. Photo by Alan Crook.

*Gobiosoma horsti* (Y) sitting on the lip of the osculum of an unidentified sponge at Whale Cay, Berry Islands, Bahamas.

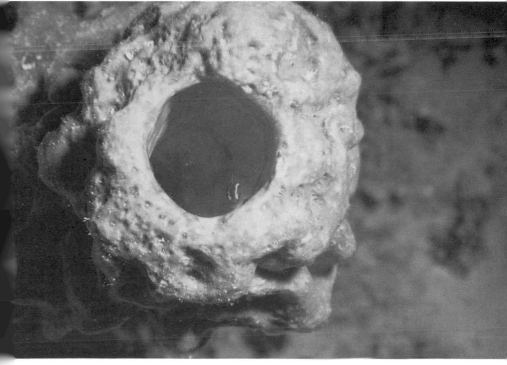

*Coloration:* No life color notes were included in the original description. The colored lateral stripe starts on the dorsal portion of the eye and extends to the basal portion of the caudal fin rays. The stripe is yellow and narrower than the diameter of the pupil. The posterior portion of the stripe becomes somewhat greenish in the region of the pectoral fin, but yellow is the predominant color. The posterior portion of the colored stripe widens slightly in the region near the end of the hypural plate and in about one half of the individuals examined there is a definite break in the colored stripe just anterior of this point. In individuals which have this break, the posterior portion of the stripe resembles a separate elongate yellow spot. Such breaks are evident even in preserved specimens and have been seen on live specimens as small as 15 mm S.L. Both sexes may possess the break in the colored stripe.

The lateral dark stripe is well developed and wide, extending from the ventral end of the pectoral fin base to the lower portion of the caudal fin where it forms a distinct oval black spot centered slightly below the dorsal-ventral midline of the fin and peduncle. Its edges are very distinct and contrast sharply with the remaining clear portion of the caudal fin and the yellow lateral stripe. Dorsal to the colored stripe the body is dusky, not quite as dark as the lateral dark stripe.

The snout has a large oval yellow spot starting just anterior to the eyes and reaching nearly to the upper jaw. The most pointed portion of the oval is usually oriented anteriorly. The rest of the snout area is very dark. The anterior portion of the upper jaw is dark, and the posterior portion of the upper jaw, lower jaw, chest, and belly are pale. All fins except the caudal fin are clear.

Bohlke and Robins (1968) did not record the presence of the oval snout spot, but it can be observed in many preserved specimens.

*Distribution: Gobiosoma atronasum* is known only from Exuma Sound, Bahamas. It is known from southwestern Eleuthera Island, Little San Salvador, Highborn Cay (Exuma Chain) and northwestern Long Island. It has been observed and collected between 6 and 35 m depth.

*General Habits: Gobiosoma atronasum* often has been observed hovering in mixed groups close to vertical faces with numerous holes and around undercut ledges. The species occurs singly and in groups of at least 100 individuals, and is a midwater particulate feeder. Many individuals were observed using a sigmoid flexure of the body to propel themselves forward. This sigmoid flexure may compensate for the lack of protrusible jaws, as are found on most particulate plankton feeding fishes (Davis and Birdsong, 1973), in *G. atronasum.*

The species often rests on living corals in groups of as many as 20 individuals. Collection UMML 30349 consists of 12 specimens out of nearly

20 observed resting on a coral head (*Montastrea cavernosa*) one-half meter in diameter. Several *G. evelynae* (Y) also occupied the same coral. Tyler and Bohlke (1972) report that the young of *G. louisae* dwell on corals, and this record almost surely refers to *G. atronasum* since at the time of the observations by C.R. Gilbert it was not known that *G. atronasum* possessed a yellow oval spot on the snout, an important field character for identifying *G. louisae.*

This species apparently does not engage in cleaning behavior. Several times large fishes were observed to pass near groups of *G. atronasum* which, although not fleeing, made no attempt to engage in cleaning behavior or to attract passing fishes. *Gobiosoma atronasum* has not been collected or observed in association with any sponges.

At night it shelters on living, expanded coral heads as do the other species of *Gobiosoma* commonly associated with corals.

*Food Habits:* Five specimens from UMML 31360 were examined for gut contents. All had material in the gut, and 2 were fully packed. The only identifiable items were copepod crustaceans, supporting the supposition that *G. atronasum* feeds on zooplankton. For fishes in which at least two hours had elapsed between live collection and preservation, the guts were empty. The gut of *G. atronasum* is very short, being scarcely longer than the distance between the mouth and the anus. The stomach appears very sac-like and is very thin walled. The species also possesses a swim bladder, an advantage in a goby which spends much of its time out of contact with the substrate.

*Reproductive habits:* Nothing is known of the reproductive habits of *G. atronasum.* No spawning or reproductive behavior has been observed in the field or in the aquarium, where several were maintained for a number of months.

*Material Examined:* Bahamas: UMML 30349 (12, 12.3-20.1), Eleuthera Island, Miller Anchorage, 23 m, PLC-B-39, 14 Dec. 1971; UMML 30350 (4, 20.9-24.5), same as above, 6 m, PLC-B-40, 15 Dec. 1971; UMML 31360 (7, 16.3-20.1), Eleuthera Island, 3 miles S of Powell Point, 12 m, RIP preserved, PLC-B-81, 18 Oct. 1973.

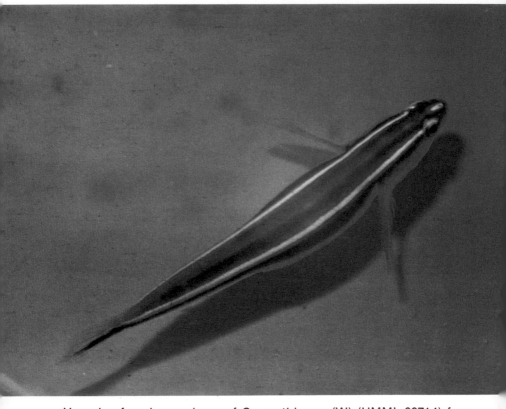

Very ripe female specimen of *G. xanthiprora* (W) (UMML 30714) from Serranilla Bank, Caribbean Sea.

Aquarium photograph of *Gobiosoma xanthiprora* (Y) from Dry Tortugas, Florida. Fish in the lower part of the photo is the greenbanded goby, *Gobiosoma multifasciatum,* and is not a member of the subgenus *Elacatinus.*

Dorsal view of a female *G. xanthiprora* (UMML 31120) from Dry Tortugas, Florida, 36.2 mm S.L.

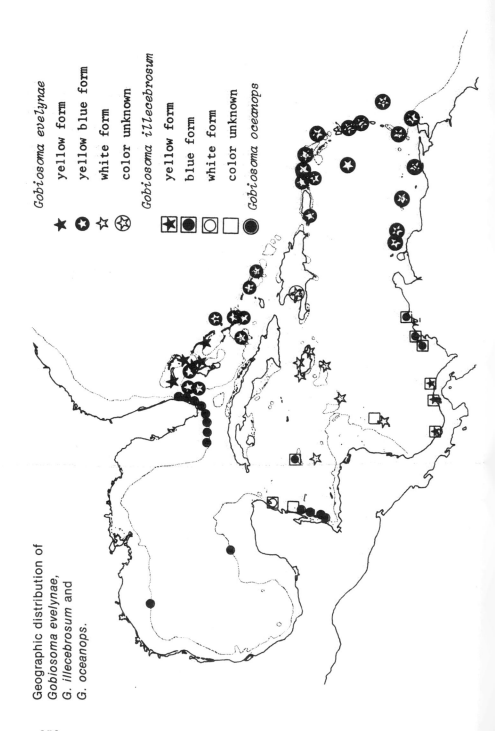

Geographic distribution of
Gobiosoma evelynae,
G. illecebrosum and
G. oceanops.

*Gobiosoma evelynae*

★    yellow form
◉    yellow blue form
☆    white form
✪    color unknown

*Gobiosoma illecebrosum*

⬚★⬚    yellow form
◼    blue form
◻    white form
□    color unknown
◐   

*Gobiosoma oceanops*

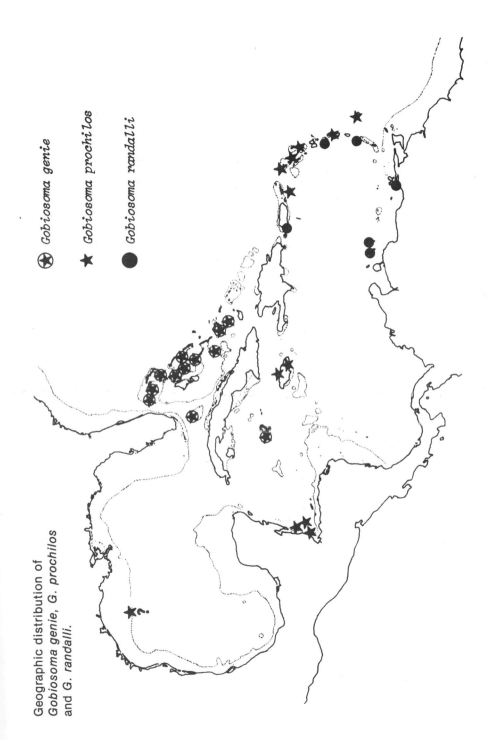

Geographic distribution of
Gobiosoma genie, G. prochilos
and G. randalli.

⊛ Gobiosoma genie

★ Gobiosoma prochilos

● Gobiosoma randalli

*Gobiosoma xanthiprora* (Y) from Dry Tortugas, Florida, showing the terminal position of the mouth typical of sponge-dwelling *Gobiosoma*.

Two male individuals of *G. xanthiprora* (W) from Serranilla Bank. One (UMML 30714, 34.6 mm S.L.) has the faint blue line on the cheek sometimes seen in this species. The other specimen is guarding eggs in the tube and has the dusky coloration characteristic of brooding male *Gobiosoma*.

*Gobiosoma xanthiprora* (Y) dwelling in the sponge *Callyspongia plicifera* at Dry Tortugas, Florida (depth 12 m).

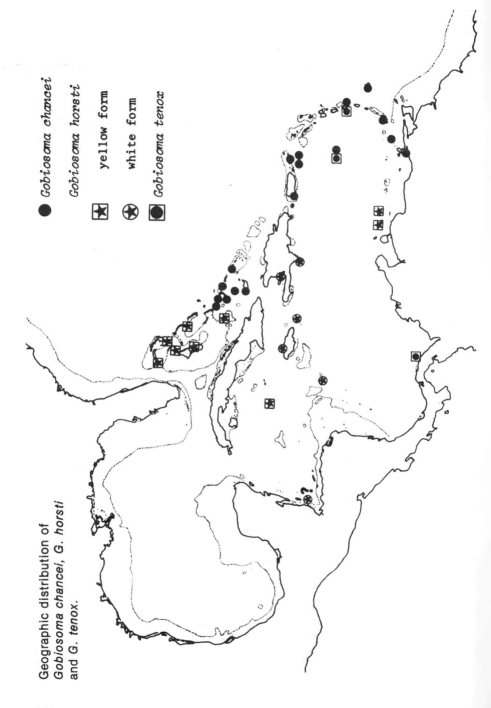

Geographic distribution of
*Gobiosoma chancei*, *G. horsti*
and *G. tenox*.

Geographic distribution of
*Gobiosoma chancei*, *G. horsti*
and *G. tenox*.

● *Gobiosoma chancei*

*Gobiosoma horsti*

⊞ yellow form

⊛ white form

◉ *Gobiosoma tenox*

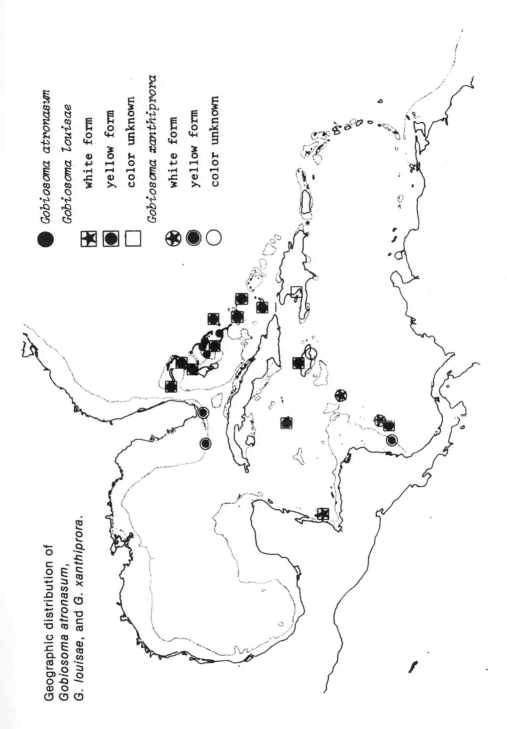

Geographic distribution of
Gobiosoma atronasum,
G. louisae, and G. xanthiprora.

*Gobiosoma atronasum*

● *Gobiosoma atronasum*

*Gobiosoma louisae*

⊞ white form
⊡ yellow form
□ color unknown

*Gobiosoma xanthiprora*

⊛ white form
◉ yellow form
○ color unknown

155

Aquarium photograph of *G. louisae* (Y) from Discovery Bay, Jamaica, showing the rounded end of the dark lateral stripe.

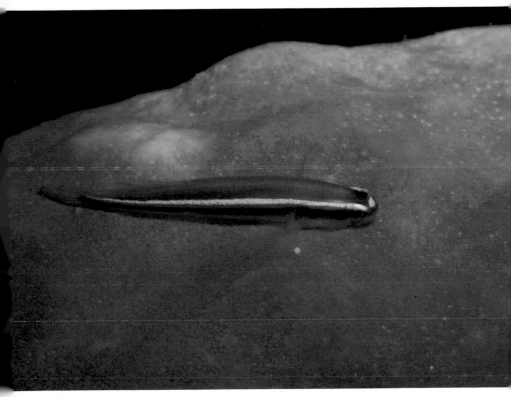

The goby *G. louisae* (Y) on the sponge *Agelus* sp. at Discovery Bay, Jamaica. The oval snout marking and rounded end of the dark lateral stripe are plainly visible in this specimen.

Specimen of *G. louisae* (Y) in fright coloration.

# FIELD AND LABORATORY
# COMPARATIVE STUDIES

This section deals with field studies on the ecology of species of *Elacatinus* at various localities in the western North Atlantic and laboratory studies on reproductive biology and larval development. The zoogeography and relationships of the group are also considered in this section.

## DENSITY, SPACIAL DISTRIBUTION AND BATHYMETRIC DISTRIBUTION

Little has been published regarding the abundance of reef fishes in the western North Atlantic, particularly small fishes. Reef fish populations were estimated by making direct counts of fishes on reefs by Odum and Odum (1955) for Eniwetok and Bardach (1959) for Bermuda. Randall (1963), using ichthyocides, compared populations of fishes on natural and artificial reefs at St. John, Virgin Islands. Emery (1968b) compared direct counting and poison stations for determining density of Pomacentridae at Alligator Reef, Florida. He swam transects and counted fishes 1 m on either side of him, then poisoned the transect area. The area covered by the poison station was much greater than that covered by transects, but population estimates obtained by direct counting were at least 20 times those obtained by poisoning. Poisoning also killed selectively, making relative comparisons between species collected at a station difficult. Smith and Tyler (1972) determined abundance of many species on an isolated small patch reef during extensive observations, then collected from that reef using ichthyocides. They obtained nearly equal numbers of individuals of many species when comparing direct observation and poison collections. Wary, free-swimming fishes were much more abundant in visual counts than in poison stations because they probably leave the area when it is disturbed.

The problems of visual censuses of reef fishes include: 1) fishes that are free-swimming and in motion are difficult to count accurately; and 2) some fishes are so secretive that they cannot be observed by divers. Fortunately, neither problem is of major importance in determining abundance of species of *Gobiosoma*. All are relatively sedentary, moving only a few meters in normal movements, and they are not particularly frightened by divers. Most individuals are not secretive and are visible on coral heads or inside their host sponges. For these reasons the species of *Gobiosoma* are perhaps ideal reef fishes for censuses of density, bathymetric distribution, and long term fluctuation of populations. If all coral heads are slowly and carefully checked, all sponges examined thoroughly, and rock ledges scanned, it is reasonably certain that most, if not all, *Gobiosoma* in a limited area can be censused; such data are more accurate than that obtained from poison stations. For example, Smith and Tyler (1972: 131) observed 10 individuals of *G. evelynae* (YB) on their study reef, always on well exposed living coral, during their two weeks of observation, but the terminal rotenone collections only produced 6 specimens.

One problem is encountered in comparing values obtained in the quadrat surveys. The size of the quadrat ((10 m) sq.) is determined by vertical projection of this square and does not consider the actual surface area of the bottom, which may be greater than 100 square meters due to channels, large coral heads, or other variations in relief. It does not consider the ratio of hard (coral rock) substrate to soft (sand) substrate, or the number or area of coral heads and the number of sponges present. Generally quadrats were selected in areas considered "typical" of wider reef areas observed during early survey dives.

Methods of quantitatively describing a limited area of a coral reef are still extremely crude. Most problems stem from the reef surface being a complex and diverse substrate (Stoddart, 1972).

The quadrat size of (10 m) square was chosen for several reasons. This size quadrat would in most cases contain a number of individuals, but not so many that the number present would be difficult to determine. The size was sufficiently large that most individuals except those on the perimeter were undisturbed during the laying out of the quadrat. The setting out of a square of (1m) square or (3 m) square would have disturbed most of the individuals present. But the (10 m) square quadrat was sufficiently small that it could usually be surveyed during the course of one dive.

At Discovery Bay, Jamaica, a total of 10 quadrats was surveyed. The reefs near Discovery Bay are the best known reefs in the western Atlantic (Goreau and Wells, 1967; Wells and Lang, 1973; Kinzie, 1973), but a definitive quanitative work on the ecology of these reefs has not yet been produced. Many aspects of the biology of the reefs are well known, however, and of interest in the present study (Reiswig, 1970, 1971a, 1971b; Wells, 1973).

A permanent transect line was established on one finger of the reef, termed "dancing lady reef" from a depth of 7 m to 23 m, a distance of ap-

Juvenile specimen of *G. louisae* (Y), 17.4 mm S.L. from San Salvador, Bahamas.

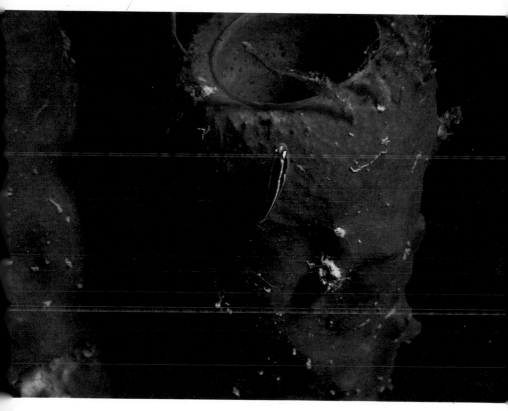

Individual of *G. louisae* (Y) on the outer surface of the sponge *Verongia fistularis,* Highborn Cay, Exuma Islands, Bahamas; depth 24 m (80 feet).

Noctural coloration of *G. louisae* (Y) from the Bahamas.

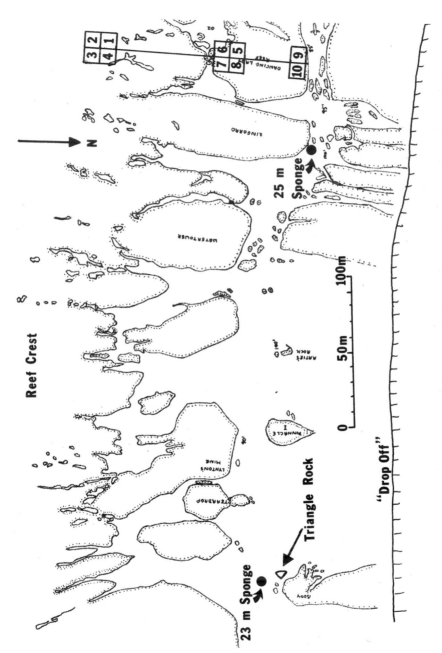

Map of the reefs offshore from the Discovery Bay Marine Laboratory, Discovery Bay, Jamaica.

proximately 120 m. Also located on the map are other areas referred to in subsequent discussion. The area of the reef that was studied appeared typical of the entire shallow portion of the reef. The plan was to sample the various zones along the transect. Goreau (1959) described species composition and zonation of a reef on the north coast of Jamaica near Ocho Rios and most, but not all, of his description is applicable to the Discovery Bay reef. Kinzie (1973) dealt with the Discovery Bay reef and has descriptions and photographs of the various zones. Basically, on the reef there is a shallow zone characterized by *Acropora palmata,* elkhorn coral. Below this zone is an area of mixed corals, particularly the massive corals *Montastrea* and *Colpophyllia.* Seaward and slightly deeper is a zone consisting largely of the coral *Acropora cervicornis* with some other coral heads. A steep slope (about 45°) is encountered at the end of the *A. cervicornis* zone where the depth drops from 15 to 24 m.

Quadrats 1-4 were located in the mixed zone at 9 m depth. Quadrats 5-8 were in the *A. cervicornis* zone at 12 m, and quadrats 9-10 were on the escarpment at 17-24 m.

Qualitatively these quadrats were similar to other areas in their respective zones. Although both *G. prochilos* and *G. louisae* occur along the north coast of Jamaica, neither was encountered in the quadrats. *Gobiosoma prochilos* is relatively rare on the north coast, and *G. louisae* is usually encountered deeper than the study area. Information was recorded for the coral-dwelling goby *Coryphopterus lipernes,* often found with *Gobiosoma,* since it offers interesting comparisons. The number of individuals and stations was recorded. A station was a single contiguous coral colony or sponge or a localized area of rock substrate. Two fishes on adjacent coral heads, although close to one another, were recorded as occupying separate stations because of uncertainty in deciding whether such individuals are associated with each other.

At Curacao, Netherlands Antilles, the seven quadrats surveyed formed a continuous transect, 10 m wide, of the steeply sloping reef from a depth of 4.5 to 40 m. The study area was located about 1 km west of the Caribbean Marine Biological Institute on the south (leeward) coast of Curacao. This transect was resurveyed a year later and the two surveys compared. Roos (1964 and 1971) has dealt with the stony corals found in the study area. The reef area in Curacao is not so easily divided into zones as that at Discovery Bay, but because the shelf at Curacao is narrow, the entire width available to *Gobiosoma* could be surveyed.

A gently sloping bottom is found running 50-100 m offshore from the beach or rock cliffs to a depth of 8-10 m, with the outer portion having numerous coral heads. The bottom then slopes quickly (approximately 30° angle) to at least 65-70 m depth. Then a slightly sloping sandy

Aquarium photograph of *G. louisae* (Y). The individual in the plastic tube is a male with the lateral colored stripe confluent with the oval snout marking.

*Gobiosoma louisae* on the outer surface of a tubular *Verongia* sponge, Exuma Sound (Eleuthera Island), Bahamas, depth 21 m (70 feet).

A male *G. louisae* in the sponge *Agelus* sp. at Discovery Bay, Jamaica.

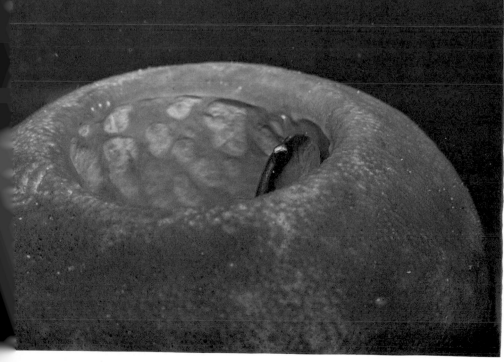

# TABLE 3

## RESULTS OF QUADRATS SURVEYED AT DISCOVERY BAY, JAMAICA, AUGUST 1-20, 1971

| Quadrat Number | Individuals of G. evelynae (W) | Individuals of G. horsti (W) | Individuals of C. lipernes | Stations with G. evelynae (W) | Stations with G. horsti (W) | Stations with C. lipernes | Stations with G. evelynae (W) and C. lipernes | Depth (m) |
|---|---|---|---|---|---|---|---|---|
| 1 ... ... | 8 | 2 | 3 | 7 | 2 | 3 | 1 | 9 |
| 2 ... ... | 8 | 0 | 4 | 6 | 0 | 2 | 1 | 9 |
| 3 ... ... | 8 | 0 | 2 | 6 | 0 | 1 | 1 | 9 |
| 4 ... ... | 3 | 0 | 3 | 2 | 0 | 3 | 0 | 9 |
| 5 ... ... | 9 | 2 | 34 | 8 | 1 | 20 | 3 | 12 |
| 6 ... ... | 10 | 2 | 22 | 8 | 1 | 17 | 4 | 12 |
| 7 ... ... | 5 | 0 | 18 | 5 | 0 | 13 | 1 | 12 |
| 8 ... ... | 5 | 0 | 11 | 4 | 0 | 9 | 1 | 12 |
| 9 ... ... | 9 | 1 | 55 | 9 | 1 | 38 | 2 | 17–24 |
| 10 ... ... | 8 | 0 | 31 | 8 | 0 | 19 | 5 | 17–24 |

plain about 30-50 m wide is encountered at the study area, and at its outer edge (75 m) the bottom again slopes away steeply. The reef slope from
8 to 40-50 m has an abundant coral fauna which changes in both species
composition and abundance with depth. Species of *Montastrea* are most
abundant on the upper reaches of the slope (above 20-30 m), and species
of *Agaricia* are predominantly deeper.

Qualitatively, the surveyed area appeared typical of large sections of
the south coast. The differences in quadrat populations of *Gobiosoma* are
probably reflective of differences in coral growth within the quadrats.

Two quadrat surveys were carried out in the Bahamas; the first consisted of 6 quadrats at Grand Bahama Island and the second of 4 quadrats at Acklins Island. The two areas were different in coral growth within the quadrats and will be described separately.

The quadrats at Grand Bahama Island were surveyed along the
south shore near the "Hydro-lab" underwater habitat. This area was chosen not due to the habitat being used, but because information was avail-

able about the area. Bunt *et al.* (1972) present a descriptive and pictoral representation of the area located about 1.7 km offshore at a depth of 15 m. The quadrats were surveyed in an area of rocky reef formations that produced finger-like projections rising about 2 m above the sand. Living coral was relatively sparse, covering no more than 5-10% of the bottom. Some massive sponges, such as *Xestospongia muta,* were present. During the study (May, 1972) *G. evelynae* (Y) was the only form of this species present at Grand Bahama Island. However, *G. evelynae* (YB) has been found there at a later date.

## TABLE 4

## RESULTS OF QUADRATS SURVEYED AT CURACAO, NETHERLANDS ANTILLES NEAR PISCADERA BAAI

## JULY 1971

| Quadrat Number | Individuals of G. evelynae (YB) | Individuals of G. horsti (Y) | Individuals of G. randalli | Individuals of C. lipernes | Stations with G. evelynae (YB) | Stations with G. horsti (Y) | Stations with G. randalli | Stations with C. lipernes | Stations with both G. evelynae (YB), G. randalli | Stations with both G. evelynae (YB), C. lipernes | Stations with both G. randalli, C. lipernes | Depth (m) |
|---|---|---|---|---|---|---|---|---|---|---|---|---|
| 1 … … | 31 | 1 | 1 | 2 | 17 | 1 | 1 | 2 | 1 | 2 | 0 | 4.5–6.5 |
| 2 … … | 26 | 0 | 3 | 8 | 11 | 0 | 2 | 7 | 2 | 5 | 2 | 6.5–9.0 |
| 3 … … | 30 | 0 | 1 | 17 | 13 | 0 | 1 | 5 | 1 | 5 | 0 | 9.0–14.0 |
| 4 … … | 7 | 0 | 0 | 2 | 3 | 0 | 0 | 2 | 0 | 2 | 0 | 14.0–20.0 |
| 5 … … | 5 | 0 | 0 | 1 | 3 | 0 | 0 | 1 | 0 | 1 | 0 | 20.0–27.0 |
| 6 … … | 0 | 0 | 0 | 0 | 0 | 0 | 0 | 0 | 0 | 0 | 0 | 27.0–36.0 |
| 7 … … | 2 | 0 | 0 | 0 | 2 | 0 | 0 | 0 | 0 | 0 | 0 | 36.0–40.0 |

All the quadrats were similar qualitatively. The number of individuals was fairly consistent and probably reflected the similarity of the quadrats.

Four quadrats were surveyed at Acklins Island, Bahamas about 1 km from shore on the west side (leeward) of the island near the south tip. This area was 15-17 m deep and located about 15 m from the edge of a steep drop-off into Exuma Sound. The reef on the edge of the dropoff is about 150 m wide with scattered patches of reef inshore for a short distance. The reef is relatively flat with abundant *Acropora cervicornis* and scattered heads of massive corals.

On the west coast of Barbados about 1 km south of and 1 km offshore from the Bellairs Research Institute in St. James, 5 quadrats were surveyed. The reef here is rather unusual for the West Indies because it is separated from the shore by an area of deep water, often more than 50 m

Typical habitat of *Gobiosoma louisae* on the deep fore reef at approximately 40 m at Discovery Bay, Jamaica. Isolated coral heads on a steep sandy slope include large Demospongiae such as *Verongia gigantea* (yellowish, barrel-like sponge) and other species of *Verongia* and *Agelus*.

Dorsal view of a freshly killed specimen of *G. tenox* from Aves Island (UMML 30701). The yellow lateral stripe and snout bar have already faded to a nearly black color.

Lateral view of *G. tenox* (UMML 30701) showing the very dusky color of this species. The lateral stripe, running from the eye to the pectoral fin base, has faded in this freshly killed individual.

# TABLE 5

## RESULTS OF QUADRATS SURVEYED AT GRAND BAHAMA ISLAND, BAHAMAS, OFF LUCAYA HARBOR, 15m DEPTH

### MAY 1971

| Quadrat Number | Individuals of *G. evelynae* (Y) | Individuals of *G. genie* | Individuals of *G. horsti* (Y) | Individuals of *C. lipernes* | Stations with *G. evelynae* (Y) | Stations with *G. genie* | Stations with *G. horsti* (Y) | Stations with *C. lipernes* | Stations with *G. evelynae* (Y) and *C. lipernes* | Stations with *G. genie* and *C. lipernes* | Stations with *G. evelynae* (Y), *G. genie* and *C. lipernes* |
|---|---|---|---|---|---|---|---|---|---|---|---|
| 1 ... | 7 | 4 | 5 | 0 | 3 | 3 | 4 | 0 | 0 | 0 | 0 |
| 2 ... | 3 | 4 | 1 | 0 | 2 | 3 | 1 | 0 | 0 | 0 | 0 |
| 3 ... | 14 | 3 | 1 | 2 | 5 | 2 | 1 | 1 | 1 | 1 | 1 |
| 4 ... | 5 | 3 | 3 | 0 | 4 | 3 | 2 | 0 | 0 | 0 | 0 |
| 5 ... | 14 | 4 | 5 | 3 | 11 | 3 | 3 | 2 | 0 | 1 | 0 |
| 6 ... | 5 | 3 | 2 | 0 | 5 | 3 | 2 | 0 | 0 | 0 | 0 |

deep, but the coral bank rises to 12 m. A series of these "coral banks" is found in deeper water, probably representing Pleistocene coral reefs. The quadrats were on the upper part of this coral bank, which is relatively flat. On either side the bank slopes relatively steeply (10°-30°). While some patch reefs are found along the shore, this coral bank is the area of maximum coral growth on the west coast. Although the coral growth is abundant, the reef structure is much less developed and complex than an area such as Discovery Bay, Jamaica. Large specimens of the sponge *Xestospongia muta* were common in most of the quadrats with specimens of *Gobiosoma*, particularly *G. prochilos*, found on them.

At St. Croix, Virgin Islands, two quadrats were surveyed. These were located inside of the Tague Bay barrier reef on the north side of the island near its east end.

The final quadrat surveys were carried out at Galeta Island, Panama, offshore from the Galeta Marine Laboratory of the Smithsonian Tropical Research Institute. The area differed considerably from the

## TABLE 6

## RESULTS OF QUADRATS SURVEYED AT JAMAICA BAY, ACKLINS ISLAND, BAHAMAS, 17m DEPTH

### APRIL 1972

| Quadrat Number | Individuals of G. evelynae (YB) | Individuals of G. chancei | Individuals of G. louisae (Y) | Individuals of C. lipernes | Stations with G. evelynae (YB) | Stations with G. chancei | Stations with G. louisae (Y) | Stations with C. lipernes | Stations with G. evelynae (YB) and C. lipernes | Stations with G. chancei and G. louisae (Y) |
|---|---|---|---|---|---|---|---|---|---|---|
| 1 ... ... | 15 | 5 | 2 | 10 | 9 | 5 | 2 | 8 | 3 | 2 |
| 2 ... ... | 10 | 5 | 0 | 15 | 5 | 3 | 0 | 10 | 4 | 0 |
| 3 ... ... | 10 | 4 | 2 | 14 | 9 | 4 | 1 | 12 | 3 | 1 |
| 4 ... ... | 5 | 1 | 1 | 8 | 4 | 1 | 1 | 6 | 0 | 1 |

## TABLE 7

## RESULTS OF QUADRATS SURVEYED AT BARBADOS OFF THE BELLAIRS RESEARCH INSTITUTE

### JULY 1972

| Quadrat Number | Individuals of G. evelynae (YB) | Individuals of G. prochilos | Individuals of G. chancei | Individuals of C. lipernes | Stations with G. evelynae (YB) | Stations with G. prochilos | Stations with G. chancei | Stations with C. lipernes | Stations with G. evelynae (YB) and C. lipernes | Stations with G. evelynae (YB) and G. prochilos | Stations with G. prochilos and C. lipernes | Stations with G. evelynae (YB), G. prochilos and C. lipernes | Depth (m) |
|---|---|---|---|---|---|---|---|---|---|---|---|---|---|
| 1 ... | 14 | 1 | 1 | 10 | 6 | 1 | 1 | 8 | 3 | 0 | 0 | 0 | 13 |
| 2 ... | 9 | 5 | 2 | 12 | 8 | 1 | 2 | 9 | 1 | 0 | 0 | 0 | 13 |
| 3 ... | 31 | 89 | 5 | 58 | 16 | 9 | 3 | 24 | 5 | 6 | 4 | 2 | 16 |
| 4 ... | 13 | 37 | 6 | 2 | 9 | 18 | 4 | 2 | 2 | 3 | 0 | 0 | 18 |
| 5 ... | 4 | 14 | 5 | 5 | 4 | 3 | 4 | 4 | 0 | 2 | 0 | 0 | 20 |

Several specimens of *G. atronasum* resting temporarily on the coral *Montastrea cavernosa*. Exuma Sound, Eleuthera, Bahamas (depth 20 m).

Specimen of *G. atronasum*) sheltering beneath the expanded polyps of *Montastrea cavernosa* at night. Photographed at Eleuthera Island, Exuma Sound, Bahamas, 20 m depth.

*Gobiosoma atronasum* is restricted to Exuma Sound, Bahamas, where it is found hovering along steep reef faces and occasionally resting on corals.

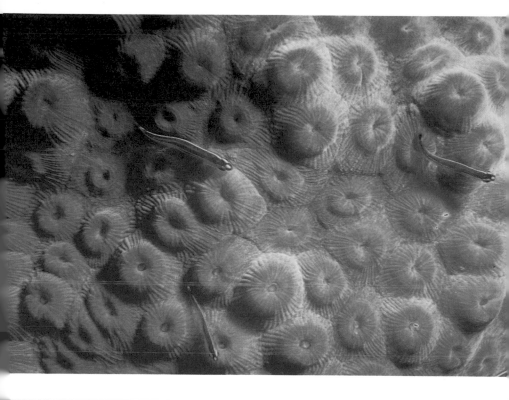

## TABLE 8

## RESULTS OF QUADRATS SURVEYED AT TAGUE BAY, ST. CROIX, VIRGIN ISLANDS, DEPTH 1–3 m. JUNE 1972

| Quadrat Number | Individuals of *G. evelynae* (YB) | Individuals of *G. prochilos* | Stations with *G. evelynae* (YB) | Stations with *G. prochilos* | Stations with *G. evelynae* (YB) *G. prochilos* |
|---|---|---|---|---|---|
| 1 ... ... ... | 12 | 4 | 10 | 3 | 1 |
| 2 ... ... ... | 3 | 1 | 3 | 1 | 0 |

others that were surveyed and had by far the least abundant reef corals, particularly below 10 m depth. The small number of *G. illecebrosum* (Y) was probably due to the poor reef development. Qualitative observations at localities such as Portobello and the San Blas Islands indicate much larger populations at those sites. The quadrats consisted of 3 transects 10 m wide that were immediately adjacent to one another. They effectively covered the entire width of the reef for a distance of 30 m and form a single quadrat (30 m) at 1-11 m depth. A single quadrat was in shallower (0.5-1.0 m) water.

Some data are available from other studies for comparison with present data. Smith and Tyler (1972) found 10 individuals of *G. evelynae* (YB) on their study reef, which was triangular in shape and approximately 3 m on a side with some small isolated satellite patches. Their reef was 1.6 m high, and its size more or less compares with the reef found within (10 m) square quadrats that contained some sand substrates. Their value of 10 individuals is comparable to values obtained in the present quadrat surveys. Dammann (1969) found one individual of *G. evelynae* on a reef of approximately 800 square meters that was poisoned in the Virgin Islands. Randall (1963) found many *Gobiosoma* on two natural reefs that were poisoned for comparison with artificial reefs, but he did not identify gobiids to species and listed only the number of individuals for the entire family. Visual and poison stations cannot be directly compared because of discrepancies in population assessments (Emery, 1968b; Smith and Tyler, 1972).

The number of individuals found on a single station also was examined. A station was defined as a continuous single coral colony or sponge, regardless of its size or number of tubes, or a limited area of rock surface usually delimited by adjacent features such as coral heads or sand, but never more than 1-2 m in any dimension. The data concerning numbers of individuals found per station include data from quadrats and general surveys of abundance, numbers, and substrate inhabited. Usually only a few per cent of stations are occupied by more than 5 individuals. The total numbers of individuals at stations occupied by two individuals is greater than the number of individuals at stations occupied by one individual. The methods used cannot underestimate the number of stations occupied by a single individual if the individual is not hiding. The number of stations occupied by more than one individual can be underestimated because an individual may move to a nearby coral head during a survey, causing one station with two individuals to be recorded as two stations with one individual each.

## TABLE 9

## RESULTS OF QUADRATS
## SURVEYED AT GALETA ISLAND, PANAMA
## SEPTEMBER 1971

| Quadrat Number | Individuals of *G. illecebrosum* (Y) | Individuals of *G. saucrum* (*Tigrigobius*) | Stations with *G. illecebrosum* (Y) | Stations with *G. saucrum* (*Tigrigobius*) | Stations with *G. illecebrosum* (Y) *G. saucrum* (*Tigrigobius*) | Depth (m) |
|---|---|---|---|---|---|---|
| 1 ... ... | 0 | 0 | 0 | 0 | 0 | 0.5–1.0 |
| 2 ... ... | 2 | 3 | 1 | 3 | 0 | 1.0–7.0 |
| 3 ... ... | 5 | 5 | 1 | 4 | 1 | 7.0–9.0 |
| 4 ... ... | 0 | 2 | 0 | 1 | 0 | 9.0–11.0 |
| 5 ... ... | 0 | 3 | 0 | 2 | 0 | 1.2–7.0 |
| 6 ... ... | 1 | 10 | 1 | 7 | 0 | 7.0–9.0 |
| 7 ... ... | 0 | 6 | 0 | 3 | 0 | 9.0–11.0 |
| 8 ... ... | 3 | 1 | 1 | 1 | 0 | 1.8–5.0 |
| 9 ... ... | 1 | 1 | 1 | 1 | 0 | 5.0–8.5 |
| 10 ... ... | 1 | 7 | 1 | 3 | 1 | 8.5–11.0 |

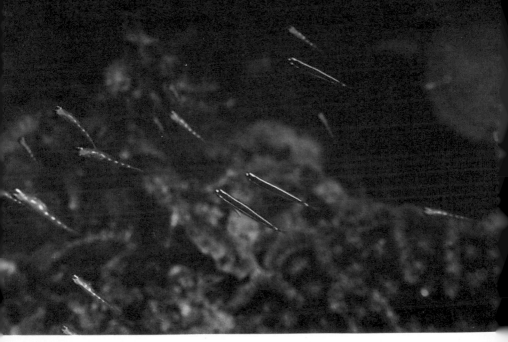

*Gobiosoma atronasum* occurs in aggregations with planktivorous reef fishes such as these *Gramma loreto.*

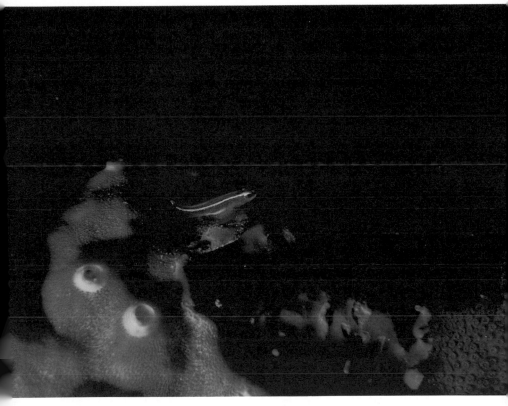

*Gobiosoma atronasum* resting on an unidentified sponge. See comments on lower plate, page 181.

Masked gobies, *Coryphopterus personatus*, commonly occur along steep faces with *G. atronasum.* The *G. atronasum* show the break in the lateral colored stripe near the caudal peduncle found in many individuals of this species.

## TABLE 10

### RANGE, MEAN AND STANDARD DEVIATION†
### OF NUMBERS OF INDIVIDUALS/m² OF SPECIES OF GOBIES AT VARIOUS LOCALITIES

| | Discovery Bay Jamaica | Piscadera Baai Curacao | Grand Bahama Island | Acklins Island Bahamas | St. James Barbados | St. Croix Virgin Islands | Galeta Island Panama |
|---|---|---|---|---|---|---|---|
| Number of Quadrats | 10 | 7 | 6 | 4 | 5 | 2 | 10 |
| *Gobiosoma evelynae* (all color forms) | 0.03–0.10 0.07 (0.02) | 0.00–0.31 0.14 (0.11) | 0.05–0.14 0.08 (0.04) | 0.00–0.15 0.10 (0.03) | 0.04–0.31 0.16 (0.09) | 0.03–0.12 0.07 | — |
| *Gobiosoma genie* | — | — | 0.03–0.04 0.03 (0.005) | — | — | — | — |
| *Gobiosoma prochilos* | — | — | — | — | 0.01–0.89 0.29 (0.29) | 0.01–0.03 0.02 | — |
| *Gobiosoma randalli* | — | 0.00–0.02 | — | — | — | — | — |
| *Gobiosoma illecebrosum* (Y) | — | — | — | — | — | — | 0.00–0.05 0.01 (0.01) |
| *Gobiosoma horsti* (all color forms) | 0.00–0.02 0.01 (0.01) | 0.00–0.01 | 0.01–0.05 0.03 (0.02) | — | — | — | — |
| *Gobiosoma chancei* | — | — | — | — | 0.01–0.05 0.03 (0.01) | 0.01–0.06 0.04 (0.02) | — |
| *Gobiosoma saucrum* (*Tigrigobius*) | — | — | — | — | — | — | 0.00–0.10 0.04 (0.03) |
| *Coryphopterus lipernes* | 0.03–0.58 0.18 (0.16) | 0.00–0.17 0.04 (0.4) | 0.00–0.03 0.01 (0.01) | 0.08–0.15 0.12 (0.03) | 0.02–0.58 0.17 (0.04) | — | — |

† Standard deviation in parentheses.

# TABLE 11

## OBSERVED PERCENTAGES OF STATIONS AT VARIOUS LOCALITIES WITH CERTAIN NUMBERS OF FISHES PRESENT

| | Number of Individuals Present at Station | | | | | | | | | | | Number of Individuals | Mean No. Ind./Sta. |
| | 1 | 2 | 3 | 4 | 5 | 6 | 7 | 8 | 9 | 10 | 11–20 | | |
|---|---|---|---|---|---|---|---|---|---|---|---|---|---|
| *Gobiosoma evelynae* | | | | | | | | | | | | | |
| yellow form (Y) | 54 | 28 | 3.2 | 4.8 | 6.3 | — | — | — | 3.2 | — | — | 126 | 2.00 |
| yellow blue form (YB) | 68 | 19 | 3.4 | 2.9 | 1.9 | 2.4 | — | 0.5 | 1.4 | — | — | 349 | 1.69 |
| white form (W) | 78 | 18 | 1.2 | 1.2 | — | — | — | 0.6 | — | 0.6 | — | 201 | 1.22 |
| *Gobiosoma genie* | 73 | 23 | 2.1 | — | — | 1.0 | 1.0 | — | — | — | — | 131 | 1.36 |
| *Gobiosoma illecebrosum* | | | | | | | | | | | | | |
| yellow form (Y) | 50 | 16 | 16 | — | 16 | — | — | — | — | — | — | 13 | 2.17 |
| *Gobiosoma oceanops* | 42 | 25 | 1.5 | 6.2 | 3.1 | 6.2 | 1.5 | 1.5 | 1.5 | — | 12.2 | 263 | 4.05 |
| *Gobiosoma prochilos* | 58 | 25 | 1.7 | 3.4 | 3.4 | — | 1.7 | 5.1 | 1.7 | — | — | 125 | 2.11 |
| *Gobiosoma randalli* | 75 | 5 | 15 | 5 | — | — | — | — | — | — | — | 30 | 1.50 |
| *Coryphopterus lipernes* | 68 | 20 | 4.7 | 2.2 | 3.6 | 0.8 | 0.5 | 0.3 | 0.3 | — | — | 587 | 1.61 |

179

The teardrop shape of the snout marking in *G. atronasum* is apparent in this dorsal view.

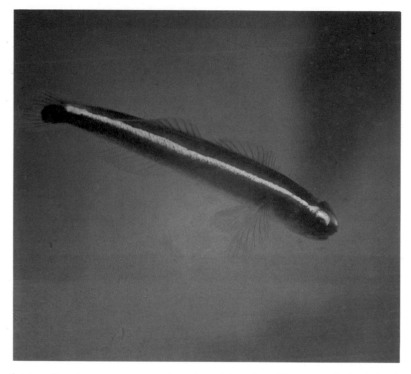

Large *G. atronasum* hovering in mid-water. The rounded end of the dark lateral stripe and the position of the mouth are visible in this individual which does not have the break in the colored stripe at the caudal peduncle.

Individual of *G. atronasum* resting on an unidentified sponge, Exuma Sound, Bahamas. Photographed after completion of the text, this is the sole record of *G. atronasum* on sponges. The fish just in front of it is *Coryphopterus personatus*.

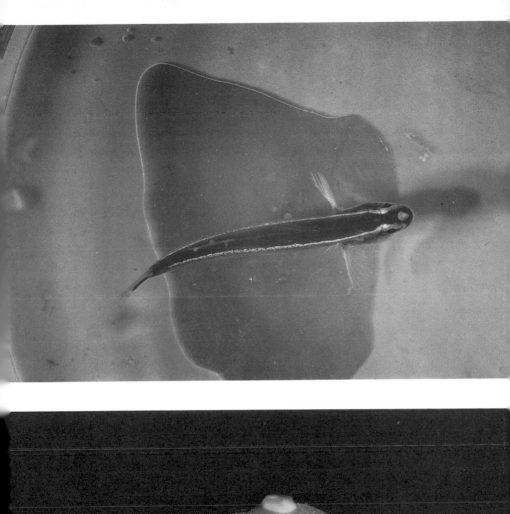

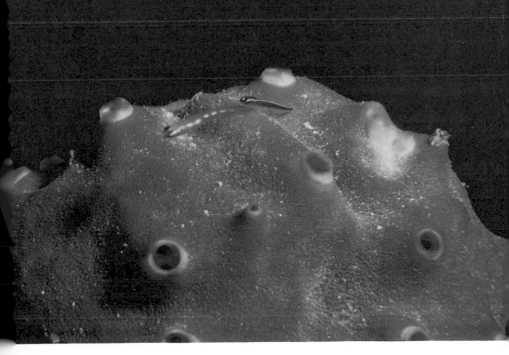

Coral area off the west coast of Barbados about 1.5 km southwest of the Bellairs Research Institute. Although the coral growth is not particularly luxurious, the highest densities of species of *Gobiosoma* were found in such areas.

An interesting comparison can be made utilizing "Triangle Rock," a small patch reef at 24 m depth at Discovery Bay, Jamaica. Approximately 150 coral heads or "stations" exist on the patch reef, determined from photographs, and it was surveyed several times over a two year period to determine the populations of *Gobiosoma*. Three surveys involved sufficient numbers of individuals to test whether individuals were randomly distributed on the stations or congregating. In all three cases the distributions were significantly different (beyond the 0.05 level) from that expected if the individuals were randomly distributed. Evidently a social component is operating causing individuals to congregate at stations.

It is difficult to make a similar comparison of the number of fishes per station per quadrat, but unoccupied stations greatly outnumbered individuals of *Gobiosoma* and no more than 10-20% of stations were occupied. Again individuals apparently were not randomly distributed, but clumped, although there are no statistical data to support this contention for the quadrat surveys.

The species of corals most commonly inhabited by *Gobiosoma* were *Montastrea annularis* and *M. cavernosa*. The corals inhabited by *Gobiosoma* are discussed more in the section on coral dwelling.

In certain areas it seemed that there was a depth zonation of some ecologically similar species of *Gobiosoma*. Both Bohlke and Robins (1968: 112) and Bohlke and Chaplin (1968: 614) state that in the Bahamas *G. genie* usually occurs in shallower areas than *G. evelynae*. An effort was made to test this, particularly since *G. genie* is found with two different color varieties of *G. evelynae*. *G. genie* usually is found shallow-

TABLE 12

PERCENTAGE OF INDIVIDUALS OF VARIOUS SPECIES OF *Gobiosoma* OBSERVED WITHIN CERTAIN DEPTH RANGES IN COMPARISON WITH THE TOTAL INDIVIDUALS OBSERVED IN THAT DEPTH RANGE AT VARIOUS LOCALITIES

A.—Northern Bahamas (Grand Bahama Is., Great Abaco Is., Eleuthera Is.). Only the yellow form of *G. evelynae* was present. Numbers in parentheses refer to numbers of individuals observed.

| Depth (m) | G. evelynae (Y) | G. genie |
|---|---|---|
| 0–10 | 5(1) | 95(20) |
| 11–20 | 87(65) | 13(10) |
| 21–30 | 95(37) | 5(2) |
| 31–40 | 100(2) | 0 |

B.—Other Bahamian localities. Both the yellow and yellow-blue form of *G. evelynae* were present. Numbers in parentheses refer to numbers of individuals observed.

| Depth (m) | G. evelynae (Y) | G. evelynae (YB) | G. genie |
|---|---|---|---|
| 0–10 | 0 | 38(17) | 62(28) |
| 11–20 | 40(48) | 51(60) | 9(12) |
| 21–30 | 69(9) | 32(3) | 8(1) |

Laboratory reared hybrid *Gobiosoma* (*G. oceanops* [female] x *G. evelynae* (W) [male]) 17.5 mm S.L. White spheres on the posterior half of the body are caused by a parasitic infection.

Mixed aggregation of *G. atronasum* and *Coryphopterus personatus* at Eleuthera Island, Bahamas. In the background is the squirrelfish *Holocentrus rufus*.

Aerial view of one of the islands, termed the Pedro Cays, on the
Pedro Bank, located south of Jamaica. The reef crest has waves
breaking on it and the bottom drops sharply toward the upper left
corner.

er than either color form of G. *evelynae*. Data from the geographic area where only G. *evelynae* (YB) occurs with G. *genie* have not been included in analysis since there is systematic confusion regarding G. *genie* in this area. There is a differential distribution with depth of G. *evelynae* (YB) and (Y), the yellow form being more abundant in deeper water. It is impossible to interpret abundance of one species or compare abundance between species for the different depth ranges because observations of equal duration or covering equal area were not made.

A similar situation regarding differential depth distribution was also believed to exist for some of the sponge-dwelling gobies. *Gobiosoma louisae* occurs with the northern population of G. *horsti* (Y), G. *horsti* (W), and the northern reaches of G. *chancei*. Observation records of these species were compared for different depth ranges, in terms of percentage of each species observed within that depth range. In all three instances, G. *louisae* occupies a deeper range than the other species even though they are found in the same species of sponges, and at intermediate depths may occupy the same individual sponge. Where G. *louisae* does not occur, the bathymetric range of the other species may be expanded at its lower limit. At St. Croix, where G. *louisae* does not occur, individuals of G. *chancei* were taken several times at 45 m and once at 65 m depth.

## TABLE 13

PERCENTAGE OF TOTAL SPONGE-DWELLING *Gobiosoma*
OF VARIOUS SPECIES OBSERVED AT VARIOUS DEPTHS
IN THE NORTHERN BAHAMAS

NUMBER OF INDIVIDUALS IN PARENTHESES

| Depth (m) | G. evelynae (Y) | G. louisae (Y) |
|-----------|-----------------|----------------|
| 0–10      | 100(2)          | 0              |
| 11–20     | 100(19)         | 0              |
| 21–30     | 27(11)          | 73(26)         |
| 31–40     | 0               | 100(6)         |
| 41–50     | 0               | 100(8)         |

## TABLE 14

### PERCENTAGE OF TOTAL SPONGE-DWELLING *Gobiosoma* OF VARIOUS SPECIES OBSERVED AT VARIOUS DEPTHS ON THE NORTH COAST OF JAMAICA

### NUMBERS OF INDIVIDUALS IN PARENTHESES

| Depth (m) | G. horsti (W) | G. louisae (Y) |
|-----------|---------------|----------------|
| 0–10 | 100(2) | 0 |
| 11–20 | 100(37) | 0 |
| 21–30 | 90(45) | 10(5) |
| 31–40 | 47(17) | 53(19) |
| 41–50 | 25(3) | 75(9) |
| 51–60 | 0 | 100(4) |

Practically no quantitative information exists regarding variation in coral-reef fish populations over the seasons. Areas at Discovery Bay, Jamaica and Curcao, Netherlands Antilles were resurveyed periodically to determine any changes in the numbers of fishes. Each area will be considered separately.

At Discovery Bay, the major, long term survey area was an isolated patch reef, called "Triangle Rock" due to its shape, located at a depth of 25 m on the fore reef slope. This particular location was chosen because: 1) there are few isolated patch reefs at Discovery Bay small enough to practically survey repeatedly; 2) the reef was in an area of high coral diversity, with rich coral growth; 3) conditions here were thought to be nearly ideal for species of *Gobiosoma* and should show maximum population stability.

Underwater slates with a line drawing of the site were constructed in the following manner. From photographs a line drawing of the site was made; this drawing was transferred to the back surface of a thin piece of sanded acrylic plastic in reversed form. The lines were inked and the surface sprayed with gray enamel. The front surface was also sanded so that an ordinary pencil could be used to write on it. This produced a small, accurate map of the site on which notes could be taken repeatedly. With such aids, the entire survey of "Triangle Rock" could be carried out in 30 minutes or a single dive at 25 m depth. All species of *Gobiosoma* and *Co-*

The British Honduras (Belize) barrier reef is one of the longest in the world and an ideal location for various species of *Gobiosoma.*

Northwest Cay on the southern side of the Pedro Banks, South of Jamaica, with waves breaking on the fringing reef. Fishermen's shacks are built on the island.

Aerial view across the British Honduras (Belize) barrier reef. Waves break on the shallow reef crest from the open Caribbean Sea (lower portion); the lagoon (upper portion) separates the reef from the mainland (upper corner) by several miles.

## TABLE 15

PERCENTAGE OF TOTAL SPONGE-DWELLING *Gobiosoma*
OF VARIOUS SPECIES OBSERVED AT VARIOUS DEPTHS
AT HOGSTY REEF AND ACKLINS ISLAND, BAHAMAS

| Depth (m) | *G. chancei* | *G. louisae* (Y) |
|---|---|---|
| 11–20 | 82(28) | 18(6) |
| 21–30 | 29(6) | 71(15) |
| 31–40 | 0 | 100(1) |


## TABLE 16

RESULTS OF SURVEYS OF NUMBERS OF INDIVIDUALS OF
VARIOUS SPECIES OF FISHES ON TRIANGLE ROCK AT
DISCOVERY BAY, JAMAICA OVER A PERIOD OF TWO YEARS
NUMBER OF STATIONS OCCUPIED IN PARENTHESES

| Time of Survey | *G. evelynae* (W) | *G. horsti* (W) | *C. lipernes* |
|---|---|---|---|
| Feb. 1971 | 24(15) | 0 | no data |
| Aug. 1971 | 25(19) | 0 | 5(4) |
| Feb. 1972 | 1(1) | 0 | 0 |
| June 1972 | 17(10) | 1 | 20(10) |
| Feb. 1973 | 9(9) | 0 | 10(9) |

## TABLE 17

NUMBERS OF INDIVIDUALS PRESENT AND THEIR SIZES
ON A SPONGE AT 25 m DEPTH AT VARIOUS TIMES AT
DISCOVERY BAY, JAMAICA

| Time of Survey | G. horsti (W) | Size of Individuals Present |
|---|---|---|
| Aug. 1971 | 13 | medium to large |
| Oct. 1971 | 13 | medium to large |
| Jan. 1972 | 0 | —— |
| July 1972 | 12 | small to medium |
| Feb. 1973 | sponge gone, destroyed | |

*ryphopterus lipernes* were noted, as were the numbers of individuals on any coral head. Species of corals that were inhabited were recorded.

The results of 5 surveys of "Triangle Rock" cover a 2-year period at nearly 6-month intervals from February, 1971 through February, 1973. Both *Gobiosoma evelynae* (W) and *C. lipernes* showed an extreme decrease in abundance during February 1972 which was not seen in the winters of either 1971 or 1973. No data for *C. lipernes* are available for February, 1971. "Triangle Rock" has an area of approximately 25 m square when viewed from above, but has a height of 2 m above the bottom and a minimum surface area of about 60-75 square meters. "Triangle Rock" populations can be compared with population densities from other areas. The density values of approximately 0.4 individuals / m-square for *G. evelynae* (W) and 0.3-0.4 individuals / m-square for *C. lipernes* were among the highest obtained in the study.

Some other locations at Discovery Bay were surveyed more than once. A large sponge, *Neofibrularia massa*, was located at a depth of 25 m at the base of an escarpment from the shallow reef immediately north of the reef finger called "zingaro." The sponge was chosen because of its large size and the large number of *G. horsti* (W) originally observed on it. Extensive observations were carried out at this sponge to ascertain if *G. horsti* engaged in cleaning behavior and to determine general habits of the species. All individuals present in October 1971 were of medium to large size but were gone in January 1972. On July 1972, 12 *G. horsti* (W) were present but all were of small to medium size and were obviously

Stilt houses on the lagoon side of the British Honduras barrier reef near Belize City.

Shallow reef (8 m) at Discovery Bay, Jamaica, with large colonies of
*Acropora palmata* in the foreground and the lower, more delicately
branched *A. cervicornis* below it. A variety of mixed coral heads are
visible in the background.

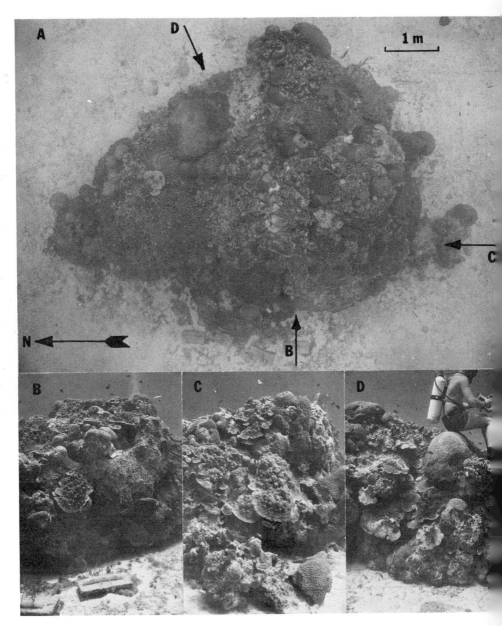

View from above of "Triangle Rock," a patch reef located at a depth of 25 m at Discovery Bay, Jamaica. The lettered arrows refer to views of the sides shown in B, C, and D.

## TABLE 18

NUMBERS OF INDIVIDUALS PRESENT AND THEIR
SIZES ON A SPONGE AT 23 m DEPTH AT VARIOUS
TIMES AT DISCOVERY BAY, JAMAICA

| Time of Survey | G. horsti (W) | Size of Individuals Present |
|---|---|---|
| Feb. 1971 | 6 | small |
| Aug. 1971 | 0 | — |
| Jan. 1972 | 0 | — |
| June 1972 | 1 | small |

from newly metamorphosed larvae. Unfortunately this entire sponge was destroyed in February 1973 and was lost for further long term studies.

A second sponge goby site, termed "Sponge Rock," located at 23 m depth near "Triangle Rock," was observed on numerous occasions. A large red head of the coral *Montastrea cavernosa* was surveyed on two occasions. In February, 1971, 10 individuals of *G. evelynae* (W) and in February, 1972, 8 individuals of the same species were found on this prominent cleaning station.

At Curacao, Netherlands Antilles, a transect of the reef from depths of 5 to 42 m was surveyed twice, in July, 1971 and July, 1972. The transect, located approximately 1 km west of the Caribbean Marine Biological Institute on the south coast of Curacao, consisted of seven (10 m) square quadrats which covered the entire transect of the reef from 5 to 42 m. These are the same quadrats reported from Curacao in the population density considerations; however, only the 1971 survey was considered in that section. The members of *Gobiosoma* in the area were *G. evelynae* (YB), *G. randalli*, and *G. horsti* (Y). The coral-dwelling goby *C. lipernes* was also abundant. The numbers of *Gobiosoma* were surprisingly alike in the two surveys. The observed differences are considered as valid and not artifacts of survey techniques. *Caryphopterus lipernes* was considerably more abundant in 1972 than in 1971.

These data indicate that populations of *Gobiosoma* in limited localities do show some, often considerable, variation over periods on the order of the life span (1 year) of individual fishes. No gross changes could be ob-

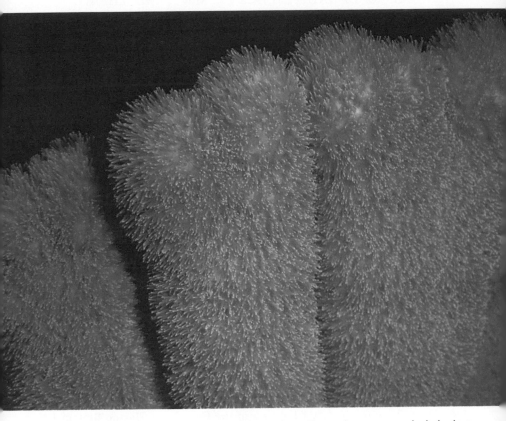

Pillar coral, *Dendrogyra cylindricus*, has the polyps expanded during daylight and is one of the few species of Atlantic corals with which *Gobiosoma* does not associate.

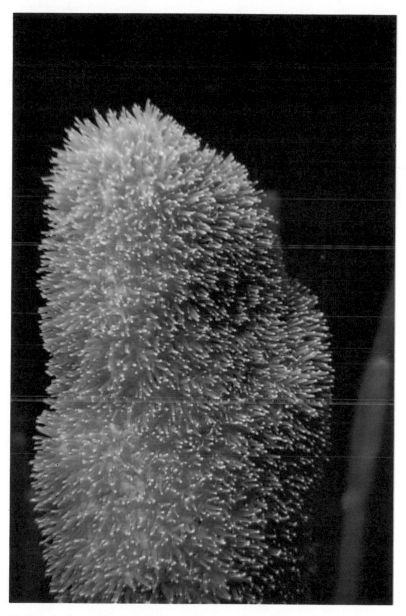

Closer look at the pillar coral, *Dendrogyra cylindricus*, with expanded polyps. At night these polyps retract.

served in any of the localities where these long-term observations were made. As far as *Gobiosoma* and *C. lipernes* are concerned, space does not seem to be an important limiting factor at the densities that were observed. Other factors, such as larval survival or environmental conditions, probably are more important. Most coral heads and a significant percentage of large sponges are not occupied by any *Gobiosoma*.

## TABLE 19

## RESULTS OF TWO QUADRAT SURVEYS ONE YEAR APART (JULY 1971: JULY 1972) AT PISCADERA BAAI, CURACAO

| Quadrat Number | Individuals of *G. evelynae* (YB) 1971 | Individuals of *G. evelynae* (YB) 1972 | Individuals of *G. randalli* 1971 | Individuals of *G. randalli* 1972 | Individuals of *G. horsti* (Y) 1971 | Individuals of *G. horsti* (Y) 1972 | Individuals of *C. lipernes* 1971 | Individuals of *C. lipernes* 1972 |
|---|---|---|---|---|---|---|---|---|
| 1 | 31 | 18 | 1 | 0 | 1 | 1 | 2 | 0 |
| 2 | 26 | 30 | 3 | 2 | 0 | 2 | 8 | 19 |
| 3 | 30 | 30 | 1 | 0 | 0 | 0 | 17 | 61 |
| 4 | 7 | 11 | 0 | 0 | 0 | 0 | 2 | 35 |
| 5 | 5 | 10 | 0 | 0 | 0 | 0 | 1 | 14 |
| 6 | 0 | 0 | 0 | 0 | 0 | 0 | 0 | 4 |
| 7 | 2 | 4 | 0 | 0 | 0 | 0 | 0 | 8 |
| Totals | 101 | 103 | 5 | 2 | 1 | 3 | 30 | 141 |

# CORAL DWELLING IN SPECIES OF *GOBIOSOMA*

That various species of *Gobiosoma* occur on living corals has been known for some time. Jordan (1904) recorded *G. oceanops* from coral heads. Seven species of *Gobiosoma* (*G. oceanops; G. evelynae* (Y), (YB), and (W); *G. illecebrosum* (Y), (B), and (W); *G. genie; G. randalli; G. prochilos;* and *G. atronasum*) have been collected from living coral heads. All sizes from newly metamorphosed juveniles to large adults have been observed on corals. These species also inhabit other substrates. Most have been observed on rock or on the surface of massive sponges. A comparison of western Atlantic reef corals with the species of *Gobiosoma* which have been observed on them is presented. The list of corals is from Wells and Lang (1973), but some species are not included because of their small size, or they have been combined into a larger group if they could not be easily identified in the field. For example, the six species of *Agaricia* were not distinguished.

This does not reflect relative abundance of corals. All of the coral-dwelling species of *Gobiosoma* have been observed, usually in large numbers, on such extremely abundant corals as *Montastrea annularis, M. cavernosa, Diploria* spp., *Siderastrea* spp., and *Colpophylia natans.* The various species of *Gobiosoma* have seldom or never been observed on some common, abundant stony corals. In only one instance was an individual of *G. genie* observed on *Acropora palmata,* yet *A. palmata* is so abundant in many localities that various zones of the reef are termed the "*Acropora* zone" by ecologists. Coral-dwelling species of *Gobiosoma* have not been observed on the other two species, *A. cervicornis* and *A. prolifera.* Large fleshy corals, such as the multipolyped *Mussa angulosa* and the single polyped *Scolymia lacera* and *S. cubensis,* are not utilized by *Gobiosoma.* These polyps may be over 100 mm in diameter. Pillar coral, *Dendrogyra cylindricus,* also is not used by *Gobiosoma.* This coral is unusual because its polyps are expanded during the day.

All the coral-dwelling *Gobiosoma* species shelter at night on coral heads with expanded polyps. Schroeder (1964: 142-143) published a color photograph of two individuals of *G. oceanops* on an expanded brain coral.

All species of *Gobiosoma* resting on corals, both during the day and at night, are apparently immune to nematocysts of the coral polyps. This relationship is not understood, but may be similar to some other coelenterate-fish relationships. The association of fishes of the genus *Amphiprion* with sea anemones in the tropical Indo-Pacific is probably the best documented relationship (Allen, 1972; Mariscal, 1966). It has been determined that a chemical factor in the mucus of the fish prevents the dis-

Corals of the genus *Mycetophyllia* are occasionally used by cleaning members of *Gobiosoma*.

Large *Neofibrularia massa* sponge on the fore-reef, Discovery Bay, Jamaica. This sponge often contains *Gobiosoma* and is noxious for humans to handle.

Close-up view of *Mycetophyllia* showing the individual polyps. Photographed at 20 m (66 feet) depth, Discovery Bay, Jamaica.

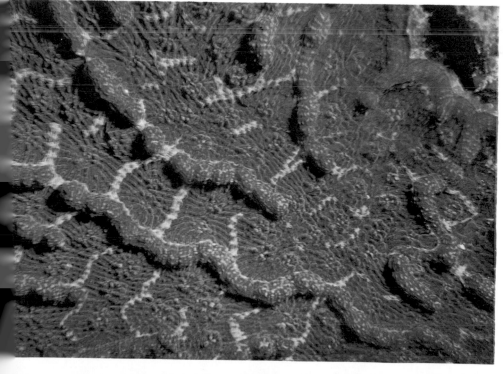

## TABLE 20

## OCCURRENCE OF CORAL-DWELLING GOBIES ON COMMON WESTERN ATLANTIC CORALS

| Coral Species | G. oceanops | G. evelynae (YB) | G. evelynae (Y) | G. evelynae (W) | G. illecebrosum | G. genie | G. randalli | G. prochilos | Coryphopterus lipernes |
|---|---|---|---|---|---|---|---|---|---|
| Stephanocoenia michelinii | — | X | X | X | — | — | — | X | X |
| Madracis spp. (4) ... | — | — | — | — | — | — | — | — | — |
| Acropora palmata ... | — | — | — | — | — | X | — | — | — |
| A. cervicornis ... ... | — | — | — | — | — | — | — | — | — |
| A. prolifera ... ... | — | — | — | — | — | — | — | — | — |
| Agaricia spp. (6) ... | X | X | X | X | X | — | — | — | X |
| Helioseris cucullata ... | — | — | — | — | — | — | — | — | — |
| Siderastrea spp. (2) ... | X | X | X | X | X | X | X | X | X |
| Porites asteroides ... | — | X | — | X | — | — | — | X | X |
| P. porites ... ... | — | X | — | — | — | — | — | — | — |
| Porites spp. (4)... ... | — | — | — | — | — | — | — | — | — |
| Favia fragum ... ... | — | — | — | — | — | — | — | — | — |
| Diploria labyrinthiformis | X | X | X | X | — | X | X | X | X |
| D. clivosa ... ... | X | X | X | X | X | X | X | X | X |
| D. strigosa ... ... | X | X | X | X | X | X | X | X | X |
| Manicina areolata ... | — | X | X | X | — | — | — | — | X |
| Colpophyllia natans ... | X | X | X | X | X | X | X | X | X |
| Cladocera arbuscula ... | — | — | — | — | — | — | — | — | — |
| Montastrea annularis ... | X | X | X | X | X | X | X | X | X |
| M. cavernosa ... ... | X | X | X | X | X | X | X | X | X |
| Solenastrea hyades ... | — | — | — | — | — | — | — | — | — |
| Oculina diffusa... ... | — | — | — | — | — | — | — | — | — |
| Dichocoenia stokesii ... | — | X | — | — | — | — | — | — | — |
| Dendrogyra cylindricus | — | — | — | — | — | — | — | — | — |

X = Positive Occurrence

## TABLE 20—Continued

| | G. oceanops | G. evelynae (YB) | G. evelynae (Y) | G. evelynae (W) | G. illecebrosum | G. genie | G. randalli | G. prochilos | C. lipernes |
|---|---|---|---|---|---|---|---|---|---|
| Mussa angulosa | — | — | — | — | — | — | — | — | — |
| Scolymia lacera | — | — | — | — | — | — | — | — | — |
| S. cubensis | — | — | — | — | — | — | — | — | — |
| Isophyllia sinuosa | — | X | — | X | — | — | — | — | — |
| Isophyllastrea rigida | — | — | — | — | — | X | — | — | — |
| Mycetophyllia lamarckana | — | X | — | X | X | — | — | — | X |
| Eusmilia fastigiata | — | — | — | — | — | — | — | — | — |
| Tubastrea aurea | — | — | — | — | — | — | — | — | — |

X = Positive Occurrence.

Coral list taken from Wells and Lang, 1973. This is not a complete list, but reflects species which could be easily distinguished in the field. A few uncommon species have been omitted.

charge of the nematocysts of the anemone. This chemical inhibition is lost if the fish is removed from anemones for some time, but is reacquired within a few days or hours through an acclimatization process. Abel (1960) described a facultative relationship between the goby *Gobius buc-chichii* and an anemone, *Anemonia sulcata*, in the Mediterranean.

Two species of the pomacentrid genus *Dascyllus* (*D. trimaculatus* and *D. albisella*) also have been reported to associate occasionally with sea anemones (Stevenson, 1963). Recently, two species of cardinalfishes (Apogonidae) have been reported in association with two species of sea anemones in the West Indies (Colin and Heiser, 1974). In this relationship the fishes lack immunity to the anemone nematocysts but congregate closely around the anemone for protection.

Davis and Cohen (1968) described a new species of goby, *Cottogobi-us yongei*, and a palaemonid shrimp, both of which lived on an antipath-arian coelenterate, *Ceripathes* sp., in Borneo and Hawaii. Other examples are the association of the fish *Nomeus gronovii* with the Portuguese man-of-war, *Physalia*, and association of various small individuals of several species with large jellyfish, *Rhizostoma* and *Cyanea*, by sheltering beneath the bell of the jellyfish (Mansueti, 1963).

*Colpophyllia natans* is one of the commonest massive corals on Atlantic reefs and is often utilized by coral-dwelling *Gobiosoma*.

*Meandrina meandrites*, with its large septa, is an easily recognized "brain" coral often having associated *Gobiosoma*.

An individual of
*Coryphopterus*
*lipernes* resting
on the coral
*Colpophyllia*
*natans.*

A number of different western Atlantic fishes, including *Elacatinus*, *Gobiosoma* (*Tigrigobius*) *saucrum*, *Coryphopterus lipernes*, *C. personatus*, *Coryphopterus* (species undetermined, Florida), *Emblemaria diaphana*, *E. signifera* (Smith and Tyler, 1972), and *Derilisus nanus*, are found at least occasionally on coral heads. Certainly this list will be expanded, particularly by the Clinidae of the *Emblemaria* complex and related genera for which few life observations are available.

Coral-dwelling fishes can be divided into two groups. The first group is strikingly colored and conspicuous when resting on coral heads. These include members of *Elacatinus*, *Coryphopterus lipernes*, and some others. The second blends well with coral backgrounds, often being nearly transparent and difficult to observe in life. This second group includes *G. saucrum* and *Emblemaria diaphana*. Other *Emblemaria* are similarly colored but have not been identified to species.

The nature of any immunity that *Gobiosoma* may possess to nematocysts of corals is unknown and should be studied. At night corals are capable of capturing reasonably large organisms. This can be demonstrated by attracting plankton to a light held next to a coral head at night. The large "plankters," often 10-15 mm in length, are captured if they contact the coral and are apparently held by the discharge of nematocyst-type cells of the corals.

Food habits of coral-dwelling species other than *Elacatinus* have not been examined closely. *Coryphopterus personatus* is a hovering forager which preys on small organisms near the subtrate (Davis and Birdsong, 1972: 302), and *C. lipernes* has also been observed hovering above coral heads apparently eating plankton.

The table summarizes the species of coral-dwelling *Elacatinus* which have been observed to share the same coral head. This table essentially reflects geographic co-occurrence, except for *G. atronasum* and *G. genie*, which could occur together but have not been observed so in the field. This is probably due to the relatively few observations of *G. atronasum* on corals. *Coryphopterus lipernes* and *G. saucrum* have been observed sharing coral heads with all species of *Elacatinus* occupying their geographic ranges, except for *G. atronasum*.

## TABLE 21

## CO-OCCURRENCE OF CORAL-DWELLING GOBIES ON THE SAME CORAL HEAD

| | G. atronasum | G. evelynae (Y) | G. evelynae (YB) | G. evelynae (W) | G. genie | G. illecebrosum | G. oceanops | G. prochilos | G. randalli |
|---|---|---|---|---|---|---|---|---|---|
| *Gobiosoma atronasum* ... | — | X | — | — | — | — | — | — | — |
| *G. evelynae* (Y) ... | X | — | X | — | X | — | — | — | — |
| *G. evelynae* (YB) ... | — | X | — | — | X | — | — | X | X |
| *G. evelynae* (W) ... | — | — | — | — | — | — | — | X | — |
| *G. genie* ... ... | — | X | X | — | — | — | — | — | — |
| *G. illecebrosum* ... ... | — | — | — | — | — | — | — | — | — |
| *G. oceanops* ... ... | — | — | — | — | — | — | — | X | — |
| *G. prochilos* ... ... | — | — | X | X | — | — | X | — | — |
| *G. randalli* ... ... | — | — | X | — | — | — | — | — | — |
| *G. saucrum ( Tigrigobius)* | — | — | X | X | — | — | — | X | — |
| *Coryphopterus lipernes*... | — | X | X | X | X | — | X | X | X |

X = Positive Occurrence.

*Agaricia tenufolia* largely occurs in "thickets" in fairly shallow water and rarely has *Gobiosoma* associated with it.

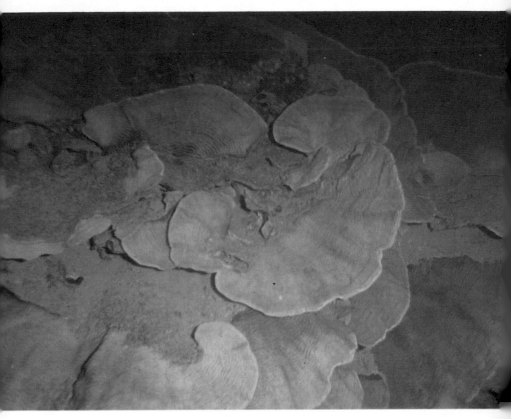

In deeper water, corals of the genus *Agaricia* form large foliate plates which are extremely fragile. While coral-dwelling *Gobiosoma* do not regularly associate with *Agaricia* in shallow water, they apparently occur on it more often in deeper depths where other corals are not as abundant.

Lettuce coral, *Agaricia agaracites,* is a common reef coral which *Gobiosoma* associates with only occasionally.

Individuals of
*C. personatus*
temporarily
resting on the
coral
*Montastrea
cavernosa.*

## CLEANING BEHAVIOR AND ECOLOGY OF *GOBIOSOMA*

Cleaning, a widely recognized phenomenon in the sea, involves the removal of ectoparasites, foreign material, and unwanted tissue from hosts, termed cleanees, by other organisms termed cleaners. Cleaning behavior is well known in terrestrial situations and is becoming increasingly known in the aquatic environment. Longley (1918: 81) was the first to observe and record cleaning behavior in the sea, but he did not interpret his observations as ectoparasite removal until later (Longley and Hildebrand, 1941). He described cleaning behavior by *G. oceanops* as follows:

"The tiny, blue-striped *Elacatinus oceanops* may be seen at almost any time creeping over the bodies of larger fishes such as grunts and groupers. Its jerky movement seems a source of minor irritation commonly borne with indifference or an air of hopeless resignation, even when the little fellows slip almost within their hosts capacious jaws. The severence of relations between the two usually occurs in stereotyped fashion: the larger grows restless and with a characteristic movement halfway between jump and shrug rids itself of its visitor, which then goes back to its accustomed station near the coral heads, or rests upon their vertical faces."

Beebe (1928) is generally credited in the literature as the first to observe cleaning behavior in the sea, in that case of an unidentified wrasse cleaning parrotfish. Longley and Hildebrand (1941) published the first detailed *in situ* observations of cleaning symbiosis and recorded three species in three families as cleaners (*Anisotremus virginicus*, Pomadasyidae; *Thalassoma bifasicatum*, Labridae; *Gobiosoma oceanops*, Gobiidae). During the late 1940's and the 1950's numerous observations were made on cleaners, both fishes and invertebrates, and these were summarized by Limbaugh (1961). Eibl-Eibesfeldt (1955) published an account of cleaning activities in the Caribbean and noted cleaning by gobies that he incorrectly identified as *G. oceanops*.

Feder (1966) reviewed the subject of cleaning symbiosis in the ocean. At the time of Feder's review (1966), little experimental study of cleaning relationships had been conducted. The present discussion, rather than reviewing the entire subject of cleaning in the ocean, will stress the results of recent studies which have not been summarized elsewhere. Limbaugh (1961) reported that on two small isolated Bahamian reefs all known cleaning organisms were removed, and within two weeks almost all non-territorial fishes had left; of those remaining, many had infections. This example has been cited many times (Feder, 1966: 366; Marshall, 1966; 211; Stephens, 1968: 156) as evidence for the importance of cleaning behavior in the marine environment. Youngbluth (1968) removed all but one individual of *Labroides phthirophagus*, a common Hawaiian cleaner, from a patch reef in Kaneohe Bay, Hawaii, and noted no change in the cleaning interactions between this one cleaner and other fishes. On a second reef all members of *L. phthirophagus* were removed and no changes in the reef fish population or degree of infection occurred. Losey (1972) reconsidered the ecological importance of cleaning by *L. phthirophagus* in Kaneohe Bay by repeating Youngbluth's (1968) experiments and found changes in behavior of both cleaners and cleanees in the situation in which one individual of *L. phthirophagus* remained. An increase was noted in inspection behavior by the one individual and other "occasional cleaners" spent more time engaged in such behavior. Losey (1972) used different, more precise measures of cleaning behavior than Youngbluth (1968) and thought this might be the cause of the different results. Losey (1972) felt that in this case the adaptive value of cleaning behavior was probably ectoparasite removal, but that the proximate causal factors are not related to ectoparasites.

Hobson (1969) and Youngbluth (1968) gave evidence for establishment of cleaning stations at one location for lengthy periods. Losey (1971) studied the interactions between *L. phthirophagus* and host fishes. He dealt with cleaning in both the field and aquaria and presented a

The coral *Scolymia lacera* is the largest solitary-polyped species in the western Atlantic and is not utilized by any species of *Gobiosoma*. This daytime photograph shows the polyp in its unexpanded state. Photographed at Crooked Island, Bahamas.

Expanded polyps of the coral *Mussa angulosa* at night. This coral is not utilized by coral-dwelling species of *Gobiosoma*.

A *Scolymia lacera* polyp expanded at night, photographed at 30 m (100 feet) depth, Providenciales Island, Caicos Bank.

A tiger grouper,
*Mycteroperca
tigris*, being
cleaned by
*Gobiosoma
genie* at Grand
Bahama Island.

communication system of correlated interactions. He thought that communicative signals in cleaning symbiosis were less specialized than those in vertebrate social behavior, but the communication system indicated cleaning symbiosis was more than a casual relationship.

Hobson (1968) described cleaning behavior by *Gobiosoma* (*Tigrigobius*) *digueti* and stated that as many as 20 individuals of this diurnal species could be found cleaning large fishes in rocky caves in the Gulf of California. He also noted that the species will land on humans who enter these caves. Hobson (1969) considered several generalizations about tropical and temperate cleaners, particularly those put forth by Feder (1966), and thought that there were no data to support them. Hobson (1971) dealt further with cleaning symbiosis in California shore fishes. Potts (1968) described the ethology of *Crenilabrus melanocercus*, a European labrid, and reported on its cleaning behavior. Potts (1973) studied cleaning symbiosis among British fishes.

De Lisle (1969) studied the cleaning biology of *G. evelynae* in Puerto Rico. De Lisle's work may be criticized because he makes unwarranted assumptions based on poorly designed experiments and worked almost totally in laboratory aquaria, but rather freely extrapolated his results to the field situation. However, one interesting finding by De Lisle (1969) was that host fishes in aquaria presented with models of *G. evelynae* in a

214

sequence that progressed from models least like to most like *G. evelynae* responded by "displaying" most often to the most realistic models, but the "intensity" (duration of display) was not related to the realism of the model. Neither the shape nor striping of the model was critical in producing "displaying" by a host fish.

Losey (1974) recently ran 173 m of transects off Puerto Rico, during which he crossed 96 coral heads, 9 of which had cleaning stations with 1 to 3 *G. evelynae*. Fishes in this study area had higher levels of ectoparasite infestations, and the cleaning fish (*G. evelynae*) were more abundant than those Losey observed in Hawaii. He believed that at his study area cleaning may play a vital ecological role as Limbaugh's (1961) early experiment had indicated. Losey's preliminary results are intriguing and point to the need for an adequate, long term study of cleaning ecology in the western Atlantic.

Darcy *et al.* (1974) found that individuals of *Gobiosoma* (*G. evelynae* (YB), *G. prochilos*, or both) cleaned piscivorous and nonpiscivorous fishes, but young *Thalassoma bifasciatum* cleaned only herbivorous fishes in the field. In aquarium experiments, individuals of *Gobiosoma* spp., *T. bifasciatum*, and an anchovy were added to aquaria containing piscivorous fishes. The anchovies were eaten first, then the wrasses and the gobies were either not eaten or taken after a considerable period had elapsed. Darcy *et al.* thought predators recognized members of *Gobiosoma*, but not *T. bifasciatum*, as cleaners. Darcy *et al.* did not eliminate the possibility that *Gobiosoma* are relatively immune to predation due to noxious properties, rather than its cleaning behavior. Some species of *Gobiosoma* (*G. chancei* and *G. horsti*) are noxious and other species (*G. evelynae* (YB)) may be.

Collette and Talbot (1972) noted that *G. evelynae* (YB) from St. John, Virgin Islands, cleaned 14 species of fishes and that the cleaning period extended from early morning to late afternoon. Smith and Tyler (1972) listed 7 species cleaned by *G. evelynae* (YB). Some cleanees were not residents of their study reef, but "seemed to visit it only for the purpose of being cleaned."

The present study was not intended to deal with cleaning ecology, but some observations were made and are summarized here. They do not answer basic questions regarding cleaning symbiosis, but do provide some background information for a detailed study of cleaning behavior by species of *Gobiosoma*.

Six species of *Gobiosoma* are known to engage in cleaning behavior. They are: *G. evelynae* (Y), (YB), (W); *G. genie*; *G. illecebrosum* (Y), (B), (W); *G. oceanops*; *G. prochilos*; and *G. randalli*. All color varieties of these species have been observed cleaning. All dwell on living coral

A barred hamlet, *Hypoplectrus puella,* emerging from the sponge *Mycale* sp., which is occasionally inhabited by *Gobiosoma*. The barred hamlet is a small predator which is not restricted from entering sponge oscula of sufficient size.

The coral *Mussa angulosa* photographed at night. Note the extremely large polyps of this species. Perhaps this is why it is avoided by species of *Gobiosoma*.

The sponge *Mycale* sp., which is occasionally inhabited by *Gobiosoma*.

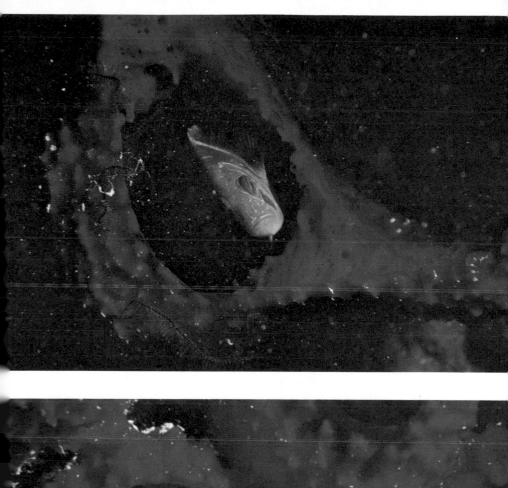
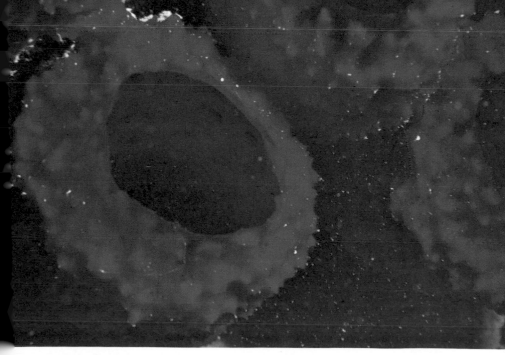

heads, but no species is restricted to living corals. They are occasionally observed on rock or on live sponges, but they have not been observed to enter the sponges. All of the substrates (coral, rock and sponges) are inhabited by gobies engaged in cleaning, and cleaning stations are not limited to prominent coral heads.

*Gobiosoma atronasum*, occasionally found on corals, does not engage in cleaning behavior. It is a plankton feeder and spends most of its time hovering near steep reef faces.

In all cleaning species of *Gobiosoma*, the lateral colored stripe runs the length of the body from anterior of the eye to the caudal fin.

No species of *Gobiosoma* associated solely with sponges (*G. chancei, G. horsti, G. xanthiprora, G. louisae* and *G. tenox*) has been observed to clean. Although such species often are clearly visible on the top and outer surfaces of sponges, none exhibited any behavior interpretable as soliciting host fishes for a cleaning interaction. No host species has attempted to solicit cleaning behavior by sponge-dwelling *Gobiosoma* under natural conditions.

Cleaning stations are occupied for long periods of time as reported by several authors. Several stations were maintained on certain coral heads at Discovery Bay for 2 year periods and for 1 year at Curacao. Not all cleaning stations, however, are stable. Several noted at both Discovery Bay and Curacao were visited months later and no cleaning gobies were present, probably reflecting fluctuations of local populations over time. Cleaning stations that remain stable probably have a regular influx of new cleaners, particularly if the site is in a superior location because of its prominence or other features.

The species of fishes observed being cleaned in the field by *Gobiosoma* are recorded, based on observations in the present study and on literature records. A wide variety of fishes (51 species of 20 families) is cleaned, and this list will increase with additional observations. The species of fishes cleaned are of the same type from locality to locality.

One to several individuals of *Gobiosoma* will clean a single host fish. All sizes of *Gobiosoma*, from newly metamorphosed to very large individuals, will engage in cleaning behavior. Where two cleaning species occur together, both species may be found at a single cleaning station and will clean the same fish simultaneously. No behavior considered competitive has been observed between species that were simultaneously cleaning the same fish.

All cleaner species of *Gobiosoma* entered the mouths and gill chambers of larger fishes. There seems to be no specialization among sympatric cleaning species for restriction and division of cleaning behavior to a particular portion of the body of the host fishes.

## TABLE 22

## SPECIES OF FISHES OBSERVED BEING CLEANED BY VARIOUS SPECIES OF *Gobiosoma*

| Species Being Cleaned | *G. oceanops* | *G. evelynae* (YB) | *G. evelynae* (Y) | *G. evelynae* (W) | *G. illecebrosum* | *G. genie* | *G. randalli* | *G. prochilos* | Location* | Other Source |
|---|---|---|---|---|---|---|---|---|---|---|
| **Muraenidae** | | | | | | | | | | |
| *Gymnothorax moringa* | X | — | — | X | — | — | — | — | 3, 6 | |
| *G. funebris* | X | X | — | X | — | — | — | — | 1, 3 | |
| **Aulostomidae** | | | | | | | | | | |
| *Aulostomus maculatus* | — | X | — | X | — | — | — | — | 2, 3 | |
| **Holocentridae** | | | | | | | | | | |
| *Holocentrus rufus* | — | X | X | — | — | — | — | — | 2 | |
| *Myripristis jacobus* | — | — | — | — | — | — | — | — | | Collette and Talbot, 1972 |
| **Serranidae** | | | | | | | | | | |
| *Epinephelus cruentatus* | X | X | — | X | — | X | X | X | 1, 2, 3, 5, 6 | |
| *E. fulva* | X | X | X | — | X | — | X | — | 4, 5, 7, 8 | |
| *E. guttatus* | X | X | — | — | — | X | — | — | 2, 4 | |
| *E. striatus* | X | X | X | — | X | X | — | — | 1, 2, 7 | |
| *Mycteroperca bonaci* | X | — | X | — | — | X | — | — | 1, 2 | |
| *M. interstitialis* | — | X | — | — | — | — | — | — | 2 | |
| *M. tigris* | — | X | X | — | — | X | — | — | 2 | |
| **Grammistidae** | | | | | | | | | | |
| *Rypticus saponaceus* | — | X | — | — | — | — | — | X | 6 | |
| **Priacanthidae** | | | | | | | | | | |
| *Priacanthus cruentatus* | — | — | — | X | — | — | — | — | 3 | |
| **Carangidae** | | | | | | | | | | |
| *Caranx ruber* | — | — | — | — | — | — | — | — | | Collette and Talbot, 1972 |
| **Lutjanidae** | | | | | | | | | | |
| *Lutjanus griseus* | X | — | — | — | — | — | — | — | 1 | |
| *L. apodus* | — | — | — | — | — | X | — | — | 2 | |
| **Pomadasyidae** | | | | | | | | | | |
| *Haemulon flavolineatum* | X | X | — | — | — | — | — | — | 1, 2 | |
| *H. sciuris* | X | — | — | — | — | — | — | — | 1 | |
| **Sparidae** | | | | | | | | | | |
| *Calamus* sp. | — | X | — | — | — | X | — | — | 2 | |

*Verongia fistularis*, a common tubular sponge of many reef areas, is often occupied by *Gobiosoma*. Photographed at 12 m (40 feet) depth, Discovery Bay, Jamaica.

Two species of *Verongia* sponges on the deep fore reef, Discovery Bay, Jamaica, 40 m depth. These sponges at this depth are often inhabited by *G. louisae*.

Creole wrasse, *Clepticus parrai,* resting at night in the oscular opening of the sponge *Callyspongia plicifera*. The arms of a brittlestar are visible on the surface of the sponge and commensual zooanthids cover much of the outer surface. Photographed at Providenciales Island, Caicos Bank.

# TABLE 22—Continued

| Species Being Cleaned | G. oceanops | G. evelynae (YB) | G. evelynae (Y) | G. evelynae (W) | G. illecebrosum | G. genie | G. randalli | G. prochilos | Location | Other Source |
|---|---|---|---|---|---|---|---|---|---|---|
| **Mullidae** | | | | | | | | | | |
| *Mulloidichthys martinicensis* | — | X | — | — | — | — | — | — | 5 | |
| *Pseudupeneus maculatus* | — | — | — | — | — | — | — | — | | Collette and Talbot, 1972 |
| **Pomacanthidae** | | | | | | | | | | |
| *Holacanthus bermudensis* | X | — | — | — | — | — | — | — | 1 | |
| *Pomacanthus arcuatus* | X | — | — | — | X | X | — | — | 2, 7 | |
| **Pomacentridae** | | | | | | | | | | |
| *Chromis cyanea* | X | X | — | X | — | — | — | — | 1, 3, 5, 6 | |
| *C. insolatus* | — | X | — | — | — | — | — | — | 2 | |
| *C. multilineata* | — | X | — | X | — | X | X | — | 2, 3, 5, | |
| *Microspathodon chrysurus* | — | — | — | X | — | — | — | X | 3, 6 | |
| *Pomacentrus fuscus* | X | X | — | X | — | — | — | — | 1, 3, 5 | |
| *P. partitus* | X | X | — | — | — | — | — | — | 1, 5 | |
| *P. leucostictus* | — | X | — | — | — | — | — | — | 4 | |
| *P. variabilis* | — | X | — | — | — | — | — | — | | Collette and Talbot, 1972 |
| **Labridae** | | | | | | | | | | |
| *Bodianus pulchellus* | X | — | — | — | — | — | — | — | 1 | |
| *B. rufus* | — | X | — | — | — | — | — | — | | Collette and |
| *Clepticus parrae* | — | X | X | — | — | — | X | — | 2, 5, 6 | Talbot, 1972 |
| *Halichoeres garnoti* | — | — | — | X | — | — | — | — | 3 | |
| *H. maculipinna* | X | — | — | — | — | — | — | — | 1 | |
| *Lachnolaimus maximus* | X | — | — | — | — | — | — | X | 8 | |
| **Scaridae** | | | | | | | | | | |
| *Scarus coeruleus* | — | — | X | — | — | — | — | — | 2 | |
| *S. coelestinus* | — | — | — | — | X | — | — | — | | Böhlke and McCosker, 1973 |
| *S. croicensis* | — | — | X | — | — | — | — | — | 2 | ,, ,, |
| *S. guacamaia* | — | — | — | — | X | — | — | — | | ,, ,, |
| *S. vetula* | — | — | X | — | X | — | — | — | 2 | ,, ,, |
| *Sparisoma viride* | — | — | X | X | X | — | — | X | 2, 3 | ,, ,, |
| *S. rubripinne* | — | — | — | — | X | — | — | — | 2 | ,, ,, |
| **Blenniidae** | | | | | | | | | | |
| *Ophioblennius atlanticus* | — | X | — | — | — | — | — | — | | Collette and Talbot, 1972 |

# TABLE 22—*Continued*

| Species Being Cleaned | G. oceanops | G. evelynae (YB) | G. evelynae (Y) | G. evelynae (W) | G. illecebrosum | G. genie | G. randalli | G. prochilos | Location | Other Source |
|---|---|---|---|---|---|---|---|---|---|---|
| **Acanthuridae** | | | | | | | | | | |
| *Acanthurus bahianus* | X | — | X | — | X | — | — | — | 1, 2, 7 | |
| *A. chirurgus* | — | — | — | — | X | — | — | X | | Böhlke and McCosker, 1973 |
| *A. coeruleus* | — | — | — | — | X | — | — | X | | ,,          ,, |
| **Ostraciidae** | | | | | | | | | | |
| *Lactophrys triqueter* | — | X | — | — | — | — | — | — | 4 | Smith and Tyler, 1972 |
| **Diodontidae** | | | | | | | | | | |
| *Diodon hystrix* | — | X | — | — | — | — | — | — | 4 | |
| **Balistidae** | | | | | | | | | | |
| *Balistes vetula* | — | — | — | X | — | — | — | — | 9 | |

*Key to Locations: 1—Florida, 2—Bahamas, 3—Jamaica, 4—Virgin Islands, 5—Curacao, Bonaire, 6—Barbados, 7—Colombia, 8—Belize, 9—Serranilla Bank.

*Gobiosoma* cleaned species of fishes that have or can have noxious properties in their skin. In Barbados, both *G. evelynae* (YB) and *G. prochilos* on separate occasions cleaned the greater soapfish, *Rypticus saponaceus*. Members of *Rypticus* and other genera of Grammistidae possess a toxin, grammistin, in the mucus on the body (Randall *et al.*, 1971). When *G. prochilos* was observed cleaning *R. saponaceus*, the soapfish was lying motionless on its side in a small cave at 2 m depth. The single goby worked over the body, head, caudal fin, and dorsal fin for a period of 20 minutes. The cleaner occasionally twisted its body quickly, in a nearly 180° arc laterally with the head at the center of the arc. This probably represented removal of parasites and occurred numerous times. The behavior was interrupted after 20 minutes when I attempted, without success, to collect the specimen of *G. prochilos*. The two species of *Gobiosoma* that cleaned *R. saponaceus* either avoid ingesting mucus from the fishes in the course of removing parasites, which seems unlikely, or are not much affected by the toxin in the mucus, which was shown by Randall *et. al.* (1971) to be repellent to predators.

Tubes of *Verongia fistularis* at Grand Cayman Island (12 m depth) which contained *G. horsti* (Y). Photo by Alan Crook.

Small specimen of the sponge *Verongia fistularis* at 12 m (40 feet) depth, Grand Bahama Island.

Tubes of *Verongia fistularis* on top of a colony of *Madracis* coral at Rio Bueno, Jamaica. It is debatable whether this sponge grew in the location on the coral. More likely, it fell to this position from somewhere higher on the reef.

*Gobiosoma evelynae* (YB) was observed cleaning the trunkfish *Lactophrys triqueter* at St. John by Smith and Tyler (1972: 168) and at St. Croix during the present study. When disturbed the Ostraciidae can secrete a poisonous substance from glands in the skin. This toxin is capable of killing other fishes and eventually themselves if they are confined to a small volume of water as in an aquarium. This toxin may not always be present on the surface of the skin, and *G. evelynae* may be capable of avoiding it or may not be disturbed by its presence.

There has been no research carried out on the diurnal fluctuation of cleaning activity for any western Atlantic cleaning organism. The present study gathered a small amount of quanitative information on cleaning, but the data are not comparable to other studies. Youngbluth (1968) found that cleaning rates for *Labroides phthirophagus* in Hawaii did not vary between morning and afternoon, but that the rates on different reefs varied. Losey (1972) believed that the number of cleaning interactions used by Youngbluth (1968), although easy to observe and record, was not as sensitive a measure of cleaning activity as was duration of inspection by the cleaner.

In the present study, quantitative observations on cleaning behavior were made in Curacao, Jamaica, and the Bahamas. In seven quantitative observations between 15 and 30 minutes in duration (totalling less than 3 hours), the frequency of cleaning interactions (a single continuous period of contact by the goby on the host fish) varied between 12 and 108 per hour. Although cleaning occurred in all seven periods, the highest frequency was recorded during the single morning period carried out.

Divers are also cleaned by various species of *Gobiosoma*. A hand placed near a cleaning station and held still was often approached by one or more gobies, and many times cleaning took place. Some gobies also left their substrate when a diver approached, and they swam toward the diver. This was especially true for large individuals of *G. genie*.

Host fishes may change color during cleaning, and the nature of this change shows no consistency. Such changes have been noted by Limbaugh (1961), Randall (1965), and others. At Discovery Bay, the blue chromis, *Chromis cyanea*, turned a dark blue-black immediately before moving to a cleaning station occupied by *G. evelynae* (W). On completion of cleaning, the blue chromis moved away and changed to its usual iridescent blue coloration. The next day, however, individuals remained iridescent blue during cleaning. Similar observations were made for this species in other localities.

The coney, *Epinephelus fulva*, has several different color patterns. In most patterns the body is generally of one color, often a dark brown. One phase, termed the "excitement phase" by Smith (1971: 95), is sharply dorso-ventrally bicolored. Coneys visiting cleaning stations on Bonaire

(*G. randalli*) and St. Croix (*G. evelynae* (YB)) acquired the bicolored phase shortly before or at the onset of cleaning behavior. In Belize, however, an individual remained dark brown while being cleaned by *G. oceanops* and turned sharply bicolored after it moved away from the cleaning station on the termination of cleaning. It seems unlikely that any particular color change of the host fish is consistently or uniquely associated with cleaning behavior.

Members of *Gobiosoma* clean in conjunction with other species of *Gobiosoma*, other fishes, and one crustacean. All sympatric species of *Elacatinus* clean together. Other fishes with which *Gobiosoma* cleans include the wrasses *Thalassoma bifasciatum* and *Bodianus rufus*. The only crustacean observed cleaning in conjunction with *Gobiosoma* was *Periclimenes pedersoni*.

More than one species of fish may occupy a cleaning station, but the species may not engage equally in cleaning behavior. In Jamaica and Florida, *Thalassoma bifasciatum* often cleaned much more actively than *Gobiosoma* where the two occupied the same station. In some instances a goby would leave its coral head and attempt to clean a species, such as *Clepticus parrai*, already posing for *T. bifasciatum*, and the effect of participation by *Elacatinus* caused the host fish to interrupt the cleaning behavior and swim on.

How a host fish recognizes a cleaner is not completely understood. De Lisle (1969) found in aquarium experiments that host fishes would pose for models of *G. evelynae* and that neither shape nor striping was vital. Some observations in the present study are relevant. In several locations the noxious properties of sponge-dwelling *Gobiosoma* were investigated. One method was to drop an anesthetized goby from a height of about 5 m above the reef and observe if any fishes ate or attempted to eat this goby. In one instance at Curacao an anesthetized specimen of *G. horsti* (Y) was released and, while falling slowly toward the reef, regained consciousness. The goby began swimming horizontally about 2 m above the reef. Several specimens of *Pomacentrus partitus* and *Chromis multilineata* posed for cleaning as the goby swam near to them. The goby alighted for a few seconds on one individual of *C. multilineata* which was horizontal in the water column. The *G. horsti* (Y) remained on the fish for only a few seconds and then started swimming as before. *Gobiosoma horsti* is negatively buoyant and does not swim well in open water; this individual probably landed on the *C. multilineata* to rest, not to clean, as no movements which could be construed as cleaning were observed. As the goby continued to swim, fishes also continued to pose as it passed. The *G. horsti* (Y) came to rest on a coral head and other fishes continued posing for cleaning. The goby finally retreated to a sponge, ending the series of events which occupied about 2 minutes. *Gobiosoma horsti* has

227

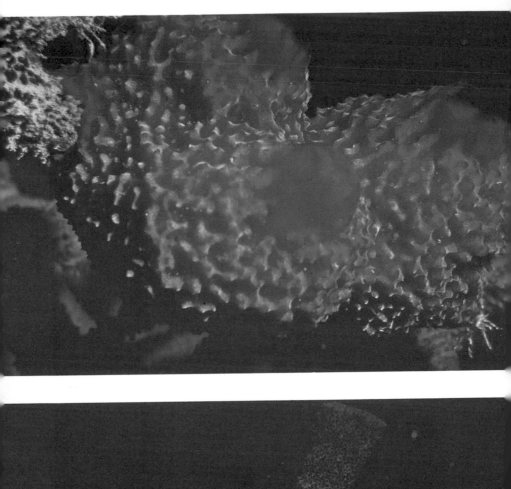

Another specimen of *Mycale* sp., photographed at Discovery Bay, Jamaica. This colorful sponge usually appears black in deep water because nearly all of the red color in sunlight penetrating the sea surface is filtered out by the water.

*Callyspongia plicifera*, occasionally utilized by *Gobiosoma*, fluoresces with a beautiful blue color. Photographed at Grand Bahama Island, 14 m (56 feet) depth.

*Callyspongia vaginalis* is occasionally occupied by sponge-dwelling *Gobiosoma*. This individual with exceptionally long tubes was photographed near Piscadera Baai, Curacao, Netherlands Antilles.

never been observed to engage in cleaning behavior or to have fishes attempt to solicit cleaning behavior by posing near the sponges that *G. horsti* usually inhabits.

Also at Discovery Bay, individuals of *Clepticus parrai* posed for cleaning by adults of *Halichoeres pictus*, a plankton-feeding species (Gomon, 1971: 73) not known to be a cleaner. Nearby a group of *Thalassoma bifasciatum* was actively cleaning other individuals of *C. parrai*. Probably because the two wrasses were colored similarly, the individuals of *C. parrai* did not distinguish between them.

The fishes most often cleaned by *Elacatinus* during the present study were *Epinephelus cruentatus, E. striatus, Mycteroperca* spp., *Chromis cyanea, C. multilineata,* and *Scarus* spp. Certain common reef fishes seem to be seldom, if ever, cleaned. No species of *Hypoplectrus,* the hamlets, has been observed being cleaned by any *Gobiosoma* in nature, even though De Lisle (1969) recorded *H. chlorurus* as having been cleaned by *G. evelynae* in an aquarium. In the field, *Hypoplectrus* often caused flight responses by *Gobiosoma,* and they were never observed to solicit cleaning behavior by posing.

In the Virgin Islands, *G. evelynae* was active from early morning to late afternoon (Collette and Talbot, 1972: 123). Apparently species of *Gobiosoma* clean at any time they are active. At Grand Bahama Island, several *G. genie* and *G. evelynae* (Y) at 5 minutes after sunset swam from their coral head to a human observer 2 m distant and proceeded to clean him. When the diver retreated the gobies returned to their coral head. Ten minutes later the diver approached and the previous behavior was repeated. At 35 minutes after sunset the coral head was revisited and several gobies were found exhibiting nocturnal color and behavior.

Every general coral-reef area in the western North Atlantic, except Berumda, has at least one cleaning species of *Gobiosoma.* In some they are scarce, and an isolated collection or set of observations may miss them. Isolated localities such as Aves Island, Barbados, and banks of the western Caribbean have cleaning species, often in surprising numbers. Bermuda may be too isolated for larvae of *Gobiosoma* to ever have reached it, or conditions may not be suitable for the survival of cleaning species of *Gobiosoma.* Bermuda has a very reduced list of gobiid species when compared to the Bahamas or the Florida Keys.

Although at least one species of cleaning goby is known from every locality visited, no more than two species exist in any one area. *Gobiosoma illecebrosum* in the Panama-Colombia region has never been collected with any other species of cleaning goby, but it is likely that it will occur with *G. prochilos* in the northern part of its range near Yucatan. *Gobiosoma oceanops* is also the only cleaning goby present in the northern part of its range. Otherwise, two species of cleaning gobies were present at all collection sites.

The presence of two closely related species in the same location, engaging in the same unusual behavior, is perplexing. Members of *Gobiosoma*, however, are not unique in this. Randall (1958: 337) reported that 3 species of *Labroides* (*L. dimidiatus, L. bicolor*, and *L. rubrolabiatus*) are frequently found near one another at several locations in the tropical Pacific. Two species would simultaneously clean the same fish, and *L. dimidiatus* was observed to briefly clean its congener, *L. bicolor*. No attempt was made to interpret the co-occurrence of these cleaners.

A closer examination of the cleaning species of *Gobiosoma* based on morphology shows that cleaners either have the mouth in the subterminal position (*G. randalli* and *G. prochilos*) or in the inferior position (*G. evelynae, G. genie, G. illecebrosum*, and *G. oceanops*). Of the inferior mouthed species, the ones that possess a rostral frenum (*G. evelynae, G. illecebrosum*, and *G. oceanops*) seem to form a natural group of 3 species. The fourth species, *G. genie*, lacks the rostral frenum and also differs in having a swim bladder. The distribution of the three species having the rostral frenum is mutually exclusive but covers nearly the entire range of the subgenus. All localities except the Cayman Islands have a single inferior mouthed species with a rostral frenum. The status of cleaning gobies at Grand Cayman is uncertain due to'confusion between systematics of *G. evelynae* and *G. genie*.

The remaining 3 species apparently also have mutually exclusive distributions, but they are not as similar morphologically as the 3 previously considered species. The distribution of these species is tentative and, although only one species has been collected at any one locality, there is some overlap in distributions. This overlap may represent isolated populations, but cannot be resolved until more collections are made.

Comparison of cleaning behavior, functional morphology, and food habits of the cleaning species of *Gobiosoma* is needed. The position of the mouth probably is important. Species with subterminal mouths may have to angle the body more to grab a parasite. In dentition, the species with inferior mouths are nearly identical, having a single row of teeth in stockade fashion on the upper jaw and a number of rows anteriorly becoming a single series laterally on the lower jaw. Males have one or two enlarged, recurved canines inside the other teeth on the lower jaw. This dentition seems highly specialized for parasite removal. The lower jaw with its numerous anterior rows can grip a parasite firmly and the upper jaw with a single, saw-like row of teeth can act as an effective nipping or cutting edge. Gobies use body leverage to remove some parasites, probably when the jaws are not strong enough to bite through the parasite. The use of

Another color form of *Callyspongia plicifera*; this individual is non-fluorescent.

The sponge *Neofibrularia massa* at 12 m depth, Discovery Bay, Jamaica. The white bodies on the inner surface of the oscular cavity are individuals of *Syllis spongicola*, the parasitic poly-chaete which sponge-dwelling *Gobiosoma* eat.

the enlarged canine teeth in males is unexplained, but probably they do not play an important role in parasite removal. Both sexes engage in parasite removal, and no differences in behavior between the two sexes could be discerned. Males prepare the spawning site, often digging in the process, and then guard the eggs until hatching. The dental dimorphism may be related to these acts.

The two species with subterminal mouths have similar but slightly different dentition. *Gobiosoma prochilos* has the teeth in the upper jaw biserial but otherwise similar to the inferior mouthed species. *Gobiosoma randalli* males have some canines on both the upper and lower jaws. Bohlke and Robins (1968: 100) state that of the species in *Elacatinus*, "*randalli* and *prochilos* approach the *oceanops* group most closely in dentition." Females of all sponge-dwelling *Elacatinus* have large canines, but females of the plankton feeding *G. atronasum* lack these as do females of all the cleaning species.

Species of *Elacatinus* in both the western Atlantic and the eastern Pacific share the habit of cleaning. Hoese (1972), in considering the eastern Pacific species of *Gobiosoma*, felt *Elacatinus* is a separate genus from *Gobiosoma* and included in *Elacatinus* the subgenus *Tigrigobius*. He reports (pers. comm.) that in the subgenus *Elacatinus* of his genus *Elacatinus* there is only one described eastern Pacific species, *E. puncticulatus*. This species is a cleaner, and two species (*E. digueti* and an undescribed related species) of the subgenus *Tigrigobius* also are cleaners.

It seems unlikely that cleaning behavior arose separately in this group in the two regions. The two oceans have been separated for at least 1-3 million years since the most recent closure of the Pan-American seaway. The western Atlantic species of the subgenus *Elacatinus* are more closely related to one another than to any eastern Pacific form. Cleaning symbiosis may be a very old behavior, though, and coral reefs have existed in their present form for millions of years. In the family Gobiidae, the largest family of marine fishes, members of *Gobiosoma* are the only known cleaners.

Other cleaning fish groups are distributed similarly. In the Pomacanthidae, the cleaners *Holacanthus passer* and *H. limbaughi* are known from the eastern Pacific, and *Pomacanthus paru* and *P. arcuatus* are known from the western Atlantic. Various butterflyfishes, family Chaetodontidae, are cleaners in the eastern Pacific and western Atlantic. Many species of the world-wide family Labridae are cleaners. Members of *Bodianus* on either side of the Panamanian land bridge are cleaners, and the cleaners of the genus *Thalassoma* are also similarly distributed, with *T. lucasanum* in the eastern Pacific and *T. bifasciatum* in the western Atlantic. In the Pomacentridae, young of the genus *Microspathodon* are cleaners (eastern Pacific, *M. dorsalis*; western Atlantic, *M. chrysurus*).

*Abudefduf saxatilis* is a cleaning member of Pomacentridae found world-wide. Some crustacean cleaners, such as *Lysmata grabhami*, are circum-tropical in distribution.

Few tropical cleaning groups are restricted to one area. Juveniles of porkfish, *Anisotremus virginicus*, of the western Atlantic are the only known cleaners in the family Pomadasyidae. *Gramma loreto* (Grammi-dae) is the only known cleaner in the serrannid-like complex of families (Eibel-Eibesfeldt, 1955). Other cleaning organisms of these groups will perhaps be discovered, but groups in which cleaning occurs are usually widely distributed.

Cleaning behavior has either arisen separately many times in the same families, which seems unlikely, or it is a relatively old phenomenon reaching at least into the Pliocene and in some instances probably Tethy-an in age. It is logical that cleaning did not have a common origin across family lines. Unless some very different mechanisms have operated in *Gobiosoma*, it seems logical that the cleaning behavior of eastern Pacific and western Atlantic species had a common origin prior to 1 to 3 million years ago.

## SPONGE DWELLING AND NOXIOUS PROPERTIES OF *GOBIOSOMA*

Sponge dwelling by fishes attracted little attention from biologists until recently. Tyler and Bohlke (1972) reviewed the subject and added considerable knowledge of these associations. They placed sponge-dwel-ling fishes in four categories: 1) morphologically specialized obligate sponge dwellers, 2) morphologically unspecialized obligate sponge dwel-lers, 3) facultative sponge dwellers, and 4) fortuitous occurrences.

In the subgenus *Elacatinus*, Bohlke and Robins (1968) recorded *G. chancei, G. horsti*, and *G. xanthiprora* as occurring in sponges and sug-gested that *G. tenox* also did so. Bohlke and Robins (1969: 14) added *G. louisae* to the list of sponge-dwelling species of *Gobiosoma*. Tyler and Bohlke (1972) added information on *G. chancei, G. horsti, G. louisae,* and *G. xanthiprora*, although they confused some records of *G. atrona-sum*, a non-sponge dweller, with *G. louisae*. Colin (1971) recorded *G. horsti* (W) on sponges in Jamaica.

Although Tyler and Bohlke (1972) record *G. chancei* and *G. horsti* as "morphologically unspecialized obligate sponge dwellers" and *G. loui-sae, G. xanthiprora*, and *G. tenox* as "facultative sponge dwellers," the present study indicates that all five species should be in the former class.

The term "obligate" should be cautiously interpreted. These five species are included in this group because 1) they have only been collect-ed in the sponge-dwelling situation, and 2) individuals of all sizes, from

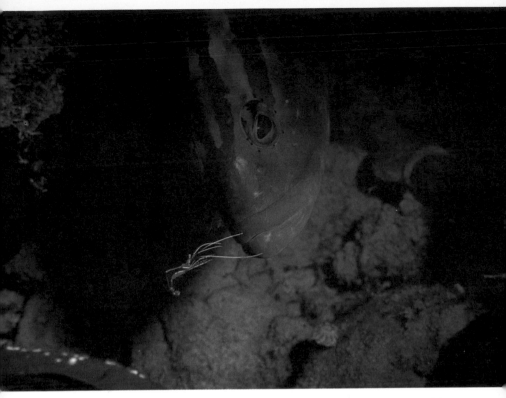

Pederson's cleaning shrimp, *Periclimenes pedersoni*, approaching a Nassau grouper, *Epinephelus striatus*, and touching the grouper's lips with its antennae before climbing onto the body of the fish. Photographed at Whale Cay, Berry Islands, Bahamas.

small juveniles to adults, are in association with sponges. However, the four species maintained in aquaria (all but *G. tenox*) live well without sponges, feed on dry tropical fish food, and spawn in artificial environments, producing fertile eggs.

In the species that were examined, all had in their gut the polychaete worm *Syllis (Haplosyllis) spongicola*. These worms are parasites of sponges and cosmopolitan in tropical seas (Imajima, 1966). Daver (1972) reported this worm to be the most abundant polychaete associated with sponges in the Gulf of Mexico. There is a close relationship between gobies, sponges, and food organisms. Reiswig (1970, 1971a, 1971b) studied the biology of tropical marine Demospongiae inhabited in some cases by *Gobiosoma*. In considering three species, *Verongia gigantea, Mycale* sp., and *Tethya crypta*, he found that the sponges' diet consists of 93 per cent particulate organic material unresolvable by direct microscopy. He be-

Greater soapfish, *Rypticus saponaceus*, which is cleaned by *Gobiosoma* even though it possesses a noxious substance in the body mucus.

The arrow blenny, *Lucayablennius zingaro*, here photographed in front of the black coral *Antipathes pennacea,* occasionally occurs with feeding aggregations of *Gobiosoma atronasum* and associated fishes. The arrow blenny is a predator in spite of its small size and lunges forward rapidly by straightening its caudal fin to strike its prey.

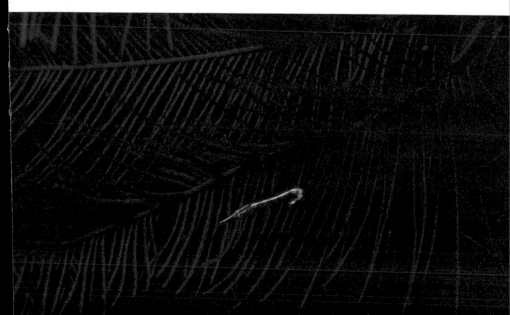

lieved that a major source of this particulate organic matter was mucus produced by corals; some bacteria produced on this mucus were also ingested. Reisiwg (1971a) mentions that of organic particles of 0.3-50 micron size, 78 per cent are retained from a volume of water passing through the sponge. Up to 5 per cent of the biomass of some sponges, such as *Verongia gigantea*, consisted of the parasitic polychaete *Syllis spongicola*, and this might account for the slow growth of *Verongia* cited by Goreau (1967).

In a 50 m wide transect at Discovery Bay, with an area of about 2300 square meters and depths of 26-51 m, Reiswig (1971a) found 17 individuals of *V. gigantea* with a total volume of 315 liters. The density of this population was 0.0075 ind. / square meter or 0.141 liter / square meter. Most species of sponges are considerably smaller than *V. gigantea*.

All species of *Verongia* at Discovery Bay (*V. gigantea, V. archeri, V. cavernosa*, and other unnamed species) contain *Syllis spongicola* (Reiswig, pers. comm.).

## TABLE 23

## OCCURRENCE OF SPECIES OF *Gobiosoma*
## ON VARIOUS SPONGES AT ALL LOCALITIES

| Sponge Species | *G. horsti* (Y) | *G. horsti* (W) | *G. louisae* (Y) | *G. xanthiprora* (Y) | *G. xanthiprora* (W) | *G. chancei* | *G. tenox* |
|---|---|---|---|---|---|---|---|
| *Agelas conifera* ... ... | X | X | X | — | — | X | — |
| *Callyspongia plicifera* ... | — | — | — | X | — | — | — |
| *C. vaginalis* ... ... | X | — | — | — | — | — | — |
| *Mycale* sp. ... ... | — | X | — | — | — | — | — |
| *Neofibrularia massa* ... | — | X | X | — | — | — | X |
| *Verongia archeri* ... ... | X | X | X | — | — | X | — |
| *V. fistularis* ... ... | X | X | X | — | X | X | — |
| *V. gigantea* ... ... | — | X | X | — | — | — | — |
| *V. lacunosa* ... ... | — | X | X | — | — | X | — |
| *Verongia* sp. ... ... | X | — | — | — | — | — | — |

X = Positive Occurrence.

# TABLE 24

## PRESENTATIONS OF SPECIES OF *Gobiosoma* TO PREDATORS AND REACTIONS OF THE PREDATORS AT CURACAO AND ST. CROIX

| Predator Species | Number of Presentations | | | Reaction of Predator | | | |
| --- | --- | --- | --- | --- | --- | --- | --- |
| | *G. horsti* (Y), Cur. / *G. chancei*, St. Cr. | *G. evelynae* (YB) | non-*Gobiosoma* | not engulfed | engulfed but rejected | eaten | see footnote |
| **Curacao** | | | | | | | |
| *Epinephelus fulva*... | 3 | 2 | 2 | — | — | 7 | a |
| *E. striatus*... | 3 | 3 | — | 5 | 1 | — | b |
| *Myripristis jacobus* | 4 | 1 | — | — | 5 | — | — |
| *Lutjanus apodus* | 2 | — | — | — | 1 | 1 | b |
| *Thalassoma bifasciatum* | 1 | — | — | — | 1 | — | — |
| *Labrisomus nuchipinnis* | 1 | — | — | — | 1 | — | — |
| **St. Croix** | | | | | | | |
| *Holocentrus rufus*... | 2 | — | — | 2 | — | — | — |
| *Epinephelus cruentatus* | 6 | — | 2 | — | — | 7 | c |

a Extreme mouth movements when *G. horsti* (Y) was ingested and no movements when non-*Gobiosoma* were eaten.

b Extreme mouth movements when engulfed.

c Ingestion of *G. chancei* was accompanied by extreme mouth movements, no mouth movements occurred after ingestion of non-*Gobiosoma*.

Reiswig (1971a, 1971b) found periodic cessation of pumping activity by *Verongia gigantea, V. archeri,* and *Agelas* sp., 3 species commonly associated with members of *Gobiosoma*. Pumping by the sponges produces a constant change in the water present in the lumen, but whether non-pumping has any effect on the behavior of *Gobiosoma* associated with a sponge is unknown. The rare, but documented, discharges of gametes (Reiswig, 1968) also might affect behavior of the associated gobies.

The yellowtail damselfish, *Microspathodon chrysurus*, acts as a cleaner when a juvenile.

The species of sponges inhabited by various species of *Gobiosoma* are listed in the table. The table includes literature records, principally from Tyler and Bohlke (1972), and records from the present study. The taxonomy of tropical marine sponges is poorly known and in some cases identification of particular sponges is not positive. Certain sponge species containing *Gobiosoma* cannot be identified at this time.

More than one species of *Gobiosoma* has been found occasionally in separate tubes of one sponge or within the same tube. When two species are present, often one will be on the outside surface of the tube and the other within the osculum. All species with overlapping geographic ranges occasionally occur on the same sponge. In their review of sponge-dwelling

The fairy basslet, *Gramma loreto,* occurs widely in the tropical Atlantic and occurs in feeding aggregations of *Gobiosoma atronasum* in Exuma Sound, Bahamas.

fishes, Tyler and Bohlke (1972) recorded *Risor ruber, Phaeoptyx xenus, Starksia lepicoelia,* and *Apogon quadrisquamatus* as occurring in the same sponges as *Gobiosoma.* In this study *Canthigaster rostrata* and *Starksia hassi,* probably fortuitous sponge-dwellers, also were collected from the same sponge as *Gobiosoma.* The shrimp *Lysmata* sp. was often found either alone or with *Gobiosoma* in the lumen of tubular sponges.

It is known that *G. horsti* (Y), *G. louisae,* and *G. xanthiprora* (W) spawn within the lumen of sponges near the base, and it is likely other sponge-dwelling species do the same. None of these species have been noted in nature to deposit eggs elsewhere. The eggs of *G. horsti, G. louisae,* and *G. xanthiprora* are similar to those of the coral-dwelling species of *Gobiosoma.* Eggs apparently are guarded by the male as in other species of *Gobiosoma,* and females have not been collected in sponges that contained brooding males. The males' coloration is dusky when brooding, and when a dusky individual was collected this was a sign to check for eggs in the sponge.

For all species of sponge-dwelling *Gobiosoma* for which information is available, the nocturnal behavior is similar. Fishes are inactive, resting near the base of the lumen, and are pale in color. Other species of fishes may be found in the sponges with members of *Gobiosoma* at night.

Few data are available, but only 60-70 per cent of apparently suitable sponges are inhabited by any species of *Gobiosoma.* For most quadrats complete data were not obtained on number and size of sponges present, but in the four quadrats surveyed at Acklins Island, Bahamas, the number and size of both occupied and unoccupied sponges were determined. Of 19 sponges comprising 39 tubes, 68 per cent of the sponges were occupied by *Gobiosoma,* with an average of 1.5 individuals per occupied sponge or 0.5 individual per sponge tube in an area of 400 square meters. These observations seem typical of those from other areas that were studied. The sponges are not "saturated" with sponge-dwelling *Gobiosoma,* and a population at least twice that commonly observed could probably be maintained.

Western Atlantic sponges are not widely used as food by fishes. Randall and Hartman (1968) found less than 10 per cent of more than 200 species of fishes they examined contained sponge material in their gut. They believed the defensive properties of sponges, such as mineralized sclerites, noxious chemical properties, and tough fibrous components, discouraged predation.

Although predation has not been observed on *Gobiosoma* under natural conditons, there is some evidence that it occurs. Smith and Tyler (1972) described an attack by the hamlet *Hypoplectrus puella* on *G. chancei* after the goby's sponge had been disturbed by divers. The goby was released after being engulfed, possibly due to noxious mucus.

Being within the sponge lumen does not assure protection from predation by fishes sufficiently small to enter the osculum. Several potential predators entered the lumen of tubular sponges, including *H. puella* and *Thalassoma bifasciatum*. Flight reactions by sponge-dwelling *Gobiosoma* sometimes occurred in response to approaches by several different species. *Gobiosoma xanthiprora* (Y) hid in a crevice between its sponge and a rock when a large *Mycteroperca* sp. grouper passed by. *Gobiosoma horsti* (W) retreated deep into the lumen of its sponge when a terminal male *Thalassoma bifasciatum* looked into the osculum, and several *G. horsti* (Y) retreated deep into their sponge when it was entered by a large pomacentrid.

Noxious properties of the polychaete worm *Syllis spongicola* have not been examined, but the following observation was made. At Discovery Bay, *S. spongicola* is common in the sponge *Neofibrularia massa* and is clearly visible inside the lumen. If the sponge was stimulated mechanically (with a pencil) or chemically (with quinaldine anesthetic), large numbers of the worms would be ejected by water currents. This "eruption" of worms and the activities of the diver causing it invariably attracted wrasses to the area. *Thalassoma bifasciatum*, a generalized opportunistic feeder (Randall, 1967), picked at a few of the worms and quickly showed no interest in eating any. It is unknown whether a connection exists between the possible noxious properties of *Syllis spongicola* and sponge-dwelling *Gobiosoma*. Deprived of sponges in an aquarium situation, sponge-dwelling *Gobiosoma* are not immune to predation but still apparently are distasteful.

In the study a series of laboratory and field trials was conducted to study noxious properties of *Gobiosoma*. Most trials used fishes in the public aquarium maintained at the Caribbean Marine Biological Institute at Piscadera Baai, Curacao. The aquarium was a ready source of tank-acclimatized predator fishes, but conditions (species present, substrate present, arrangement of material in aquarium) were different in all the aquaria used. Specimens of *G. horsti*, collected from massive sponges at Vaersenbaai and Bullenbaai using quinaldine-alcohol solution, were put in a test aquarium either anesthetized with quinaldine or unanesthetized. The predators in the aquarium were usually hungry and readily attacked any items added.

On first presentation, both anesthetized and unanesthetized *G. horsti* were rapidly attacked, engulfed, and then rejected in most cases. The mouth movements of the predators after engulfment often consisted of rapid opening of the mouth. Fine material, probably mucus, was often expelled by a water current from the mouth. In only one instance the specimen of *G. horsti* (Y) was eaten without any mouth movements of the predator (*Epinephelus fulva*), but the grouper acquired within one min-

Lateral view of *Gobiosoma saucrum* from Galeta Island, Panama. This species is one of the common coral-dwelling gobies of the Caribbean.

Individual of *Coryphopterus lipernes* on a species of *Agaricia* at Providenciales Island, Caicos Bank. This goby often occurs on corals with species of *Gobiosoma*. Depth 30 m (100 feet).

Dorsal view of *Gobiosoma saucrum* from Galeta Island, Panama. The coloration of this species serves to make it match the corals on which it rests. This is unlike the members of the subgenus *Elacatinus*, which are quite distinct on the corals they inhabit.

ute a series of pale areas on the head which remained for about a half-hour. This individual continued to eat any gobies that were offered. During two control tests when the goby *Quisquilius hipoliti* was offered, they were eaten with no subsequent mouth movements. All other first presentations of *G. horsti* (Y) resulted in the prey being rejected and, in the case of *Epinephelus striatus,* subsequent presentations elicited less response.

When *G. evelynae* (YB) was offered it was eaten, but some subsequent mouth movement always occurred. It was rejected by *Myripristis jacobus* in one case after having been ingested. Apparently *G. evelynae* (YB) is less noxious than *G. horsti* (Y). Such properties are not limited to sponge-dwelling species of *Gobiosoma* and may have significance in considering immunity from predation imparted to *G. evelynae* due to its behavior as a cleaner.

In St. Croix two predators, *Holocentrus rufus* and *Epinephelus cruentatus,* were maintained in bare aquaria and starved for 3 days before testing. *Holocentrus rufus* did not attempt to ingest either of two *G. chancei* which remained in its aquarium up to 4 hours. *Epinephelus cruentatus* attacked and ate all *G. chancei* added to its aquarium, but when predation was observed, extreme movements of the mouth accompanied ingestion. When two juvenile grunts were offered, they were readily eaten and no mouth movements occurred. Mouth movements like that described were exhibited by a starved *Hypoplectrus* sp. which ate a specimen of *G. horsti* (W) placed in its aquarium.

Specimens of *G. chancei* and *G. horsti* (Y) were maintained for up to one week in aquaria without their sponge associates, and this period of time made no difference qualitatively in the response of the predator. It seems unlikely that contact with sponges is necessary to maintain the noxious property of the skin.

Randall *et al.* (1971) reported a taste test for the skin toxin of soapfishes. The toxin grammistin has a bitter taste and is irritating to human skin. Taste tests were made on *G. horsti* (Y) mucus, but no particular taste was detectable. Mucus from *G. horsti* (Y) was spread on the author's forearm, but no effects were noted over a period of one hour.

An attempt was made to assess the reaction of fishes in the field to anesthetized sponge-dwelling species of *Gobiosoma.* Gobies were collected from sponges, anesthetized with quinaldine-alcohol, taken 5-7 m above the reef, released, and allowed to drift toward the bottom while divers observed from a distance. At Curacao 3 releases were conducted. In all instances the released *G. horsti* (Y) was not taken by any fish even though some appeared to watch the descending goby. In one case the anesthetized goby landed less than 0.2 m from a large individual of *Aulostomus maculatus,* a voracious piscivore of West Indian reefs (Randall, 1967: 686-687), but was not disturbed.

At Hogsty Reef, Bahamas, an anesthetized specimen of *G. chancei* was dropped over a school of *Lutjanus griseus*. As it descended, several snappers examined the goby, but none attempted to engulf it. An individual of *Hypoplectrus puella* picked it up off the bottom and swam to a crevice with the goby in its jaws. There a *Holocentrus* sp. took it away and apparently swallowed it. The squirrelfish showed moderate mouth movements for a period after ingestion.

Although no control trials were run with these tests, they do indicate that a noxious property of *G. horsti* (Y) and *G. chancei* is demonstrable in the field.

## TIME OF SPAWNING AND LARVAL TRANSFORMATION

The spawning season for the various species of *Gobiosoma* was determined either by collection of eggs, a relatively rare occurrence, or from the occurrence of ripe individuals. All collections at the University of Miami ichthyological collection were examined for ripe individuals and any obviously ripe females seen in the field were noted. Times at which larvae transform to juveniles were determined either by observations of newly metamorphosed individuals or by the presence of very small juveniles in collections. Young juveniles were difficult to identify, and usually identification was made by association. For example, if a small sponge-dwelling individual was found in shallow water at Discovery Bay, Jamaica, it was assumed to be of *G. horsti* (W), the common shallow-water sponge dweller. Conceivably it could have been the deeper water *G. louisae*, but it is believed that these fishes move little, if any, after metamorphosis, and it seems less likely that *G. louisae* would metamorphose in shallower water than *G. horsti* (W). Juveniles of species with a V marking on the snout show this within a few days of metamorphosis, and this aids field identification.

From the data, only the times during which spawning was occurring or larvae were transforming can be determined. The absence of ripe individuals or juveniles in the samples does not necessarily mean that spawning and larval transformation are not taking place at that time. Except for *G. oceanops*, insufficient collections are available to determine when spawning is not occurring.

Lack of sufficient collections is a problem. Most species in this study have been collected at only one or two times of the year. Although there are many specimens of *G. oceanops* in the collections of the University of Miami, most were taken during the summer months, and for several months (February, November, December) there are no collections. The minimum size of any ripe female observed was recorded also.

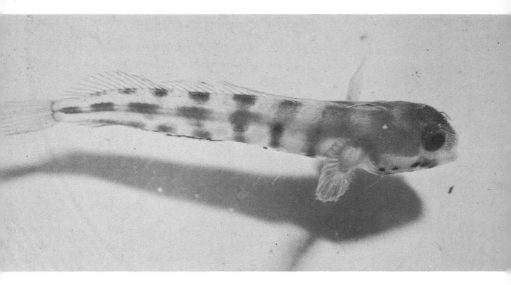

The clinid blenny *Acanthemblemaria rivasi* from Galeta Island, Panama, occurs in holes in coral heads. These heads often have *G. illecebrosum* associated with them.

A masked goby, *Coryphopterus personatus*, resting at night on the dead portion of a colony of *Montastrea cavernosa* adjacent to the living, expanded polyps, Acklins Island, Bahamas.

The goby *Coryphopterus lipernes* resting on star coral, *Montastrea annularis.* Photo by Carl Roessler.

Species of emblemarid blenny on *Montastrea cavernosa* at Whale Cay, Berry Islands, Bahamas. Many emblemarids are nearly transparent and blend well with the surface of the corals they inhabit.

# TABLE 25

## TIME OF SPAWNING AND LARVAL SETTLEMENT
## OF SPECIES OF *Gobiosoma*

| Species | Occurrence of Ripe Females | Smallest Ripe Female | Occurrence of Small Juveniles |
|---|---|---|---|
| *G. atronasum* | No information | — | No information |
| *G. chancei* | July | 23.3 | Bahamas, April; St. Croix, June; Barbados, July |
| *G. evelynae* (Y) | Dec. | 21.2 | Dec., March, May |
| *G. evelynae* (YB) | Bahamas, Dec. Virgin Is., Oct. Nov., Feb. others June-Aug. | 22.8 | Bahamas, March, April; Virgin Is., June others July |
| *G. evelynae* (W) | Feb.-Aug. | 21.8 | Jan.-June |
| *G. genie* | July | 25.5 | May |
| *G. horsti* (Y) | March, July | 28.8 | May, July |
| *G. horsti* (W) | Oct. | 27.8 | Feb., June |
| *G. illecebrosum* | July-Oct. | 19.6 | Sept. |
| *G. louisae* (Y) | Bahamas, Dec., April; Jamaica, July | 18.8 | Bahamas, Sept.; Jamaica, Feb., June |
| *G. oceanops* | Fla., Jan.-May | 26.9 | Fla., Feb.-Aug. |
| *G. prochilos* | Barbados, July | 20.2 | Barbados, July; Brit. Honduras, Oct. |
| *G. randalli* | June-Aug. | 18.0 | June-Aug. |
| *G. tenox* | Aug. | 31.4 | No information |
| *G. xanthiprora* (W) | Oct. | — | No information |
| *G. xanthiprora* (Y) | No information | — | No Information |

Feddern (1967) reported that spawning by *G. oceanops* in Florida was almost exclusively confined to February, March, and April. In the present study ripe individuals were found from January to May. The lack of any ripe females from June through September based on the large number of females that were examined suggests that spawning must occur very rarely, if at all, during this period in Florida.

The spawning season of other species of *Gobiosoma* differs. Some species are in spawning condition nearly every month. Several species, principally *G. evelynae, G. genie,* and *G. randalli,* are ripe during the summer. The spawning season lasts at least a few months (*G. evelynae, G. horsti, G. illecebrosum, G. louisae,* and *G. randalli*) and probably all species have an extended spawning period.

*Gobiosoma oceanops* inhabits areas with the lowest temperatures of any *Elacatinus* and also inhabits the area with the greatest annual temperature range. Its spawning season includes the coldest portion of the year (February), and the first three months of its spawning season have the coldest water temperatures of any quarter of the year. Species that live in areas with the warmest and most stable water temperatures often spawn during the summer, the warmest part of the year. *Gobiosoma evelynae* may spawn year round since it is found in areas of stable temperatures (3°-5° C. annual variation), while *G. oceanops* is closely tied to a particular temperature regime requiring variation, perhaps as a spawning stimulus, of considerable magnitude (6°-10° C. annual variation).

## TABLE 26

TIME OF OCCURRENCE OF RIPE FEMALES OF *Gobiosoma oceanops* ON THE FLORIDA REEF TRACT*

| Month of Collection | Number of Female Individuals in Collection | Number of Ripe Females | Percentage |
|---|---|---|---|
| January ... ... | 2 | 2 | 100 |
| February ... ... | — | — | — |
| March ... ... | 1 | 1 | 100 |
| April ... ... | 11 | 5 | 45 |
| May ... ... | 9 | 1 | 11 |
| June ... ... | 17 | 0 | 0 |
| July ... ... | 10 | 0 | 0 |
| August ... ... | 24 | 0 | 0 |
| September ... | 1 | 0 | 0 |
| October ... ... | — | — | — |
| November ... | — | — | — |
| December ... | — | — | — |

*Only the material of *G. oceanops* in the University of Miami Ichthyological Collection (UMML) was utilized and only females over 20.0 mm S.L. were considered in percentage determinations.

The goby *Coryphopterus lipernes* resting on the coral *Stephanocoenia michelinii*. The red spots are contracted zooanthids living with the coral.

The spotfin hogfish, *Bodianus pulchellus*, is a cleaner found in deeper waters along Atlantic reefs. Photographed at 25 m (84 feet), Cosgrove Light, Florida Keys.

Small individual of *G. evelynae* (Y) on *Agaricia* at 40 m (133 feet) depth, Eleuthera Island, Bahamas.

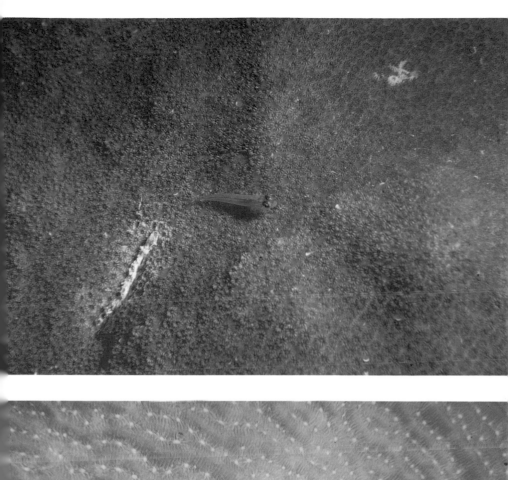

The spawning period of the Belize population of *G. oceanops* should be compared with that of the Florida population, for Belize has a more stable temperature regime in its coastal waters.

The minimum size of ripe females is shown in the table. More material no doubt will lower these limits somewhat. Most species appear to have a minimum spawning size around 18.0-22.0 mm S.L. There is no correlation between life habits and minimum spawning sizes.

Recently metamorphosed individuals of *Elacatinus* are present on reefs throughout the spawning period. Observations were made during the present study on occurrence of newly metamorphosed (2-4 days after metamorphosis) individuals of various species with time of year and locality. Newly metamorphosed specimens are found associated with the substrate (sponges or corals) normally frequented by larger juveniles and adults.

Individuals which have metamorphosed no more than 2 or 3 days previously are easily recognized in the field by size and color pattern. The coloration and behavior of newly metamorphosed individuals of *Gobiosoma* are discussed in the section on rearing of larvae. The size frequency distribution of *G. oceanops* from Florida in the UMML collection shows

## TABLE 27

## PERCENTAGE OF INDIVIDUALS OF *Gobiosoma oceanops* OF VARIOUS SIZES FROM THE FLORIDA REEF TRACT BY MONTH

| Month | | 10.0 | 10.0 14.9 | 15.0 19.9 | 20.0 24.9 | 25.0 29.9 | 30.0 34.9 | 35.0 39.9 | Number of Individuals |
|-------|---|------|-----------|-----------|-----------|-----------|-----------|-----------|-----------------------|
| January | ... | 0 | 0 | 0 | 0 | 33 | 67 | 0 | 3 |
| February | ... | 0 | 0 | 0 | 0 | 0 | 0 | 0 | 0 |
| March | ... | 0 | 0 | 0 | 0 | 50 | 50 | 0 | 2 |
| April ... | ... | 3 | 21 | 30 | 18 | 12 | 9 | 6 | 33 |
| May ... | ... | 4 | 26 | 22 | 22 | 7 | 7 | 12 | 27 |
| June ... | ... | 0 | 2 | 25 | 32 | 23 | 11 | 4 | 46 |
| July ... | ... | 0 | 3 | 17 | 34 | 31 | 6 | 3 | 29 |
| August | ... | 0 | 4 | 14 | 39 | 39 | 4 | 0 | 49 |
| September | ... | 0 | 0 | 0 | 0 | 67 | 33 | 0 | 3 |
| October | ... | 0 | 0 | 0 | 0 | 50 | 50 | 0 | 2 |
| November | ... | 0 | 0 | 0 | 0 | 0 | 0 | 0 | 0 |
| December | ... | 0 | 0 | 0 | 0 | 0 | 0 | 0 | 0 |

Standard Length in mm

that small individuals are found on Florida reefs from April through August. This correlates well with the observed spawning period of *G. oceanops* (January-May), if a larval period of 1-2 months is normal and if some of the 10.0-14.9 mm S.L. individuals are 4 or more weeks post-metamorphosis. Unfortunately too few specimens were available to determine whether young individuals are also present from September through March.

Other species of *Gobiosoma* seem to follow the general trends of their spawning period with regard to presence of newly metamorphosed larvae. Lengthy seasons of larval settlements, often during the summer months, seem to be common among species of *Gobiosoma*.

## SPAWNING AND LARVAL DEVELOPMENT

For most species it was impossible to get information on reproductive behavior in the field, so an effort was made to obtain such information in the laboratory.

The fertilized eggs of three species, *G. horsti* (Y), *G. louisae,* and *G. xanthiprora* (W), were obtained from near the base of the lumen of tubular sponges they inhabit. In all three instances a single large male was found with the eggs, presumably guarding them. In one instance it appeared that more than one female *G. horsti* (Y) had spawned because many eggs in two distinct developmental stages were present. In the other cases it appeared that only a single female had spawned.

The eggs of the coral-dwelling species have not been obtained in the field. They are probably deposited in rock crevices or holes and would be more difficult to collect than those found in sponges. Males of some coral-dwelling species of *Gobiosoma* remove material, such as sand, from holes and crevices both in the field and the laboratory, and apparently perform this activity in nest preparation. Digging was carried out with the mouth alone.

Spawning usually occurs in pairs, and in aquaria a pair will continue to spawn periodically for some months. The presence in nature of "mated pairs" which spawn together consistently over a period of time has not been proved. Often large individuals of the coral-dwelling species are found in pairs, and these pairs are invariably male-female.

Little is known about the reproductive biology of any species in the field. Field collections can provide some information, especially regarding spawning season and larval transformation. Some additional information has been obtained for *G. oceanops* because of the numerous collections available. Of *G. oceanops* from Florida larger than 20.0 mm S.L., a size at which sex can be confidently determined, the ratio of males to females is 4:5, (134 individuals). Few data are available except in the

The masked goby, *Coryphopterus personatus,* in its typical habit of hovering in and around reef caves and ledges, Discovery Bay, Jamaica.

Unidentified goby of the genus *Coryphopterus* resting on the head coral *Colpophyllia natans.*

months of April-August. Where there are adequate data the curves for each month are unimodal. Individuals apparently mature within one year (20-25 mm S.L.) and may well reach considerably larger sizes in this time. Aquarium observations indicate that some individuals live beyond one year, hence the number of large individuals in April, May, and June may be one year old. Whether they live to 2 years, through the second winter, is unknown. Localized populations can undergo sizeable changes over short periods of time, probably due to changes in environmental conditions. Many small marine shore fishes have short life spans and could almost be termed annual fishes (Rosenblatt, 1963). Although species of *Elacatinus* may not be annual in the strict sense of the word, they probably do not live beyond 2-3 years and can reproduce in less than one year. As Rosenblatt (1963) noted, such a short life span is one of the factors promoting rapid speciation.

Both Valenti (1972) and Feddern (1967) briefly described the spawning behavior of *G. oceanops* in aquaria. Valenti (1972) described preparation of the spawning site by the male through rubbing with the pelvic fins and removing any loose particles with the mouth. A brief courtship was observed with side to side quivering motions. Spawning occurred ½ to 1 hour after courtship. Feddern (1967) reported that the male took the initiative in courtship by first making violent swimming motions which were restrained by the pelvic cup attached to the bottom. The male butted the female in the head and genital region with his snout and slapped the female in the head with his caudal fin.

## TABLE 28

## SUMMARY OF LABORATORY SPAWNINGS
## OF SPECIES OF *Gobiosoma*

| Species | Number of Spawnings | (C°) Temperature Range | Average Time and Range in Days Between Spawnings |
|---|---|---|---|
| *G. evelynae* (YB) | 2 | 20–23 | 21 |
| *G. evelynae* (Y) | 1 | — | — |
| *G. evelynae* (W) | 7 | — | 14 (9–20) |
| *G. genie* | 5 | 25.7–26.7 | 9 (8–10) |
| *G. horsti* (Y, W) | 5 | 25.6–29.6 | — |
| *G. louisae* (Y) | 2 | — | — |
| *G. oceanops* | 3 | — | — |
| *G. xanthiprora* (Y) | 20 | 24.1–25.7 | 12 (7–14) |

Although no detailed analysis was attempted, the other coral-dwelling species of *Gobiosoma* that spawned in the laboratory (*G. evelynae,* all forms, and *G. genie*) had similar courtship activities. Courtship behavior was not observed for any sponge-dwelling species of *Gobiosoma* that spawned in the laboratory (*G. horsti*, all forms, *G. louisae*, and *G. xanthiprora* (W)). Males of *G. horsti* (Y) chased other fishes from the vicinity of a tube in which spawning later took place. The female that spawned the eggs was not chased.

In the laboratory, the fishes were provided one inch inside diameter (2.54 cm) polyvinyl chloride plastic tubes as shelter. They also spawned in these tubes. Sponge-dwelling species adapted well to the plastic tubes and behaved as they might in sponges by sitting in or on the tube and fleeing to its lumen when disturbed. Polyester drafting film was cut in rectangular pieces, rolled and inserted in these tubes. As the film unrolled, it formed an inner lining to the tube. The gobies spawned readily on this surface and the film with attached eggs could be easily removed for any experiments or observations.

Unfortunately only limited information comparing spawning of species in aquaria is available because temperature and other conditions in the aquaria were uncontrollable. Some species such as *G. evelynae* (YB) and *G. horsti* spawn over a wide range of temperatures. The time between spawnings for pairs is variable, but probably temperature dependent.

The number of eggs produced per spawning varies, depending on the size of the female and the prespawning conditions. Often subsequent spawnings would have fewer eggs than previous spawnings and consisted of as few as 10-20 eggs. The maximum number of eggs probably lies near 1000, since laboratory spawnings containing 300-500 eggs from moderate sized females are common. Eggs of all western Atlantic *Elacatinus* are

**A.** *Gobiosoma xanthiprora* (W). Egg approximately 24 hours after being laid. Egg capsule length is 1.9 mm.

**B.** *Gobiosoma xanthiprora* (W). Egg approximately 49 hours after being laid.

**C.** *Gobiosoma xanthiprora* (W). Egg approximately 72 hours after being laid.

**D.** *Gobiosoma xanthiprora* (W). Egg approximately 100 hours after being laid.

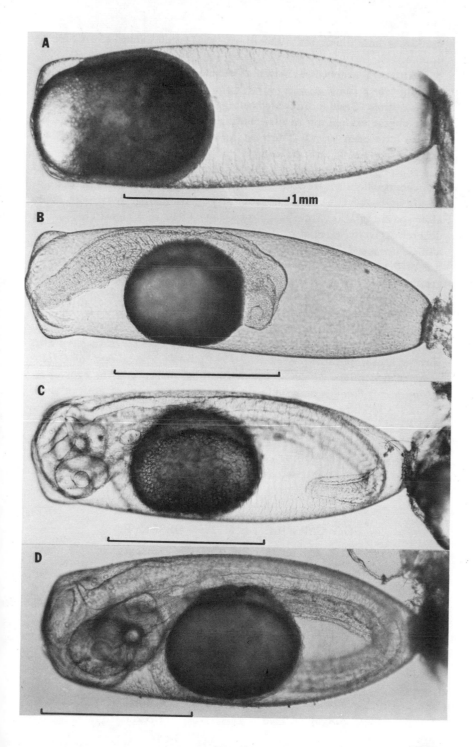

A

B

1mm

C

D

similar to those illustrated by Feddern (1967) and Valenti (1972) for *G. oceanops*.

Although a complete series of developing eggs and larvae is not available for a single species, some stages of developing eggs and larvae are illustrated. Besides differences in egg capsule size between species, no other characters serving to differentiate eggs and larvae of the various species have been found. The best series of eggs obtained and photographed was for *G. xanthiprora* (W).

The egg development of *G. xanthiprora* (W) corresponds to that of *G. oceanops* detailed by Valenti (1972). The eggs were incubated at approximately 24° C. A late gastrula-early neurula stage occurs 24 hours after spawning and is comparable to stage 11-12 of Valenti (1972). No differences were detected in the development of eggs of *G. xanthiprora* and *G. oceanops*. The other species of *Gobiosoma* have similar eggs, but it is difficult to make comparisons from preserved material and photographs. The eggs of *G. genie* are similar to eggs of *G. xanthiprora* (W) and *G. oceanops*.

All species of *Elacatinus* which spawned in the laboratory laid elliptical eggs with 5 or 6 protuberances on the end opposite the holdfast. All gobies lay elliptical eggs, but this is the only group known to have eggs with such protuberances. Breder (1942) figured elliptical eggs of *Gobiosoma* (*Garmannia*) *robustum* and Kuntz (1916) recorded the eggs of *G.* (*Gobiosoma*) *bosci* as being elliptical also, but the eggs of both of these related gobies are quite different from those of *Elacatinus*. Egg shape may be characteristic for the subgenus *Elacatinus*. More information is needed regarding the eastern Pacific species of *Elacatinus* and others within *Gobiosoma* regarding egg morphology.

## TABLE 29

## EGG CAPSULE LENGTHS OBSERVED
## FOR VARIOUS SPECIES OF *Gobiosoma*

| Species | Observed Egg Capsule Length |
|---|---|
| *G. evelynae* (W) ... ... | 1.8–1.9 |
| *G. genie* ... ... ... | 2.5 |
| *G. horsti* (Y) ... ... ... | 2.7–3.0 |
| *G. horsti* (W) ... ... ... | 2.0–2.1 |
| *G. louisae* (Y) ... ... ... | 2.8–2.9 |
| *G. oceanops* ... ... ... | 3.3 |
| *G. xanthiprora* (W) ... ... | 1.7–2.0 |

260

Most spawnings hatched in about one week, but hatching took up to 12 days due to cool (about 18°-20° C.) temperatures. No attempt was made to compare hatching times among species because temperatures in the spawning aquaria could not be controlled closely.

In the one instance larvae were reared through metamorphosis; they were hybrids and what effect, if any, their hybrid origin had on suitability for aquarium rearing is unknown. This rearing took place in a 120-liter all-glass aquarium with a single tube, Gro-lux fluorescent lighting fixture. The aquarium was illuminated 24 hours per day, and zooplankton of 56-200 micron size fraction, collected from the School of Marine and Atmospheric Sciences pier, was added every 8-12 hours. The aquarium water, from Bear Cut, was aerated and maintained at approximately 24° C and about 32% salinity. Freshly hatched *Artemia salina* were included in the foods added to the aquarium 14 days after hatching. Metamorphosis occurred 26 days after hatching.

Rearing was attempted in smaller aquaria (40 liters) with less success, but it is not known that aquarium size was a limiting factor. Usually spawns were deposited in 1-inch diameter (2.54 cm) polyvinyl chloride plastic tubes. If removed from the guarding male, it was necessary to pass a flow of water over the eggs if development and hatching were to occur. This was accomplished by an airlift which provided a flow of water through the tube. Actually, a flat rock or large clam shell provides a better object for the spawning since a simple airstone could then be used to agitate the eggs. However, when the plastic tube is used with a polyester film lining, the eggs can be removed and easily divided into experimental groups by cutting the film into sections with scissors.

The newly hatched larvae of all species of *Elacatinus* are similar. There is some variability in the amount of yolk still present when the eggs hatch, but this is probably related to incubation conditions and may not be species dependent. It is unknown how much variability in larval length at hatching occurs among species or within the same species.

The swim bladder of all species hatched was inflated a few hours after hatching. I did not observe larvae swimming to the surface to take in air at any time between hatching and bladder inflation, and it appears that the bladder is inflated while larvae are submerged. When the yolk has been completely absorbed the larvae begin to attempt to feed. If suitable food is present, they can be seen to flex the body and strike, probably toward food organisms in the water. Feeding is evident from material visible in the gut in the area posterior to the swim bladder.

The larvae apparently are photopositive. Agitation and aeration of the aquarium water is provided by an airstone. Before death, most individuals go through a behavior termed "top skimming" in which the larva swims strongly along the surface of the water with the head pointed up-

## TABLE 30

### COMPARISON OF SPAWNING OCCURRENCES OF
### HYBRID PAIR AND CONTROLS OF
*Gobiosoma oceanops* AND *G. evelynae* (W)

| | | | | |
|---|---|---|---|---|
| **HYBRID PAIR** | | | | |
| *G. oceanops* × *G. evelynae* (W) | 10–XII–71 | | | |
| | 14– II–72 | ... ... ... | | 67 |
| **CONTROL PAIR** | | | | |
| *G. evelynae* (W) × *G. evelynae* (W) | 28– XI–71 | | | |
| | 18–XII–71 | ... ... ... | | 21 |
| | 1– I–72 | ... ... ... | | 14 |
| | 26– I–72 | ... ... ... | | 25 |
| | 17– II–72 | ... ... ... | | 22 |

Mean Days Between Spawnings
For Control Pair... ... ... 20.5

ward. In groups of larvae where many individuals exhibited this behavior, all usually died within 24 hours.

The only observations on behavior of individuals during and after metamorphosis involved hybrids. A piece of living coral, *Montastrea cavernosa*, was placed in the aquarium about 1 day before metamorphosis. The premetamorphic larva progressively developed a full complement of fin-rays and a complete pelvic fin cup before metamorphosis. The first apparent evidence of metamorphosis is the appearance of the dark lateral stripe which, when viewed dorsally, forms a Y-shape. There is a break in this stripe near the caudal peduncle, and the posterior bit of black appears as a small spot.

Nine individuals metamorphosed. Metamorphosing individuals were capable of resting on the live coral colony in the aquarium, but still spent part of their time swimming. The most developed individuals often chased other less developed individuals off the coral. Premetamorphic, pelagic larvae were not chased when they swam near the coral. Within one day of the appearance of the dark stripe, the colored stripe began to appear and its color could be determined. All nine individuals that metamorphosed eventually occupied the one coral colony in the aquarium. The standard length of the larvae at metamorphosis was approximately 8 mm S.L.

Potential hybridization situations were arranged in 40-liter aquaria with a male and female of different species. In two cases hybridization occurred. A male *G. evelynae* (W) from Isla de Providencia spawned twice with a female *G. oceanops* from Florida. The eggs were viable and young from one spawning were reared past metamorphosis. A long period between the two spawnings of the hybrid pair may reflect differences in the reproductive cycles of the two species.

Nine hybrid individuals metamorphosed; the largest and last surviving juvenile was preserved 55 days after metamorphosis (81 days after hatching). This specimen (UMML 30359) is 17.5 mm S.L. and has fin-element counts within the overlapping ranges of both parent species. In certain pigmentary characters, the 9 metamorphosed hybrids were intermediate to the parents.

Hybridization also occurred between a female *G. evelynae* (W) from Isla de Providencia and a male *G. genie* from the Bahamas. *Gobiosoma genie* is known only from the Bahamas and Grand Cayman Island, although it probably also occurs in Cuba. The pair spawned twice with 20 days between spawnings. Viable larvae were produced, but no attempt was made to rear them.


## TABLE 31

### COMPARISON OF PIGMENTARY CHARACTERS OF TWO SPECIES OF *Gobiosoma* AND RESULTING HYBRIDS

| Species | Snout Marking | Snout Marking Color | Lateral Stripe Color |
| --- | --- | --- | --- |
| *Gobiosoma evelynae* (W) | Lateral Stripes Form V | White | Bluish White |
| Hybrid *G. evelynae* (W) × *G. oceanops* | Lateral Stripes End Just Anterior of Eye, Inturned in Dorsal View | Bluish White | Pale Iridescent Blue |
| *G. oceanops* | Lateral Stripes End at Anterior Preorbital Pore | Iridescent Blue | Iridescent Blue |

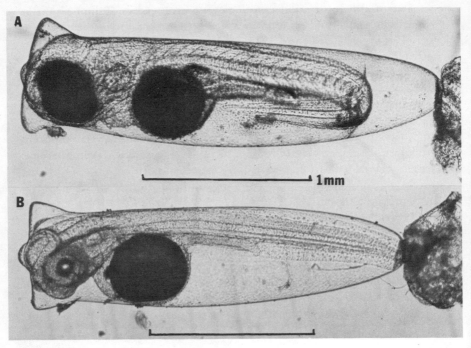

**A.** The egg of *Gobiosoma genie.*

**B.** The egg of *Gobiosoma genie.*

**A.** Newly hatched larva of *Gobiosoma evelynae* (W).

**B.** Newly hatched larva of *Gobiosoma louisae* (Y).

**C.** Newly hatched larva of hybrid spawning of *G. evelynae* (W) and *G. oceanops.*

**D.** Newly hatched larva of *Gobiosoma oceanops* (approximately 24 hours after hatch).

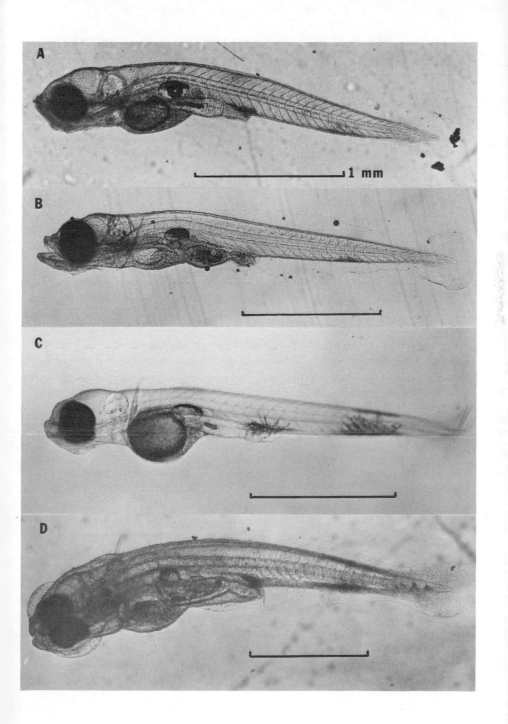

The instance of hybridization between *G. evelynae* (W) and *G. oceanops* involved allopatric species. In the case of *G. evelynae* (W) and *G. genie, G. evelynae* (W) is allopatric with *G. genie*, although the other two color varieties of *G. evelynae* commonly occur with *G. genie* over at least part of its range.

No hybridization occurred between species of the *"horsti"* complex, as described by Bohlke and Robins (1968), which are mostly sponge dwellers. One particular attempt was made to hybridize this group. The females of two spawning pairs of gobies, *G. horsti* (Y) and *G. xanthiprora* (W), were switched 10 days after their last previous spawning, which had occurred on the same day for each pair. Neither mixed pair spawned even though both females had been spawning regularly with the male of their own species.

Rubinoff and Rubinoff (1971) dealt with laboratory hybridization among Panamanian gobies of the genus *Bathygobius*, and their results suggest that laboratory experiments on non-choice hybridization between fishes should be extrapolated cautiously to field situations. However, it appears that closely related but allopatric members of the *"oceanops"* complex (Bohlke and Robins, 1968) of *Elacatinus* are interspecifically fertile and under laboratory non-choice conditions are not reproductively isolated. Although natural hybrids of *Elacatinus* are unknown, there is some evidence that different color forms of the same species may occasionally cross in the narrow areas where both forms occur.

**A.** 16 day after hatch larva  of *G. evelynae* (YB).

**B.** 23 day after hatch larva  of hybrid spawning of *G. evelynae* (W) and *G. oceanops*, near metamorphosis.

**C.** Caudal fin development of 16 day after hatch larva  of *G. evelynae* (YB).

**D.** Caudal fin development of 23 day after hatch larva  of hybrid spawning of *G. evelynae* (W) and *G. oceanops*.

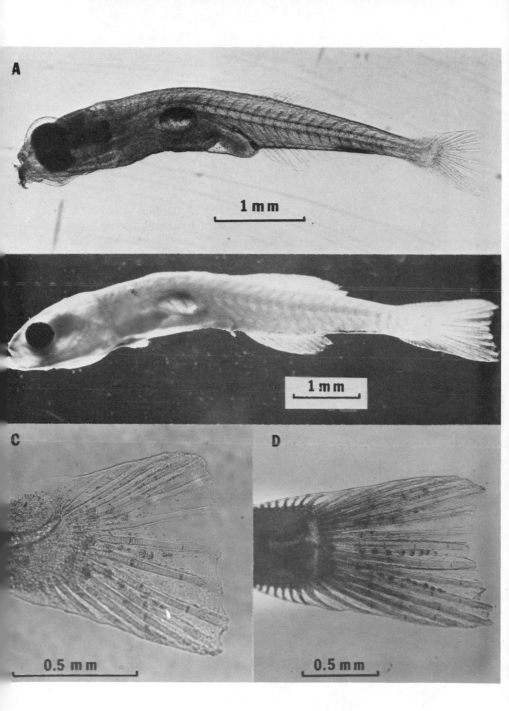

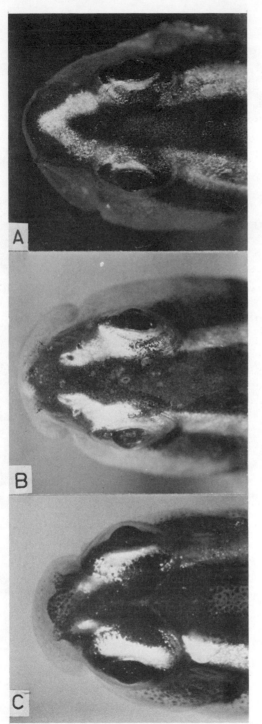

**A.** Dorsal view of the head of a specimen of *G. evelynae* from Isla de Providencia.

**B.** Dorsal view of the head of a specimen of *G. oceanops* from Florida.

**C.** Dorsal view of the head of a 17.5 mm S.L. hybrid of *G. evelynae* (W) and *G. oceanops.*

# ZOOGEOGRAPHY OF SPECIES OF THE SUBGENUS *ELACATINUS* IN THE WESTERN NORTH ATLANTIC

Geographic distribution of the various species of *Elacatinus* has been described for each species in an earlier section. No species of *Elacatinus* is found throughout the range of the subgenus. The geographic distribution of *Elacatinus* has been examined in relation to other species of fishes, and possible mechanisms that produced the distributions are discussed.

The present knowledge of the distribution of shore fishes in the tropical western Atlantic is far from complete. Only in the last 20 years have truly definitive faunal studies been carried out in the area (Robins, 1971). At present the best known localities in the western Atlantic are the Florida Keys (Starck, 1968), the Bahamas (Bohlke and Chaplin, 1968), and Venezuela (Cervigon, 1966 and subsequent work), particularly Cubagua Island and Margarita Island. The U.S. Virgin Islands, Cayman Islands, and Tortugero Lagoon, Costa Rica are also reasonably well known.

Western Atlantic shore fishes do show some patterns of distribution. There are species which are ubiquitous, found throughout the tropical western Atlantic. These species evidently are tolerant of a wide variety of conditions and amount to a considerable portion of the fish fauna of the area. Certain species have more restricted distributions, and these Robins (1971) termed continental and insular. Robins (1971) felt it was ecological rather than physical barriers which restricted the ranges of these species. The continental fauna lives in environments where change is a way of life. Temperature, salinity, and turbidity vary greatly with the seasons and also within shorter time spans.

The insular fish fauna requires clear water, constant environmental conditions, and bottoms composed largely of calcium carbonate. Such conditions are found from the Bahamas to the islands off Venezuela and in the western Caribbean. Coral and massive sponge growth is best in these areas, and the species of *Elacatinus* are mostly found in the insular type areas. Intergradation of continental and insular faunas can be found, and numerous examples of these distributions are presented by Robins (1971).

The distribution of a number of small, specialized shore fishes fits into this general scheme, but these species may occupy a range far less than that which seems potentially available in terms of the environmental conditions they require. The species of *Elacatinus* have such distributions.

Small size and specialized habits of fishes immediately introduce problems in defining their geographic ranges. They may seldom be taken

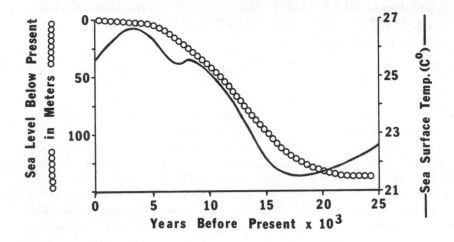

Sea level and temperature curves for the past 25,000 years.

in the usual collections or may exist in sponges, deep drop-off areas, or wave-tossed rocky shores, habitats that are seldom collected. Many such species have been described, often known only from the type specimens or from such limited areas that any discussion of zoogeography would be foolish. Only in those groups where widespread specialized collections have been made, such as those for *Elacatinus*, or recent comprehensive reviews have been carried out, can meaningful comparisons be made.

Past oceanographic conditions are important in considering pres-ent day fish distributions. The major climatic, geological, and oceano-graphic "event" during the Pleistocene was the repeated glacial-intergla-cial periods. The gross effect of these conditions, particularly the cold glacial periods, on the fish fauna of the western North Atlantic possibly was the extermination of numerous forms, particularly the most special-ized groups. Although connected via a Central American seaway as little as 1-3 million years ago, the eastern Pacific and western Atlantic have rel-atively few species of fishes in common (Rosenblatt, 1967). Until the Plio-cene the faunas on either side of the Americas had a great deal in com-mon (Rosenblatt, 1963). Today there are many families of shore fishes common between the Indo-Pacific and the Atlantic.

Glaciation also can exert other influences on fish faunas; first, by the lowering of sea surface temperature, and second by the lowering of sea level due to large amounts of water being incorporated into the polar ice

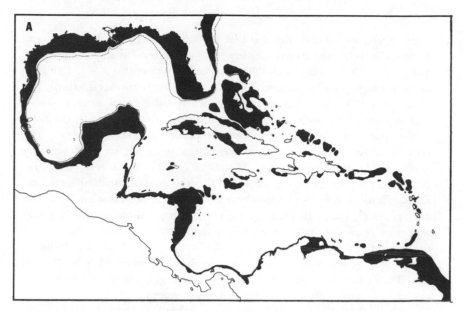

A. Shallow water (less than 50 m depth) and emergent land areas during the present time in the tropical western North Atlantic Ocean.

B. Shallow water (less than 50 m depth) and emergent land areas during the last glacial period (about 20,000 years before present) in the tropical western North Atlantic Ocean.

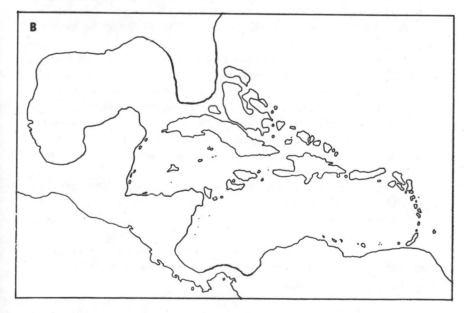

caps. A sea-level curve for the last 25,000 years (from Milliman and Emery, 1968) has the maximum lowering of sea level as about 130 m below present; that occurred 16,000 years before present (y.b.p.). The Holocene transgression began about 14,000 y.b.p. and continued rapidly until about 7,000 y.b.p. Large areas presently submerged were exposed, and in some areas, such as the Bahama Banks, this resulted in the solution of platform limestone and the formation of sinkholes, caves, and other features. Submerged reefs have been reported on by MacIntyre (1967, 1972) and Anglejan and Mountjoy (1973). MacIntyre (1967) reported that submerged coral banks off the west coast of Barbados are very similar in form to reefs present there today. Although most authors have not accurately dated these features, there is general consensus that they represent reefs that probably were actively growing during low water periods in the Pleistocene. Newell et al. (1959) reported that the Bahama Banks, emergent during low sea levels, were first flooded 4000-5000 years ago. They cited the drowned sinkholes, submerged mangrove peats, and age of aragonite sediments on the bank as evidence.

The large shallow water banks of the Bahamas, and many other places in the Caribbean, were eliminated as marine environments by lowered sea level, and the area occupied by coral reefs also decreased. The shallow water (less than 50 m depth) area 20,000 years ago with a sea level of 135 m was less than 10 per cent of the area today. The true value may be near 5 per cent or less. These values were obtained by measuring the area between various depths by cutting out and weighing the area between either 0-50 m or 100-150 m depth while knowing the area present per unit weight throughout the western Atlantic from bathymetric charts.

Today most of the coasts of the islands in the western Atlantic and parts of the continental coast have steeply sloping or vertical faces below a depth of 50-75 m. These are the "drop-off" areas and are widespread. Ginsburg and James (1973), Colin (1974), Milliman (1967), Bunt et al. (1972) and U.S. Naval Oceanographic Office (1967) have illustrations of profiles of such areas. While some areas do not have vertical slopes below 50-100 m, probably most coastlines in the tropical western North Atlantic have steep aspects at these depths.

There must have been less area occupied by coral reefs 20,000 years ago. This example is taken from Discovery Bay, Jamaica, which has a narrow fringe of reef (about 300 m wide). There are many other locations where the well developed reefs are of much greater extent. Considering the entire western North Atlantic area, but not considering effects of temperature decrease, the area occupied by reefs was at most 20-30 per cent of that occupied today.

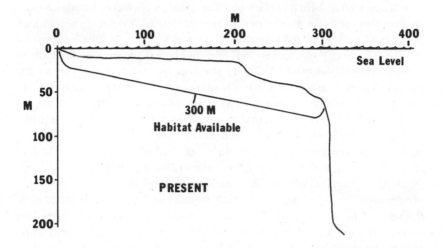

**A.** The width of a narrow shelf available for coral reef habitat during the present interglacial period. This example is taken from the shelf off Discovery Bay, Jamaica and assumes 50 m as the effective depth limit of coral growth.

**B.** The width of a narrow shelf available for coral reef habitat during the glacial period about 20,000 years ago with a sea level approximately 150 m below present. A depth of 50 m is assumed as the lower limit of effective coral growth.

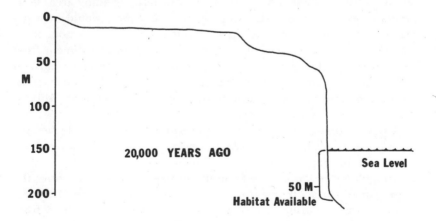

Rather than broad, relatively flat areas with waves breaking on a shallow reef crest, the glacial period reef presented a vertical escarpment both above and below the water's surface and very precarious location for extensive coral colonies to develop. Sedimentation patterns were changed considerably (Lynts *et al.*, 1973) by the lack of broad shallow areas that produce calcareous sediment from sources such as the alga *Halimeda*. Although no comparable situation exists today and it is difficult to reconstruct a paleo-glacial reef, corals were alive and present in some areas during low sea levels. Ginsburg and James (pers. comm.) dated a coral sample collected from a vertical face at 140 m at Belize as 12,700 years old. The presence of a coral colony of that age indicates that some corals must have existed on these faces (sea level should have been approximately 75 m below present and somewhat below the beginning of the vertical face at this locality). Many coral-reef organisms, including fishes, are tied to microhabitats of the coral-reef environment, and changes as drastic as those caused by sea level changes must have had great effects in many areas.

The lowering of sea level also changed the "aquatic morphology" of various areas which may have affected water circulation and physical properties. As an example, consider the emergent land on the Great Bahama Bank and shallow-water areas both today and 20,000 years ago. The deep-water basins, Tongue-of-the-Ocean and Exuma Sound, today are connected to other areas by 1) shallow-water areas of the Bahama Banks, 2) a deep opening with a depth of at least 1000 fathoms (1829 m), and 3) in the case of Exuma Sound a shallow sill (20 m depth) connection with the Atlantic Ocean. A lowering of sea level by 50 m would cause all communication of these two bodies of water with surrounding areas to be eliminated except through the deep opening and there would be a decrease of adjacent shallow reef areas. Lynts *et al.* (1973) demonstrated that the lowering of sea level eliminated the transport of sediment from the bank east of Tongue-of-the-Ocean, caused by prevailing wind and currents, into the Tongue. Obviously surface currents in these areas must have been greatly affected and such areas may have been more isolated from others than they are today.

Extra "stepping stones" for shore fishes may have appeared when sea level was lower because sea mounts, now below the depth of coral growth, were at suitable depths during glacial low water.

In addition to low sea level conditions in the western Atlantic, the lowering of sea surface temperature operated at the same time. The temperature decrease during glaciation in the Caribbean is estimated from nearly no change to 7°-8° C. (Emiliani, 1970). There is biological information that supports fluctuating temperatures. Walters and Robins

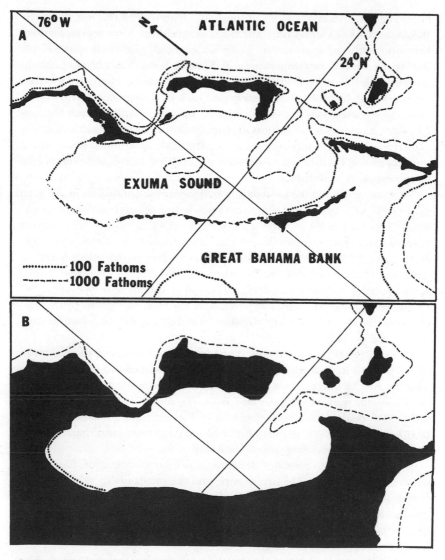

**A.** The present day distribution of emergent land and shallow water areas in the vicinity of Exuma Sound, Bahamas.

**B.** The distribution of emergent land and shallow water areas approximately 20,000 years ago in the vicinity of Exuma Sound, Bahamas with a drop of 135 m in sea level.

(1961) described a new species of toadfish, *Opsanus phobetron*, from the Bahamas, Cuba, and possibly Yucatan, and felt this form represented relict populations of a previously more widespread species. It spawns only during the winter low temperatures at Bimini, Bahamas, and is unable to establish itself on the United States coast because of competition from other species, lack of pelagic larvae, or lack of proper ecological conditions. The populations are small and well isolated, implying that the species once had a wider distribution during cool (glacial) periods. During glacial periods the northern limit of tropical conditions was pushed southward and Florida and large parts of the West Indies were temperate or sub-tropical in nature.

I have examined the present day hydrographic conditions in the area of interest and summarized recent knowledge of various phenomena. Wust (1964) reported on surface currents in the Caribbean. The surface currents and temperatures shown are taken from *U.S. Naval Occ. Off. Publ. 700*, Perlroth (1971), Jones (1973), and other sources. A reconstruction of the probable temperature distribution in the area 20,000 years ago is also shown. This reconstruction assumes the temperature decrease during glacial periods as 5° C. and sea level as -135 m from present. It is assumed that surface circulation did not significantly differ during glacial periods.

Emery (1972) discussed effects of eddies near islands on the retention of larvae, and Brucks (1971) described eddying east of the Lesser Antilles which could be a significant mechanism for transporting short-lived larvae to islands normally "upstream" from the source of the larvae. Emilsson (1971) dealt with circulation in the Cayman Sea (northern Caribbean) and pointed out the variability of currents near land masses, often opposite to the prevailing oceanic currents.

It is simplest to consider distributions of the species of *Elacatinus* within species groups. The first group, and the one for which the most detailed zoogeographic information is available, consists of the three inferior-mouthed cleaning gobies which possess a rostral frenum (*G. evelynae, G. oceanops*, and *G. illecebrosum*). At every locality at which collections have been made, only one of these three species is present. They are morphologically identical but differ significantly in pattern and color. The three species undoubtedly have a common origin and are more closely related among themselves than to any other species. The identical morphology of the three species suggests that they occupy identical ecological niches and may not be capable of occupying the same habitat concurrently. Their distributions are presently mutually exclusive, and no intermediate populations are found in areas where the distributions are adjacent, although *G. evelynae* and *G. oceanops* have hybridized in labora-

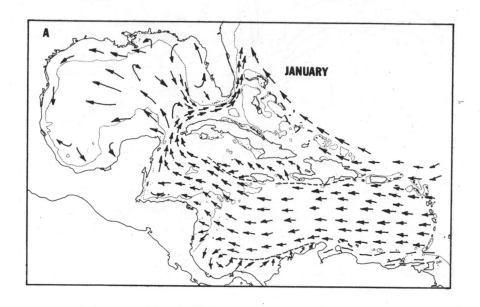

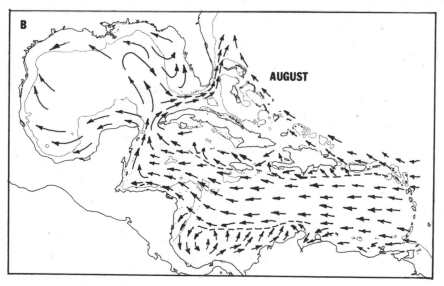

**A.** Present day surface currents of the tropical western North Atlantic Ocean during January.

**B.** Present day surface currents of the tropical western North Atlantic Ocean during August.

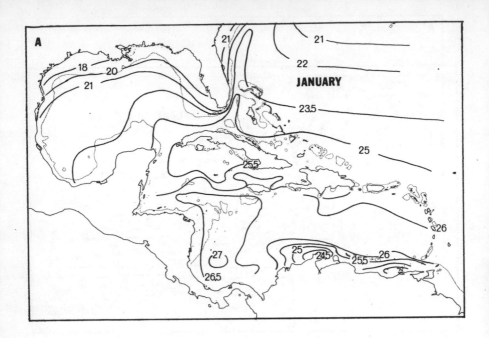

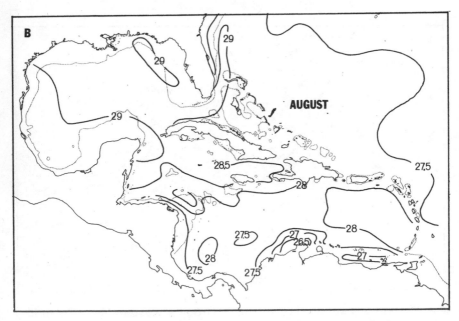

**A.** Present day distribution of surface temperature in the tropical western North Atlantic Ocean during January.

**B.** Present day distribution of surface temperature in the tropical western North Atlantic Ocean during August.

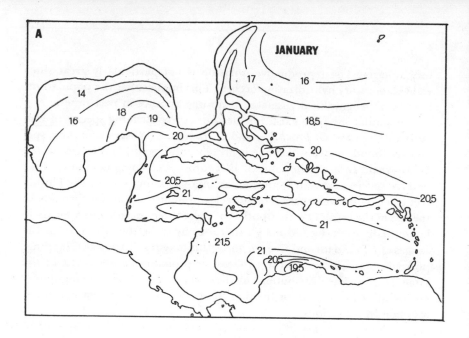

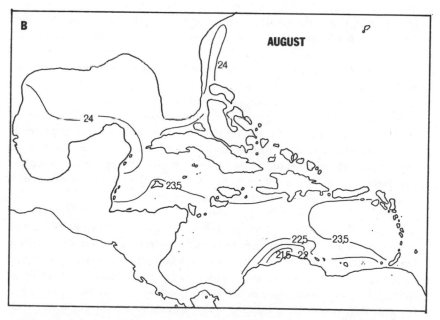

**A.** Possible distribution of surface temperature during January in the tropical western North Atlantic Ocean about 20,000 years ago during a glacial period.

**B.** Possible distribution of surface temperature during August in the tropical western North Atlantic Ocean about 20,000 years ago during a glacial period.

tory aquaria. The reproductive isolation is not particularly great since viable laboratory hybridization occurs. This implies that the populations have been geographically isolated from one another in past times.

A similar situation exists for the other three cleaning species of *Elacatinus* (*G. genie, G. prochilos,* and *G. randalli*). Where these three species are found, only a single one is present, always with a member of the *G. evelynae, G. oceanops,* and *G. illecebrosum* cleaning complex. None of these species is known from the Panama-Colombia area or the Florida reef tract. Otherwise there is one species present at localities throughout the rest of the area. The distribution of these three species also appears to be mutually exclusive. Although there seems to be some overlap of the ranges of *G. randalli* and *G. prochilos,* this may result from overlapping, isolated populations, and the two species probably do not occur at the same locality. The distributions of these three species of cleaning gobies are not as well known as for the first three species because they are not as common in collections.

Although the distributions of the two groups of three species of cleaning gobies are similar, the second group (*G. genie, G. prochilos,* and *G. randalli*) is not morphologically so similar as the first group (*G. evelynae, G. oceanops,* and *G. illecebrosum*). *Gobiosoma genie* has an inferior mouth and lacks the rostral frenum (unlike the first species group) while both *G. prochilos* and *G. randalli* have a subterminal mouth and no frenum.

*Gobiosoma atronasum* does not behave like any other known species of *Elacatinus*. While it occasionally is found resting on living corals, it spends most of its time out of contact with the substrate. The species is known only from Exuma Sound, Bahamas where it is quite common in proper habitat, and it is tempting to theorize that this species differentiated there during low sea level associated with glaciation, when Exuma Sound was more isolated from surrounding areas.

The distributions of the sponge-dwelling members of *Gobiosoma* are inadequately known except for *G. horsti* (Y) and *G. chancei.* The other three species and one color variety are known from a variety of localities but have not been collected from enough localities that a clear picture of their distributions is apparent at present. No more than two species of sponge-dwelling *Gobiosoma* occur at any one locality. If two species are present, they constitute a shallow-water species and a deeper-water species.

The distributions of *G. horsti* (Y) and (W), and *G. chancei* apparently are mutually exclusive. All three forms (*G. horsti* (Y) and (W) and *G. chancei*) occupy seemingly identical habitats and are morphologically alike except for the pattern and color of the lateral stripe. This situation parallels that in the first group of cleaning gobies.

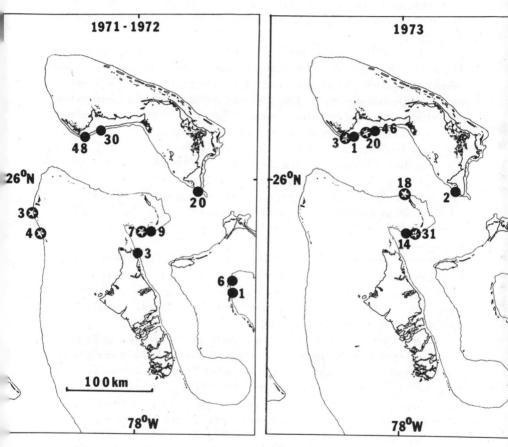

Variation in the geographic distribution of *G. evelynae* (YB) and *G. evelynae* (Y) during 1971-1973.

*Gobiosoma louisae* and *G. tenox* are deeper-water (usually below 30 m) species and, although *G. tenox* is known from only 6 collections, the two species may be mutually exclusive in their distributions. Where they occur, there is always a shallow-water sponge-dwelling *Elacatinus* also present. *Gobiosoma xanthiprora* is morphologically and ecologically more similar to the shallow-water sponge-dwellers, and its presently known distribution is mutually exclusive of both *G. horsti* and *G. chancei*.

In considering the different color varieties of the various species of *Elacatinus*, there are several instances of sharp distributional breaks between color varieties of what are considered the same species with few, if any, transitional individuals. The distributions of some color varieties are separated by physical barriers capable of isolating fishes like *Elacatinus* that have feeble means of dispersal and are tied to specialized habitats. The break between the two forms of *G. illecebrosum*, (Y) and (B), found in the southern Caribbean evidently is the Gulf of Uraba, a shallow, muddy embayment on the coast of Colombia. As Robins (1971) pointed out, the two sides of the Gulf at the mouth are ecologically very different. For other species and color varieties, there seem to be no good barriers separating populations. This is true for color varieties of *G. evelynae, G. horsti* and others.

Shown is the distribution of *G. evelynae* (Y) and (YB) in the northern Bahamas during 1971-1973. In the 1971-1972 period, the only area in which both color forms were found was the Berry Islands on the Great Bahama Bank. During this period only the yellow form (*G. evelynae* (Y)) was found on the Little Bahama Bank.

In the spring of 1973, small individuals of *G. evelynae* (YB) were found at Grand Bahama Island on the Little Bahama Bank in fairly large numbers and it appears that larvae possibly from the Great Bahama Bank had succeeded in reaching the Little Bahama Bank. Due to the short lifespan of *Elacatinus* such changes in distribution, particularly in fringe areas, are undoubtedly a normal occurrence and indicate that more than geographic isolation may be keeping these forms distinct. Some interbreeding possibly occurs in these mixed populations, but there is no quantitative information at present.

Fluctuations of distribution have a bearing on the genetic interchange between populations of the same species. It indicates that these fishes have a better ability to disperse as larvae than they do as adults. It lends more credence to the theory that the species proliferated during periods when they were more isolated with possibly smaller populations.

The isolation necessary for species differentiation may have been provided by the effects of glaciation on the marine environment. The lowering of sea level alone would have eliminated tremendous areas of suitable bottom and dramatically changed the nature of the remaining habitat for shallow-water reef fishes. Population sizes almost surely were reduced by this substrate decrease, without considering cooling of surface waters. The smaller a population is the less stable it is, particularly in a changing environment.

It is possible to theorize from a paleo-temperature distribution map where the centers of distribution of reef corals were located during glacial periods. Many areas in the West Indies probably had suitable temperatures. Much of the coast of Central and South America may have been marginal, but with tolerable temperatures. Florida was surely too cold, and there is no evidence of reef structures at depths off the Florida coastline today. The area of upwelling near the Peninsula de Guajira of Colombia was surely too cold for reef corals. Only a few areas had any extensive shallow-water areas during this period. Florida would have had a reasonably broad shallow-water belt, and off areas of Panama and Venezuela the bottom is fairly flat at -135 m. There is no evidence of what kind of reef structures, if any, existed there. The edge of the Campeche Bank would also have been relatively flat and broad.

While the change in available substrate greatly affected population size in the western Atlantic during glaciation, the barriers to dispersal of larvae probably became more pronounced. The Panama-Colombia gyre has a restricted circulation in the southern Caribbean, as described by Perlroth (1971) and, in combination with the upwelling barrier off the Peninsula de Guajira, led to isolation of this area and possibly the differentiation of species east and west of Guajira. Today this area represents a distinct faunal break with possibly only one species of *Elacatinus* common both east and west of the Peninsula. Three other species are found on one side only (*G. evelynae* (YB), *G. illecebrosum* and *G. randalli*). The populations of *G. horsti* found on either side may not be the same, since the life colors of the Panamanian population are unknown. Smith-Vaniz and Palacio (MS) report two species of the clinid genus *Acanthemblemaria* restricted to this Colombia-Panama gyre area. The occurrence of isolated populations of *G. illecebrosum* in the western Caribbean, such as at Misteriosa Bank, Banco Chinchorro, and Cozumel indicates that larvae may get into the general westward and northward drift of currents in the Caribbean. Perhaps a founder principle is involved where a particular isolated locale, like a bank or small island in mid-Caribbean, does not have a population due to previously unsuitable conditions or an unsuccessful reproductive season in which no larvae are returned to metamorphose at their point of origin. The first species to reach the locale will establish itself and be able to prevent another competing species from establishing a population until it has an unsuccessful reproductive season. This would tend to produce mutually exclusive distributions among ecologically identical species, but result in fluctuating distributions which depend on larval success every year in these short-lived fishes to maintain a population. This has been discussed for *G. evelynae* (Y) and (YB), and other species undoubtedly behave similarly.

## DISCUSSION OF RELATIONSHIPS

The western North Atlantic species of *Elacatinus*, due to their morphological similarity and ecological diversity, form an interesting group of fishes in which to attempt to determine the evolutionary relationships. In considering the various species (12 at least) and color varieties of these species (19 at least), it is difficult to assess in what direction these fishes are evolving.

In considering evolutionary history, the western Atlantic species of *Elacatinus* are more closely related to one another than to any representatives in the eastern Pacific. This implies that the group has mostly evolved in the western Atlantic, probably since the closing of the Central American seaway or in the last 1-3 million years. The group has not done well in the eastern Pacific because that region lacks extensive reefs that members of *Elacatinus* prefer. Although the eastern Pacific representatives of *Elacatinus* are poorly known, it seems unlikely that cleaning behavior in the subgenus arose independently on each side of the Isthmus of Panama. This behavior must then be at least a few million years old and must have evolved before the closure of the Central American seaway.

The historical occurrence of sponge dwelling is not documented. As Tyler and Bohlke (1972: 609) point out, most sponge-dwelling fishes are known from the western Atlantic, but this may be due to relatively greater collecting effort with special attention to this problem. In one instance where attempts were made to collect sponge-dwelling fishes on the Great Barrier Reef, few suitable sponges were located, and those that appeared suitable did not contain any fishes. The possibility exists that sponge-dwelling by fishes may be largely a western Atlantic phenomenon, but this will require more information before conclusions can be drawn.

It seems that the coral-dwelling, cleaning members and the sponge-dwelling members of *Elacatinus* evolved in two separate lines, or that the sponge-dwellers evolved from the *G. randalli-G. prochilos* line. A tentative dendrogram has been constructed, but no attempt was made to establish a time scale.

Certain groups form natural units that are difficult to consider as not having a common source. The "*oceanops* complex" of Bohlke and

Robins (1968), consisting of *G. evelynae, G. genie, G. illecebrosum,* and *G. oceanops,* is such a group. *Gobiosoma genie* differs most from other species in the group and probably differentiated somewhat earlier. The *G. horsti-G. chancei* group is a second natural grouping. Whether *G. tenox* fits into this group, although somewhat distantly, is difficult to assess. It lacks a full-length stripe, like *G. chancei,* but is different in a number of ways. *Gobiosoma louisae* differs considerably from most other species and seems to represent a distinct group. *Gobiosoma atronasum* probably is closest to *G. louisae,* although the two species are well differentiated on the basis of morphology. Both have an oval yellow spot on the snout and a dark lateral stripe ending in an oval on the caudal fin, which all other *Elacatinus* lack.

The remaining three species, *G. prochilos, G. randalli,* and *G. xanthiprora,* are so similar that they are difficult to distinguish, but they occupy very different habitats. This similarity supports the idea that the sponge-dwelling species of *Elacatinus* are closest to *G. randalli-G. prochilos.*

A dendrogram for this group probably does not give a true representation of relationships. During the Pleistocene there were many glaciations, and the alterations of the environment occurred in every glacial/interglacial cycle. With the potential for rapid speciation and the limited differences between species, the species may have been considerably altered in the last glacial cycle of 50,000 years. This does not mean that the species have evolved in a straight path from a few or single ancestral species to the present 12 species. There has probably been fluctuation in the number of species in the subgenus during the Pleistocene. Determination of relationships should be based on stable, conservative characters rather than quickly changed characters.

Color of the lateral stripe is a poor character on which to base relationships. It could be controlled by very few or even a single gene and subject to genetic drift in small isolated populations. In the cleaning gobies the entire spectrum of coloration found in *Elacatinus* is present, and the somewhat flexible nature of the host-cleaner relationship indicates that color is not critical in cleaning interactions. Any contrasting set of colors seems sufficient. Intraspecifically, the role of coloration is not known, but aquarium hybridizations between quite differently colored species have occurred.

The role of color is even less understood in the sponge-dwelling species of *Gobiosoma.* Does a brightly colored lateral stripe serve any purpose in a species which spends its life in sponges and does not engage in cleaning behavior? Two species of sponge-dwellers, *G. chancei* and *G. tenox,* have the lateral colored stripe reaching from the eye only to the

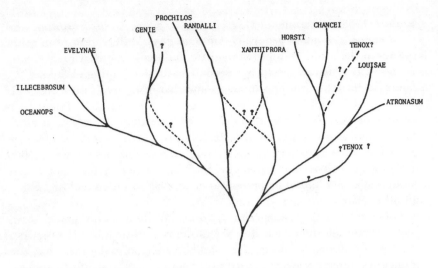

Tentative dendrogram of the western North Atlantic Ocean species of the subgenus *Elacatinus* of *Gobiosoma*.

level of the pectoral fin base. Possibly the stripe is being selected against in sponge-dwellers since it is not useful as an identifying mark, or perhaps these short-striped species represent intermediate forms between a non-striped ancestor and fully striped cleaning gobies. Bohlke and Robins (1969) point out the loss and variability of numbers of first dorsal fin spines in gobies of the genus *Evermannichthys* as a possible consequence of sponge dwelling. No hybridization has occurred between sponge-dwelling species of *Gobiosoma*, even though attempts were made. Interestingly, several species may have the same lateral stripe color in a single geographic area. In the western Caribbean, the colored stripes of *G. evelynae*, *G. horsti*, *G. prochilos*, *G. xanthiprora*, and *G. louisae* (Belize only) are white to bluish white. Is this convergence or possibly even mimicry, since certain sponge-dwelling *Gobiosoma* are known to be noxious to predators?

If coloration is a poor character on which to base relationships, the general pattern of the fish including snout markings, if any, stripe length, and width might be more reliable. Again, this appears to be a questionable character on which to base relationships because in some groups that appear to be very closely related, such as the *G. evelynae, G. illecebrosum,* and *G. oceanops* complex, there is great diversity of snout markings. Character displacement may have acted at the limits of distribution to maximize differences in snout markings where populations of species sufficiently differentiated to be valid species may contact one another and actively compete with one another.

Mouth position and dentition seem to be more conservative characters. The inferior mouth in four cleaning species of *Gobiosoma* can be considered an advanced character since it represents a specialization for cleaning behavior not found in other closely related groups of gobies. Specialized dentition also is associated with the inferior mouth position and represents another advanced character. The terminal position of the mouth apparently is not a specialized character since this is typical of most gobies and probably a primitive character.

The present level at which species have been designated in this group is probably the best possible taxonomic scheme. The present study has essentially confirmed the status of species put forth by Bohlke and Robins (1968). Each color form does not deserve rank as a separate species.

Springer (1971) reported on similar problems with the Indo-Pacific blenny genus *Ecsenius*. This group of 18 species could be divided into a number of species groups. Several of these groups consist of species which Springer (1971) could distinguish only by color pattern. If the color forms had not been collected in the same area, they were considered valid species. If, as in the case of *E. frontalis*, different color patterns of morphologically identical fishes occur together, Springer (1971) considered them color forms of a single species.

In the species of *Gobiosoma* which are considered to consist of more than one color form, the pattern does not vary, only its color. If Springer's criteria that sympatric forms are considered single species and allopatric forms are considered separate had been used, the different color varieties of *Gobiosoma* would be considered as separate species. Because the differences are strictly color and not color pattern and are probably controlled by one or a few genes, there seems to be no valid basis for considering these color forms as separate species.

The species of *Gobiosoma* which have both pattern and color differences but are morphologically nearly identical, such as *G. evelynae, G. illecebrosum,* and *G. oceanops,* are at a level of differentiation similar to that described for *Ecsenius*. Since these species of *Gobiosoma* are allopatric, the ranking of them as separate species agrees with Springer's (1971) interpretation. Further collections and study may suggest that a re-examination of these problems is necessary.

The problem of species differentiation in small tropical marine fishes needs to be examined with a variety of methods. Biochemical techniques could be used to compare populations at all levels of differentiation. *Gobiosoma* is also one of the few groups of shore fishes for which laboratory genetic experiments seem feasible with present knowledge of culture techniques for marine fishes.

## COLLECTING NEON GOBIES IN THE FIELD

In the age of jet travel, the islands and reefs of the western Atlantic are as accessible to the diving aquarist as are his local vacation areas. More people are visiting the Bahamas, Florida, and the Caribbean every year and, with today's awareness of the submarine world, more people are engaging in underwater activities on their visits. The aquarists usually long to take back some of the beauty seen, and with the proper preparation and techniques this can be very successfully done.

The gobies of the subgenus *Elacatinus* vary greatly in the amount of difficulty entailed in collecting them. The coral-dwelling species *Gobiosoma genie* is found in water only a few feet deep and is easily accessible to snorklers. The sponge-dwelling *G. tenox* and *G. louisae* are found at depths and under conditions where only experienced SCUBA divers should penetrate. Hence, this group can remain a collecting challenge for practically any aquarist or diver.

Before actual techniques are discussed, it should be emphasized that it is the duty of the collector to disturb the environment as little as possible. The removal of fishes from the reef is disturbance enough for a natural ecosystem, but the careless destruction of corals, gorgonians, and the actual rock of the reef only compounds the original disturbance by eliminating the home of the fish which would eventually replace the one collected. It is better to not even attempt to collect a specimen when there is little chance of success and a good chance of destroying part of the reef.

The easiest and, I feel, best method of collecting the coral-dwelling members of *Elacatinus* is to use a chemical anesthetic. The most commonly used anesthetic is quinaldine (2-methylquinoline), first reported as an anesthetic for fishes by Muench (1958). Other anesthetics are described by McFarland (1960), McErlean and Kennedy (1968), and Trott (1965). Randall (1963) discussed various chemical anesthetics for collecting fishes in the sea.

Quinaldine is only slightly soluble in fresh or sea water and must be combined with an organic solvent which will mix with water. Randall (1963) suggested combining about 1 part of quinaldine with 10 parts of acetone. Although this works, it is better to use alcohol as the solvent. Acetone readily dissolves many plastics and any spilled in a fiberglass boat results in marring of the finish. Isopropyl alcohol (rubbing alcohol) mixes quite well with quinaldine, is more economical than acetone and does not attack as many substances. Other alcohols, such as ethanol and methanol, also can be used but are considerably more expensive than isopropanol. A ratio of 1:10 to 1:20 quinaldine-alcohol is best. In a pinch, any high-proof alcoholic beverage could be used as a solvent. In fact,

Allen and Emery (1973:565) used quinaldine-vodka solution to collect the holotype of a new species of Pacific damselfish.

Quinaldine can be purchased from Eastman Organics*and other chemical supply houses. It is extremely irritating to human skin and eyes, poisonous if swallowed or if large amounts are absorbed through the skin, and the carcinogenic (cancer causing) properties are unknown, hence great caution should be used in handling this substance. If any is spilled on the skin it should be thoroughly flushed with water, and if contact is made with the eyes, they should be flushed with water for at least 15 minutes and medical attention sought. Despite these dire warnings, quinaldine can be effectively used for collecting marine fishes.

The anesthetic is dispensed generally from plastic squeeze bottles carried by a diver. I prefer to use a polyethylene bottle of 1 quart capacity with a curved nozzle coming out of the top, commonly called "wash bottles" in scientific catalogues. Several small lead sinkers are added inside the bottle to counteract the tendency of the bottle to float away since quinaldine-alcohol solution is lighter than water. A loop of light cord is tied around the neck of the bottle to provide a handle for the bottle. Finally a piece of aquarium air tubing is used as a plug for the delivery nozzle when not in use by first tying a simple knot in the tubing to seal it off and then forcing the tubing over the nozzle sufficiently far that it does not easily fall off and allow anesthetic to be squirted from the bottle anytime it is accidentally squeezed. The free end of this tube is usually tied to the cord around the neck so that it is not lost when the nozzle is unplugged for use. It is important to keep the anesthetic off yourself and diving gear both in the water and in boats, so a leak proof bottle is essential.

Collection of coral-dwelling *Elacatinus* usually involves use of a squeeze bottle of anesthetic in one hand and a reasonably large hand net (up to 6" x 10") in the other. The actual techniques used are difficult to explain, but the object is to get the fish to remain in a dilute cloud of the anesthetic for a sufficient period (about 10 seconds) to become nearly unconscious. This can be done in a variety of ways, usually by circling the fish with a ring of the substance or by chasing the fish into an area in which the anesthetic had previously been sprayed. The one technique which does not work is to approach the fish directly and spray the chemical right at it. The fish is irritated by the chemicals and usually flees the direction it feels is away from the irritation. The net and the hand with the bottle are used to prevent the fish from fleeing by covering any attempted escape routes. When the fish is slightly narcotized it can usually

* Eastman restricts sale of this product.

be scooped up with the net and placed in a live bucket where it quickly recovers from the anesthetic.

There has been much controversy regarding the short and long-term effects of quinaldine and other anesthetics on aquarium fishes. One school maintains that fishes collected with anesthetics ("drugged" is the normally used term) do not live long after capture, do not feed properly, and will not reproduce successfully. It is usually used as an incentive for the aquarist to purchase a more expensive "non-drugged" specimen. The other school of thought feels there are no ill effects after collection.

Allen (1972) reported no ill effects after collection on anemonefishes, and breeding pairs, collected periodically with quinaldine for measurement, continued to spawn regularly. This also seems to be the case for the neon gobies. Specimens were collected with anesthetics and maintained for over a year in aquaria. Many spawned regularly and produced viable larvae.

This is not meant to imply that quinaldine has no adverse effects on reef fishes. An excessive dose of anesthetic will kill reef fishes, and certain species seem more sensitive in this regard. Unintentional overdosage can occur easily when a fish is in restricted volumes of water and cannot easily escape the anesthetic. The yellowhead jawfish, *Opistognathus aurifrons*, is a popular aquarium fish in which this can easily occur. If quinaldine solution is squirted directly down the burrow, the fish is often dead when finally dug out of the burrow. A better method is to float a dilute cloud of the anesthetic over the burrow until the fish is narcotized. There is no evidence that use of quinaldine on the reef causes damage to corals or to other invertebrates.

It is possible, although difficult, to collect coral-dwelling *Elacatinus* without chemicals. Usually the fish is chased around its coral head with one free hand while the other hand is poised with a dip net held flat against the coral or rock. By blocking off the escape of the goby with the free hand to counter the fish's moves, the fish can sometimes be driven close to the net or actually onto the net where it can be scooped up with a very quick motion. Two people working together are even more effective using this technique.

It would be easy to collect coral-dwelling neon gobies at night when they shelter in the expanded polyps of coral heads. The gobies can be touched by the hand while resting at night and could be easily collected with a small dip net while using the free hand to almost push them into the net. Night collecting requires even more coordination than during the day to handle extra lights and avoid sea urchins which come into the open at night.

The sponge-dwelling *Gobiosoma* can be collected with a variety of techniques. Collection through placing the entire sponge in a bag, breaking its holdfast and taking it to the surface is extremely wasteful and destructive and should definitely not be done unless the sponge is to be used for some worthwhile purpose. Members of *Elacatinus* can be separated from their sponges without destroying the sponge.

The soft, tubular type of sponge is the easiest from which to collect *Elacatinus*. The sponge lumen can be squeezed closed below the goby with the hand and the goby forced outward by squeezing the sponge progressively higher until the goby must exit either into a plastic bag placed over the opening or into a waiting net. Sponges that are either too rigid to be squeezed off or noxious to the touch should have a dilute cloud of quinaldine-alcohol sprayed around them. The anesthetic is carried into the lumen by the sponge's water currents and the gobies anesthetized. Often the water currents spew the narcotized gobies out the osculum where they can be netted easily.

Members of *Elacatinus* require no special techniques for shipping; in fact, they are among the most hardy specimens for air shipment.

## MAINTENANCE AND FEEDING OF NEON GOBIES

If there is such a thing as the ideal group of aquarium fish, the neon gobies probably come as close as any group found in nature to fulfilling this ideal. They attain a length of only a few inches, are not bothered by confinement since they do not range more than a few feet in nature, are colorful and hardy, and are capable of being spawned and reared in captivity. The size of an aquarium needed to house these fishes is modest; a fully grown pair would be happy in a five gallon tank. For spawning or for larger groups, at least a ten or twenty gallon aquarium is advisable.

Any aquarium intended for neon gobies should have some bottom cover, be it a few pieces of coral or an elaborate "reef," since these fishes normally have some sort of refuge in nature. The sponge-dwelling species should be provided with a "pseudo-sponge" such as a piece of polyvinyl chloride tubing 1 or 2 inches in diameter and 4 to 8 inches long stuck nearly vertically into the aquarium sand. There should be at least one tube for each male sponge-dwelling *Elacatinus* and ideally a tube for each individual. If the males do not each have a tube they tend to become aggressive among themselves, resulting in ripped fins. No species of neon goby is aggressive toward other species of fishes, and the six cleaning species are beneficial to any aquarium set-up due to their parasite removal behavior.

Feeding in the aquarium is no problem for neon gobies. The coral-dwelling species which feed largely on crustacean fish parasites on the reef adapt well to dry foods or brine shrimp, although immediately after collection they show no interest in these "unusual" foods. After a few days hunger causes them to try various foods offered and they quickly adapt to these foods. The sponge-dwelling species which feed on parasitic poly-chaete worms found in sponges also adapt well to dry foods and brine shrimp. Breeding pairs of various species fed only dry food continued to spawn for some weeks, but it would be wise to feed brine shrimp occasion-ally to vary the diet.

The diseases of neon gobies are similar to those of other marine aquarium fishes and pose no unusual problems to the marine aquarist. Fungal and bacterial infections are generally treated with antibiotics, and other infestations such as "oodinium" are treated with copper sul-fate. Reference to a good marine aquarium manual is advisable in these cases.

## SPAWNING AND REARING OF NEON GOBIES

The species of *Elacatinus* are among the easiest species of marine aquarium fishes to breed. The species spawned by the author include *Go-biosoma oceanops, G. evelynae* (Y, YB, W), *G. genie, G. horsti* (Y, W), *G. louisae* (Y) and *G. xanthiprora* (W). There are no reports of the other 6 species having spawned in the aquarium, although they probably will do so.

The aquarist who wishes to spawn these gobies should purchase 4 or 5 individuals, unless a guaranteed breeding pair can be obtained, to have the greatest chance of success. If not sexually mature, they should be reared to a length of 20-25 mm (about 1 inch) before any reproductive activity can be expected. The aquarium for these individuals should be of at least 20 gallons and have numerous rocks, corals, and potential spawn-ing sites. A spawning pair will remain together a large part of the time and lay their eggs in a cave or on the undersurface of a rock. The male guards the eggs after spawning, and such a fish vigorously defending a spot in the aquarium, not previously defended, usually means a spawning has occurred.

Although the sponge-dwelling species of *Elacatinus* deposit their eggs within the lumen of the sponges they inhabit, they will spawn on the inner surface of plastic tubes stuck vertically into the sand of the aquari-um bottom. These tubes, termed "pseudosponges," serve as refuges and, at least in *G. louisae*, are vigorously defended by territorial males.

Sexing of neon gobies can be carried out in several ways. The most positive method is to determine the shape of the genital papilla. Males have this papilla cone-shaped and pointed. The female's is shorter and very blunt. Preserved or anesthetized specimens are easily examined with a hand lens to determine the shape of the papilla, but sexing live fishes in

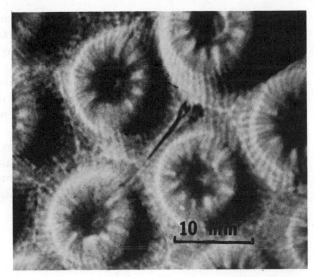

A newly metamorphosed individual of *Gobiosoma evelynae* (W) on the coral *Montastrea cavernosa* at Discovery Bay, Jamaica.

an aquarium is not as simple. In some cases the pointed papilla of the male may be visible when viewed closely from the side in an aquarium.

Males of *G. oceanops, G. evelynae, G. genie, G. illecebrosum, G. randalli,* and *G. prochilos* have one to a few enlarged recurved canine teeth on the sides of the lower jaw to the inside of the smaller teeth on the edge of the jaw. These canine teeth can occasionally be observed on aquarium specimens when the fish is facing the observer with the mouth partially open. Other species of *Elacatinus* do not have differences in dentition between sexes. In most species the females generally have the abdomen lighter in color than that of the male, but this difference is useful only in comparative situations, rather than sex determination in a single fish.

The eggs of *Elacatinus* hatch in 7-12 days, depending on temperature, and have two important requirements for their care. The first is that they be agitated while incubating. This can be done either by leaving the eggs with the guarding males who agitate them periodically or by causing water currents to agitate the eggs. Water currents can be produced by placing an airstone near the egg mass if it is on a rock or shell, or passing a gentle flow of water over the eggs in cases where they are deposited in a tube. The second care requirement is that the eggs be maintained in the same position for incubation as they were in at their laying. About 36-50 hours after laying, the embryonic goby undergoes a reorientation within the egg capsule so that the head points towards the distal end of the egg capsule, not the basal end. The larvae must exit the egg capsule head first at hatching. If the eggs are maintained inverted from the position of their laying at this time, they will not reorient and will fail to hatch.

A particularly challenging endeavor for the aquarist would be to attempt hybridization of the species and color varieties of *Elacatinus*. Individuals of different species and opposite sexes are placed in the same aquarium and hopefully spawn together.

In the present study, larval gobies were reared by feeding them zooplankton of 35-200 micron size plus brine shrimp at larger sizes. Cultured foods might be a suitable alternate, but this was not attempted in the present study. More information on rearing is in the materials and methods section.

# LITERATURE CITED

Abel, E.F. 1960. Liaison facultative d'une poisson (*Gobius bucchichii* Steindachner) et d'une anemone (*Anemonia sulcata* Penn.) in Mediterranee. Vie et Milieu, 11:517-531.

Allen, Gerald R. 1972. The Anemonefishes, their Classification and Biology. T.F.H. Publications; Neptune City, N.J. 288 pp.

Anglejan, Bruno de and Eric J. Mountjoy. 1973. Submerged reefs of the eastern Grenadines shelf margin. Bull. Geol. Soc. Amer., 84:2445-2454.

Axelrod, Herbert R. and Cliff W. Emmens. 1969. Exotic Marine Fishes. T.F.H. Publications; Neptune City, N.J. 607 pp.

———— and William Vorderwinkler. 1963. Salt-water aquarium fish. T.F.H. Publications; Neptune City, N.J., 352 pp.

Bailey, Reeve M., Ernest A. Lachner, C.C. Lindsey, C. Richard Robins, Phil M. Roedel, W.B. Scott, and Loren P. Woods. 1960. A list of common and scientific names of fishes from the United States and Canada (second edition). Amer. Fish. Soc., Spec. Pub., 2:1-102.

—————, J.E. Fitch, E.S. Herald, E.A. Lachner, C.C. Lindsey, C.R. Robins, and W.B. Scott. 1970. A list of common and scientific names of fishes from the United States and Canada (third edition). Amer. Fish. Soc., Spec. Pub., 6.

Bardach, John E. 1959. The summer standing crop of fish on a shallow Bermuda reef. Limnol and Oceanog., 4(1):77-85.

Beebe, William. 1928. Beneath Tropic Seas. Blue Ribbon Books; N.Y. 234 pp.

———— and Gloria Hollister. 1931. New species of fish from the West Indies. Zoologica, N.Y., 12(9):83-88.

———— and John Tee-Van. 1928. The fishes of Port-au-Prince Bay, Haiti. Zoologica, N.Y., 10(1):1-279.

Bohlke, James E. and Charles C.G. Chaplin. 1968. Fishes of the Bahamas and Adjacent Tropical Waters. Livingston Publ. Co.; Wynnewood, Pa. 771 pp.

———— and John E. McCosker, 1973. Two additional west Atlantic gobies (genus *Gobiosoma*) that remove ectoparasites from other fishes. Copeia, 1973(3):609-610.

––––– and John E. Randall. 1968. A key to the shallow-water west Atlantic cardinalfishes (Apogonidae), with descriptions of five new species. Proc. Acad. Nat. Sci. Philadelphia, 120(4):175-206.

––––– and C. Richard Robins. 1968. Western Atlantic seven-spined gobies, with descriptions of ten new species and a new genus, and comments on Pacific relatives. Proc. Acad. Nat. Sci. Philadelphia, 120(3):45-174.

––––– and –––––. 1969. Western Atlantic sponge-dwelling gobies of the genus *Evermannichthys*: their taxonomy, habits, and relationships. Proc. Acad. Nat. Sci. Philadelphia, 121(1):1-24.

Boyd, Dick. 1956. Spawning the neon goby, *Elacatinus oceanops*. Aquarium, 25:391-396.

Breder, Charles M., Jr. 1927. Scientific results of the first oceanographic expedition of the "Pawnee," 1925. Fishes. Bull. Bing. Oceanogr. Coll., 1(1):1-90.

–––––. 1942. On the reproduction of *Gobiosoma robustum* Ginsburg. Zoologica, N.Y., 27(3):229-232.

Briggs, John C. 1958. A list of Florida fishes and their distribution. Bull. Fla. State Mus., Biol. Sci., 2(8):223-318.

Brucks, John T. 1971. The current east of the Windward Islands, West Indies (abstract). Symposium on Invest. and Resources of the Carib. Sea and Adj. Regions, UNESCO: 31-33.

Bunt, John S., Lee, Chun C., and Michael A. Heeb. 1972. The site off Freeport intended for Hydro-Lab. Hydro-Lab Jour., 1(1):3-6, 53-56.

Caldwell, David K. 1966. Marine and freshwater fishes of Jamaica. Bull. Inst. Jamaica, No. 17, Science Ser. :1-120.

Cervigon, Fernando. 1966. Los peces marinos de Venezuela. Monograph 11, Fund. La Salle Cien. Nat. :1-385.

–––––. 1968. Los peces marinos de Venezuela, complemento 1. Mem. Soc. Cien. Nat. La Salle, 80:177-218.

Colin, Patrick L. 1971. Additions to the marine fish fauna of Jamaica, with notes on their ecology. Carib. J. Sci., 11(1-2):21-25.

–––––. 1974. Observation and collection of deep-reef fishes off the coasts of Jamaica and British Honduras. Mar. Biol., in press.

––––– and John B. Heiser. 1974. Occurrence of two species of cardinalfishes (Pisces: Apogonidae) in association with sea anemones in the West Indies. Bull. Mar. Sci., 23(3):521-524.

Collette, Bruce B. and Frank H. Talbot. 1972. Activity patterns of coral reef fishes with emphasis on nocturnal-diurnal changeover. Bull. Nat. Hist. Mus. Los Angeles Co., 14:98-124.

Dammann, Arthur E. 1969. Study of the fisheries potential of the Virgin Islands. Virgin Isl. Ecological Res. Sta. Contrib., 1:1-204.

Darcy, George H., Elizabeth Maisel, and John C. Ogden. (In press). Cleaning preferences of the gobies *Gobiosoma evelynae* and *G. prochilos* and the juvenile wrasse *Thalassoma bifasciatum*. Copeia.

Dauer, Daniel M. 1972. Polychaete fauna associated with Gulf of Mexico sponges (abstract). Program Fla. Acad. Sci. Meeting, 1972:10.

Davis, William P. and Ray S. Birdsong. 1972. Coral reef fishes which forage in the water column. A review of their morphology, behavior, ecology and evolutionary implications. Helgolander wiss. Meeresunters, 24:292-306.

————— and Daniel M. Cohen. 1968. A gobiid fish and a paleomonid shrimp living on an antipatharian sea whip in the tropical Pacific. Bull. Mar. Sci., 18(4):749-761.

DeLisle, Harold F. 1969. An analysis of cleaning symbiosis in some West Indian fishes. M.S. Thesis, Univ. of Puerto Rico.

Duarte-Bello, Pedro Pablo. 1959. Catalogo de peces Cubanos. Universidad Catolica de Santo Tomas de Villanueva, Monogr., 6:1-208.

Eibl-Eibesfeldt, Irenaus. 1955. Uber symbiosen parasitismus und andere besondere zwischenartliche Beziehungen tropischen Meerfische. Z. Tierpsychol., 19(2):165-182.

—————. 1967. Formen der Symbiose. Naturwissenschaft und Medizin, 4(16):14-27.

Emery, Alan R. 1968a. Underwater telescope. Copeia, 1968(2):627-628.

—————. 1968b. Comparative ecology of damselfishes (Pisces: Pomacentridae) at Alligator Reef, Florida Keys. Ph.D. Dissertation, Univ of Miami.

—————. 1972. Eddy formation from an oceanic island: ecological effects. Carib. J. Sci., 12(3-4):121-128.

—————. 1970. Pleistocene paleotemperatures. Science, 168:822-825.

Emilsson, Ingvar. 1971. On the upper layer circulation in the Cayman Sea. Symposium on Investigations and Resources of the Carib. Sea and Adj. Regions, UNESCO, 53-60.

Erdman, Donald S. 1956. Recent fish records from Puerto Rico. Bull. Mar. Sci. Gulf & Carib., 6(4):315-340.

Faulkner, Douglas and C. Lavett Smith. 1970. The Hidden Sea. Viking Press; N.Y. 148 pp.

Feddern, Henry A. 1967. Larval development of the neon goby, *Elacatinus oceanops*, in Florida. Bull. Mar. Sci., 17:367-375.

Feder, Henry M. 1966. Cleaning symbiosis in the marine environment. *In* Symbiosis, S.M. Henry, ed., vol. 1:327-380, Academic Press.

Fisher, Ed L. 1955. Marine tropicals. All-Pets Books, Inc.; Found du Lac, Wisconsin. 71 pp.

Fowler, Henry Weed. 1944. Results of the fifth George Vanderbilt expedition (1941) (Bahamas, Caribbean Sea, Panama, Galapagos Archipelago, and Mexican Pacific Islands). The fishes. Monogr. Acad. Nat. Sci. Philadelphia, 6:57-529.

——————. 1952. The fishes of Hispaniola. Mem. Soc. Cubana Hist. Nat., 21(1):83-115, pls. 20-26.

Ginsburg, Issac. 1933. A revision of the genus *Gobiosoma* (family Gobiidae) with an account of the genus *Garmannia*. Bull. Bingham Oceanogr. Coll., 4(5):1-59.

Ginsburg, Robert N. and Noel P. James. 1973. British Honduras by submarine. Geotimes:23-24.

Gomon, Martin F. 1971. Comparative osteology of the western Atlantic species of *Halichoeres* (Pisces, Labridae). M.S. Thesis, Univ. of Miami.

Goreau, Thomas F. 1967. Gigantism and abundance in the macrobenthos of Jamaican coral reefs (abstract). Assoc. Is. Mar. Labs. of the Carib., seventh meeting:26-27.

——————. 1959. The ecology of Jamaican coral reefs. I. Species composition and zonation. Ecology, 40:67-90.

Greenberg, Jerry and Idaz Greenberg. 1972. The Living Reef. Seahawk Press; Miami, Fla. 110 pp.

Herald, Earl S. 1961. Living fishes of the world. Doubleday and Company; N.Y. 304 pp.

——————. 1972. Fishes of North America. Doubleday and Company; N.Y. 245 pp.

Hildebrand, Henry H., Humberto Chavez, and Henry Compton. 1964. Aporte al conocimiento do los peces del Arrecife Alacranes, Yucatan (Mexico). Ciencia Mex., 23(3):107-134.

Hobson, Edmund S. 1968. Predatory behavior of some shore fishes in the Gulf of California. Fish and Wildlife Ser. Res. Rep., 73:1-92.

——————. 1969. Comments on certain recent generalizations regarding cleaning symbiosis in fishes. Pacif. Sci., 23(1):35-39.

——————. 1971. Cleaning symbiosis among California inshore fishes. Fishery Bull., 69(3):491-524.

Hoese, Douglass F. 1971. A revision of the eastern Pacific species of the gobiid fish genus *Gobiosoma*, with a discussion of the relationships of the genus. Dissertation, Univ. of Calif., San Diego.

Imajima, Minoru. 1966. The Syllidae (Polychaetous Annelids) from Japan. IV. Syllidae. Publ. Seto Mar. Bio. Lab., 14(3):219-252.

Jones, James I. 1973. Physical oceanography of the northeast Gulf of Mexico and Florida continental shelf area. *In* A summary of Knowledge of the eastern Gulf of Mexico. State Univ. System of Florida, Institute of Ocean Resources.

Jordan, David Starr. 1904. Notes on fishes collected in the Tortugas archipelago. Bull. U.S. Fish Comm., 22(for 1902):539-544.

— — — — and Joseph C. Thompson. 1905. The fish fauna of the Tortugas archipelago. Bull. U.S. Bur. Fish., 24:229-255.

— — — — —, Barton Warren Evermann, and Howard Walton Clark. 1930. Check list of the fishes and fishlike vertebrates of Noth and Middle America north of the northern boundary of Venezuela and Colombia. Rep. U.S. Comm. Fish for 1928, (2):1-670.

Kinzie, Robert A., III. 1973. The zonation of West Indian gorgonians. Bull. Mar. Sci., 23(1):93-155.

Kuntz, Albert. 1916. Notes on the embryology and larval development of five species of teleostean fishes. Bull. U.S. Bur. Fish., 34:407-430.

Limbaugh, Conrad. 1961. Cleaning symbiosis. Sci. Am., 205(2):42-49.

Longley, William H. 1918. Haunts and habits of tropical fishes. Amer. Mus. Journ.:79-88.

— — — — and Samuel F. Hildebrand. 1941. Systematic catalogue of the fishes of Tortugas, Florida. Carnegie Inst. Wash. Publ., 535: 1-331.

Losey, George S., Jr. 1971. Communication between fishes in cleaning symbiosis. *In* Aspects of the Biology of Symbiosis, T.C. Cheng, ed. University Park Press; Baltimore:45-76.

— — — — —. 1972. The ecological importance of cleaning symbiosis. Copeia, 1972(4):820-833.

— — — — —. 1974. Cleaning symbiosis in Puerto Rico with comparison to the tropical Pacific. Copeia, 1974(4).

Lynts, George W., James B. Judd and Charles F. Stehman. 1973. Late Pleistocene history of Tongue of the Ocean, Bahamas. Bull. Geol. Soc. Amer., 84(4):2665-2684.

MacIntyre, Ian G. 1967. Submerged coral reefs, west coast of Barbados, W.I. Canad. J. Earth Sci., 4:461-474.

— — — — —. 1972. Submerged reefs of the eastern Caribbean. Amer. Assoc. Petroleum Geol. Bull., 56(4):720-738.

Mansueti, Romeo. 1963. Symbiotic behavior between small fishes and jellyfishes, with new data on that between the stromateid, *Peprilus alepidotus*, and the Scyphomedusa, *Chrysaora quinquecirrha*. Copeia, 1963(1):40-80.

Mariscal, Richard N. 1966. The symbiosis between tropical sea anemones and fishes: a review. *In* The Galapagos, R.I. Bowman, ed. Univ. of California Press; Berkeley:157-171.

Marshall, Norman B. 1966. The Life of Fishes. World Publ. Co.; Cleveland and N.Y. 402 pp.

Metzelaar, Jan. 1922. On a collection of marine fishes from the Lesser

Antilles. Bijdragen tot de Dierkunde, Feestnummer 22:133-141.

Milliman, John D. 1967. The geomorphology and history of Hogsty Reef, a Bahamian atoll. Bull. Mar. Sci., 17(3):519-543.

— — — — — and K.O. Emery. 1968. Sea levels during the past 35,000 years. Science, 162:1121-1123.

Muench, Bruce. 1958. Quinaldine, a new anesthetic for fish. Prog. Fish. Cult. 20(1):42-44.

Newell, Norman D., John Inbrie, Edward G. Purdy, and David L. Thurber. 1959. Organism communities and bottom facies, Great Bahama Bank. Bull. Amer. Mus. Nat. Hist., 117(4):181-228.

O'Connel, Robert F. 1969. The Marine Aquarium for the Home Aquarist. Great Outdoors Publ. Co.; St. Petersburg, Fla.

Odum, Howard T. and Eugene P. Odum. 1955. Trophic structure and productivity of a windward coral reef community on Eniwetok Atoll. Ecol. Monogr., 25(3):291-320.

Palacio, Francisco J. 1972. Fishes collected in the Colombian Caribbean. M.S. Thesis, University of Miami.

Perlroth, Irving. 1971. Distribution of mass in the near surface waters of the Caribbean. Symposium on Investigations and Resources of the Caribbean Sea and Adjacent Regions, UNESCO:147-152.

Phillips, Craig. 1964. The captive sea. Chilton Co.; Philadelphia, Pa., 284 pp.

Potts, Geoffrey W. 1968. The ethology of *Crenilabrus melanocercus*, with notes on cleaning symbiosis. J. Mar. Biol. Assoc. U.K., 48:279-293.

— — — — —. 1973. Cleaning symbiosis among British fish with special reference to *Crenilabrus melanops* (labridae). J. Mar. Biol. Assoc. U.K., 53:1-10.

Randall, John E. 1958. A review of the labrid fish genus *Labroides*, with descriptions of two new species and notes on ecology. Pacific Sci., 12 (4):327-347.

— — — — —. 1962. Fish service stations. Sea Frontiers, 8(1):40-47, illus.

— — — — —. 1963. An analysis of the fish populations of artificial and natural reefs in the Virgin Islands. Carib. J. Sci., 3(1):31-47.

— — — — —. 1967. Food habits of reef fishes of the West Indies. Stud. Trop. Oceanogr. No. 5, Proc. Int. Conf. Trop. Oceanogr.:665-847.

— — — — —. 1968. Caribbean Reef Fishes. T.F.H. Publications Inc.; Jersey City, N.J. 318 pp.

— — — — — and Willard D. Hartman. 1968. Sponge-feeding fishes of the West Indies. Mar. Biol., 1(3):216-225.

— — — — —, Katsumi Aida, Takashi Hibiya, Nobuhiro Mitsuura, Hisao Kamiya, and Yoshire Hashimoto. 1971. Grammistin, the skin toxin of soapfishes, and its significance in the classification of the Grammistidae. Publ. Seto. Mar. Biol. Lab., 19(2,3):157-190.

Reighard, Jacob. 1908. An experimental study of warning coloration in coral reef fishes. Pap. Tortugas Lab., (103):257-325.

Reiswig, Henry M. 1970. Porifera: sudden sperm release by tropical Demospongiae. Science, 170:538-539.

— — — — —. 1971a. The physiological ecology of Porifera: a comparative study of three species of tropical marine Demospongiae. Ph.D. Dissertation, Yale University.

— — — — —. 1971b. In situ pumping activities of tropical Demospongiae. Mar. Biol., 9(1):38-50.

Robins, C. Richard. 1971. Distributional patterns of fishes from coastal and shelf waters of the tropical western Atlantic. Symposium on Investigations and Resources of the Caribbean Sea and Adjacent Regions. UNESCO, F.A.O., papers on fisheries resources:249-255.

Roos, Peter J. 1964. The distribution of reef corals in Curacao. Stud. Fauna Curacao, 20:1-51.

— — — — —. 1971. The shallow-water stony corals of the Netherlands Antilles. Stud. Fauna Curacao, 37:1-108.

Rosenblatt, Richard H. 1963. Some aspects of speciation in marine shore fishes. Systematics Assoc. Publ. No. 5:171-180.

— — — — —. 1967. The zoogeographic relationships of the marine shore fishes of tropical America. Stud. Trop. Oceanogr. No. 5, Proc. Int. Conf. Trop. Oceanogr. :579-592.

Rubinoff, Roberta W. and Ira Rubinoff. 1971. Geographic and reproductive isolation in Atlantic and Pacific populations of Panamanian Bathygobius. Evolution, 25(1):88-97.

Schroeder, Robert E. 1964. Photographing the night creatures of Alligator Reef. Natl. Geo., 125(1):128-154.

Simkatis, Helen. 1958. Salt-water fishes for the home aquarium. J.B. Lippincott Co.; Philadephia, Pa. 254 pp.

Smith, C. Lavett. 1971. A revision of the American groupers: Epinephelus and allied genera. Bull. Amer. Mus. Nat. Hist., 146(2):69-241.

— — — — —. 1973. Small rotenone stations: a tool for studying coral reef fish communities. Amer. Mus. Novitates.

— — — — — and James C. Tyler, 1972. Space resource sharing in a coral reef fish community. Bull. Nat. Hist. Mus. Los Angeles Co., 14:125-178.

Springer, Victor G. 1971. Revision of the fish genus Ecsenius (Bleniidae, Blenniinae, Salariini). Smithsonian Cont. Zool., 72: 1-74.

Starck, Walter A., II. 1968. A list of fishes of Alligator Reef, Florida with comments on the nature of the Florida reef fish fauna. Undersea Biology, 1(1):6-42.

————— and William P. Davis. 1966. Night habits of fishes of Alligator Reef, Florida. Ichthyologica, 38(4):313-356.

————— and Jo D. Starck. 1972. Probing the deep reefs hidden realm. Natl. Geo.,142(6):867-886.

Stephens, William M. 1968. Southern Seashores. Holiday House; N.Y.

Stevenson, Robert A. 1963. Behavior of the pomacentrid reef fish *Dascyllus albisella* Gill in relation to the anemone *Marchantia* (sic) *cookei*. Copeia, 1963(4):612-614.

Stoddart, D.R. 1972. Field methods in the study of coral reefs. *In* Proc. First Int. Symp. of Corals and Coral Reefs, Mar. Biol. Assoc. India, Cochin:71-80.

Straughan, Robert P.L. 1956. Salt water fishes are spawned. The Aquarium, 25(5):157-159.

—————. 1959. The salt-water aquarium in the home. A.S. Barnes and Co.; New York. 262 pp.

—————. 1964. The salt-water aquarium in the home. A.S. Barnes and Co.; New York. 304 pp.

U.S. Navy Oceanographic Office. 1967. Environmental Atlas of the Tongue of the Ocean, Bahamas. Special Publ. 94.

Valenti, Robert J. 1972. The embryology of the neon goby, *Gobiosoma oceanops*. Copeia, 1972(3):477-481.

Walters, Vladimir and C. Richard Robins. 1961. A new toadfish (Batrachoididae) considered to be a glacial relict in the West Indies. Amer. Mus. Novitates, 2047:1-24.

Wells, John W. 1973. New and old scleractinian corals from Jamaica. Bull. Mar. Sci., 23(1):16-55.

————— and Judith C. Lang. 1973. Systematic list of Jamaican shallow-water Scleractinia (appendix). Bull. Mar. Sci., 23(1):55-58.

Wickler, Wolfgang. 1962. Ei und Larve von *Elacatinus oceanops* Jordan (Pisces, Gobiiformes). Senck. biol., 43(3):201-205.

Wust, Georg. 1964. Stratification and Circulation in the Antillean-Caribbean Basins. Colombia Univ. Press; N.Y.

Youngbluth, Marsh J. 1968. Aspects of the ecology and ethology of the cleaning fish, *Labroides phthirophagus* Randall. Z. Tierpsych., 25: 915-932.

# INDEX

Page numbers printed in **bold** face refer to photos or illustrations.

**A**

Abudefduf saxatilis, 235
Acanthemblemaria rivasi, 248
Acropora cervicornis, 168, 193
  palmata, 193, 199
Agaricia, 64, 81, 208, 245, 253
  agaracites, 209
  tenufolia, 209
Agelus sp., 157, 165, 168, 238
Amphiprion, 199
Anemonia sulcata, 203
Anisotremus-virginicus, 211, 235
Antipathes pennacea, 237
Apogon lachneri, 103
  maculatus, 44
  quadrisquamatus, 242
Aulostomus maculatus, 246
Austrogobius, 9

**B**

Bathygobius soporator, 30
Belize Barrier Reef, 188, 192
Bodianus, 234
  pulchellus, 252
  rufus, 227

**C**

Callyspongia plicifera, 111, 153, 220,
  229, 232
  vaginalis, 228
Canthigaster rostrata, 242
Ceripathes sp., 203
Chromis cyanea, 226, 230
  multilineata, 227, 230
Clepticus parrai, 96, 220, 230
Colpophyllia natans, 27, 40, 54, 62, 65,
  68, 72, 101, 109, 204, 206, 256
Coral area, 182
Coryphopterus lipernes, 163, 191, 195,
  198, 206, 207, 245, 249, 253
  personatus, 37, 176, 181, 184, 206,
  207, 210, 248, 256
Cottogobius yongei, 203
Crenilabrus melanoceros, 214

**D**

Dascyllus, 203
Dendrogyra cylindricus, 196, 197, 199
Diploria labyrinthiformes, 72
  strigosa, 61, 125
  sp., 70, 78, 199

**E**

Elacatinus, 9, 18, 19
Emblemaria diaphana, 206
  signifera, 206
Epinephelus cruentatus, 230, 246
  fulva, 226, 243
  guttatus, 117
  striatus, 230, 236, 246

**G**

Garmannia, 9
Geographic distribution, 150, 151, 154,
  155, 275, 277, 278, 279, 281
Ginsburgellus, 9
Gobiosoma, 18, 81, 89, 245
Eggs of, 53
  Dendrogam of, 286
  multifasciatum, 149
  saucrum, 50, 206, 207, 214, 244
Gobiosoma (Elacatinus)
  atronasum, 142, 143, 172, 173, 176,
  177, 180, 181, 184, 237
  chancei, 82, 83, 132
  evelynae, 29, 31, 32, 35, 60, 61, 64,
  65, 68, 69, 72, 73, 76, 77, 80, 81,
  84, 85, 88, 89, 92, 93, 96, 97,
  104, 121, 129, 253, 265, 267,
  268, 293
  genie, 55, 59, 62, 105, 108, 109, 112,
  113, 116, 117, 214, 264
  horsti, 87, 90, 95, 99, 103, 133, 136,
  137, 140, 141, 144, 145
  illecebrosum, 47, 51, 54, 100, 101,
  104
  louisae, 119, 123, 127, 130, 135,
  136, 156, 157, 160, 161, 164,
  165, 168
  oceanops, 24, 25, 27, 33, 36, 37, 40,
  41, 44, 45, 48, 49, 53, 56, 57, 184
  prochilos, 66, 67, 70, 74, 120, 121,
  124, 125, 132
  randalli, 75, 78, 128, 129
  tenox, 134, 138, 169
  xanthiprora, 110, 111, 115, 148,
  149, 152, 153, 259
Gobius bucchichii, 203
Gramma loreto, 176, 235, 241
  melacara, 65
Gymnothorax moringua, 56

**H**

*Halichoeres pictus*, 230
*Holacanthus limbaughi*, 234
   *passer*, 234
*Holocentrus*, 92, 237
   *rufus*, 184, 246
*Hypoplectrus chlorurus*, 230
   *puella*, 217, 242, 243, 247
   sp., 246

**I**

*Isophyllia sinuosa*, 80

**L**

*Labroides bicolor*, 231
   *dimidiatus*, 231
   *rubrolabiatus*, 231
   *phthirophagus*, 211, 226
Localities, 14
*Lucayablennius zingaro*, 237
*Lutjanus griseus*, 247
*Lysmata grabhami*, 235
   sp., 242

**M**

*Madracis*, 225
*Meandrina meandrites*, 205
*Microspathodon chrysurus*, 234, 240
   *dorsalis*, 234
*Montastrea annularis*, 108, 120, 249
   *cavernosa*, 27, 41, 45, 60, 62, 76,
      81, 89, 93, 109, 112, 129, 172,
      173, 210, 248, 249, 293
*Mulloidichthys martinicus*, 97
*Mussa angulosa*, 199, 213, 216
*Mycale* sp., 217, 228, 236
*Mycetophyllia*, 201
*Mycteroperca tigris*, 97, 117, 214
   spp., 230
*Myripristis jacobus*, 246

**N**

*Neofibrularia massa*, 103, 145, 200, 233
*Nomeus gronovii*, 203

**P**

Pedro Bank, 185, 189
*Periclimenes pedersoni*, 227, 236
*Phaeopteryx xenus*, 242
*Physalia*, 203
*Pomacanthus arcuatus*, 104, 234
   *paru*, 234
*Pomacentrus partitus*, 227

**Q**

*Quisquilius hipoliti*, 246

**R**

Reefs, Map of, 162
*Risor ruber*, 242
*Rypticus saponaceus*, 223, 237

**S**

*Scarus*, 37, 230
*Scolymia cubensis*, 199
   *lacera*, 199, 212
*Sidastrea*, 53, 69, 73
*Starksia hassi*, 242
   *lepicoelia*, 242
*Stephanocoenia michelinii*, 253
*Syllis spongicola*, 233, 236, 237, 243

**T**

*Tethya crypta*, 236
*Thalassoma bifasciatum*, 59, 109, 211,
    215, 227, 230, 234, 243
   *lucasanum*, 234
*Tigrigobius*, 9, 234
"Triangle Rock", 182, 187, 194, 195
*Tubipora musica*, 57

**V**

*Verongia*, 164, 168, 221
   *archeri*, 237
   *cavernosa*, 237, 238
   *fistularis*, 144, 161, 220, 224, 225
   *gigantea*, 168

**X**

*Xetospongia muta*, 37, 74, 84